MORE THAN A TEARDROP

IN THE OCEAN

ALSO BY NEIL ROLDE

More Than a Teardrop in the Ocean: Volume II, More of the
Tempestuous History of the War Refugee Board

Crimes of War

Real Political Tales: Short Stories by a Veteran Politician

Breckinridge Long: American Eichmann??? An Enquiry into the Character
of the Man Who Denied Visas to the Jews

York Is Living History

O. Murray Carr: A Novel

Maine in the World: Stories of Some of Those From Here Who Went
Away

Continental Liar From the State of Maine: James G. Blaine

Maine: Downeast and Different, an Illustrated History

Unsettled Past, Unsettled Future: The Story of Maine Indians

The Interrupted Forest: A History of Maine's Wildlands

The Baxters of Maine: Downeast Visionaries

Your Money or Your Health: America's Cruel, Bureaucratic, and
Horrendously Expensive Health Care System

So You Think You Know Maine

Rio Grande Do Norte: The Story of Maine's Partner State in Brazil

Sir William Pepperrell of Colonial New England

MORE THAN A TEARDROP

IN THE OCEAN

Volume I

THE TEMPESTUOUS HISTORY
OF THE
WAR REFUGEE BOARD

Neil Rolde

Polar Bear & Company
An imprint of the
Solon Center for Research and Publishing
Solon, Maine

My gratitude to Misha Mitsel for help at the archives of the Joint Distribution Committee.

Polar Bear & Company™
Solon Center for Research and Publishing
PO Box 311, Solon, ME 04979, U.S.A.
207.643.2795, polarbearandco.org, soloncenter.org

ISBN: 978-1-882190-75-1
Cover: design by Ramona du Houx; front photo of "the first transport of Romanian children arriving in Palestine through the efforts of JDC and the U.S. War Refugee Board (1944)" courtesy American Jewish Joint Distribution Committee Archives, reference #NY_00033; back photo of Hungarian refugees in Austria 1956 © UNHCR; hope for civilization.

First print edition, first printing October 2016
Library of Congress Control Number: 2016957100
Manufactured on durable, acid-free paper in more than one country.

Contents

Explanation of My Title

After World War II, during the early 1950s, a superlative European-Jewish novelist, Manes Sperber, born in Galicia in the Austro-Hungarian Empire, wrote a trilogy of fiction that bore the overall title of *Like a Tear in the Ocean*. These words are mouthed by one of his characters, an unforgettable young rabbi in Nazi-occupied Poland, when he refuses to join the partisan resistance group his people are forming to fight back. The memorable metaphor the author has him use, to express the utter inconsequence of any action by him, highlights his devoted Hebraic fatalism honoring God's will as the ultimate determinant of all human fate, although in the end he does pick up a rifle.

I have named my history of the War Refugee Board: *More Than a Teardrop in the Ocean*. Not much more, perhaps. Yet its feat of saving some two hundred thousand targeted innocents condemned to die out of six million slaughtered, while seemingly puny, is surely worthy of respect. The nonfiction saga of the War Refugee Board is a story worthy of being told in detail and in its entirety.

Parenthetically, I recently was at a meeting of a Book Club I belong to in my hometown of York, Maine. The subject we had all agreed upon to read about and discuss was World War II. At the outset, I asked my fellow members if they had ever heard of the War Refugee Board. None had. Then, I asked if the name Raoul Wallenberg meant anything to them. All replied they knew about this heroic Swede credited with singlehandedly personally saving at least twenty thousand Hungarian Jews before vanishing mysteriously when the Russians liberated Budapest and apparently dying years later in a Russian Gulag. But not one, aside from me, knew that Wallenberg had been sent secretly to Hungary by the War Refugee Board.

There were many other heroes, generally unsung, working for the WRB, as well.

Introduction

"An idea whose time has come" is an expression I've often heard in political circles. It describes a phenomenon in the making of laws that quite literally has, one might say, *mystical overtones*. A proposed piece of legislation, rejected over and over again through many sessions, reappears once more, seemingly miraculously passes, and at last enters the legal code.

The War Refugee Board can be considered an example. But with certain deviations. First of all, although its creation was incorporated in a proposed Congressional bill, the measure was en route to dying in committee and, indeed, never reached a vote of any kind. However, here was *an idea that had to come* as World War II progressed into its final two years.

Since 1933 and the advent of Hitler, there had been a need for an instrument of U.S. government that would deal with the victims of Nazi policy. As with the proverbial frog in boiling water, the fatal effects weren't felt for a lengthy period to come. But it was obvious the Jews of Germany would be facing a persecution comparable to the harm, or worse, than what they had suffered in the Middle Ages.

Yes, it was gradual. They lost their jobs. Their businesses were taken from them. They could no longer enter or occupy certain professions. The hint that all *Juden* should pack up and leave was rapidly made crystal clear.

This was the Nazis' original intent. Make Germany *Judenrein* (Jewless). Let these hated citizens live but force them to depart, abandoning their possessions, wealth, businesses, etc., which would end up in the hands of deserving Aryans, especially Nazi followers.

Their victims weren't always Jews, either. Anyone who stood in their way—Jew and Gentile—was ruthlessly hustled off to special *Konzentrationslagers*, patterned on the British imprisonment camps for Boers in South Africa at the onset of the twentieth century.

And so in this case, while the above mentioned phenomenon was slowly gathering speed, an attempt was made by Franklin Delano Roosevelt in 1938 to provide support for the embattled Jews of Germany. A conference of thirty-two countries he masterminded at the swanky French watering resort L'Hôtel Royal in Évian-les-Bains on the French shores of Lake Geneva, however, proved worse than useless. Its do-nothing-but-speechify results, the Nazis crowed, revealed that no countries, the United States included, were willing to take Jews in any numbers. Only the Dominican Republic under Dictator Rafael Trujillo responded with more than lip service. He offered twenty-six thousand acres of his island space on which to settle a number that in the end amounted to no more than eight hundred Jews. Trujillo's unexpected largesse in this instance stemmed from his desire to offset international outrage over the deliberate massacre he ordered of thousands of Haitians who had come illegally into his country.

A follow-up equally do-nothing conference occurring on Bermuda Island after the U. S. had been in World War II for twenty-nine months was touted ahead of time to save fifty thousand Jews. Instead the number was practically zero, and in any event, the delegates were only considering helping Jews and those anti-Nazis who had already escaped the Nazis yet were still in European neutral countries.

The futility of the Bermuda Conference was pithily described as: "the results of Mr. Eden's initiative . . . held in Hamilton [away from the prying eyes of the press] . . . Hundreds of thousands of refugees died and many more thousands were exposed to threats of death and persecution while the conference adjourned in an air of satisfaction about its humanitarian ideas."

Nevertheless, pressure had kept mounting, exacerbated by the false hopes Bermuda had raised and the fiery efforts of a Palestinian Jew using the pseudonym of Peter Bergson (real name: Hillel Kook) who staged a huge star-studded rally in Madison Square Garden and continued his agitation throughout that whole year of 1943.

In April 1943, even before the Bermuda Conference, U.S. Senator "Big Ed" Johnson, a conservative Colorado Democrat, had submitted a bill to take the State Department's control of refugee matters out of the hands of the anti-immigration Assistant Secretary of State Breckinridge Long and achieve its ultimate object of creating a special emergency rescue agency. Johnson's resolution that incorporated a plea to the upcoming Bermuda meeting to take "swift action to save the remaining European Jews" did not even get out of committee.

By June 1943, Breckinridge Long was crowing in his diary: "The refugee question has died down."

In the autumn of 1943, however, the tempo again picked up to do something about saving more Jews. California Congressman Will Rogers Jr, son of the famed humorist, cosponsored a "Resolution Providing for the Establishment by the Executive of a Commission to Effectuate the Rescue of the Jewish People of Europe." Rogers was a member of the House Committee on Foreign Relations, which would hear his bill, HRes 350 and a similar measure HRes 352.

Unfortunately, the committee was chaired by New York City Congressman Sol Bloom who, although Jewish, was a patsy for Breckinridge Long, and all stops were pulled out to bottle up both pieces of legislation.

But in speaking to Bloom's committee behind closed doors, Long overreached himself. He told the members the State Department had brought in 580,000 refugees since Hitler had come to power, mostly Jews. When the committee released his testimony to the press as an excuse to kill the two bills for being unnecessary (done at Breck Long's suggestion), they unwittingly unleashed a *boomerang* effect.

Reacting to the headline about Long's figures on the front page of *The New York Times* was another New York congressman, Emanuel Celler, who represented Brooklyn/Queens. "Manny" had a German Catholic grandfather but considered himself one hundred percent Jewish. He was also one tough, gutsy, longtime congressional veteran, even having opposed the extremely popular Immigration Quota bill of 1924, still on the books today. On December 12, 1943, Celler issued a statement challenging Breck Long's numbers of 580,000 and its implication these were all Jews.

The Times buried his dissent on page eight amid the jewelry and girdle ads.

Nevertheless Celler's insistence that the 580,000 were "in the main ordinary quota immigrants coming in from all countries and the majority were not Jews" caught attention.

The most important governmental place where concern had been brewing on the issue was in the U.S. Department of the Treasury whose secretary was Henry Morgenthau Jr., Roosevelt's upstate New York pal and the sole Jewish member of the Cabinet. Sensitive about his closeness to the president, Morgenthau had stayed singularly quiet on the issue of giving favorable treatment to his co-religionists.

But not so for three of his top subordinates at the Treasury: Randolph Paul, Josiah DuBois, and John Pehle. All were Protestants. On their own, they put together a scathing indictment of Long's duplicitous activities that kept Jews in Nazi hands and outlined a proposal for saving the remainder, an idea first suggested by FDR advisor Oscar Cox, the originator of the Lend-Lease program.

Their pressure on Morgenthau to bring this parlous situation to FDR's attention included a threat by DuBois to resign and go to the press with an attack on Breckinridge Long and a plea for the substitution of a new agency to supersede his power. They demanded a meeting in the White House with the president.

So it happened in the Oval Office on Sunday, January 16, 1944, and ended with Roosevelt declaring: "We will try it."

On January 22, 1944, less than a week later, FDR issued Executive Order 9417, helpfully prepared by the Treasury guys, that declared: "It is the policy of this Government to take all measures within its power to rescue the victims of enemy oppression who are in imminent danger of death and otherwise to afford such victims all possible relief and assistance consistent with the successful prosecution of the war."

Thus began the brief stormy life of the War Refugee Board.

Chapter One

Brunswick, Maine, is a long way from the battlefields of World War II. When I first heard of the War Refugee Board, it was during a drive with a friend of mine to Portland following a board meeting we had both attended in Fort Andros, a reconverted factory building on the banks of the Androscoggin River.

My friend's name was Peter Cox. Like me, he was a strong environmentalist and both of us were trustees of the Maine Chapter of the Conservation Law Foundation. He had hitched a ride with me on my drive south to my home in York, since his wife Eunice had taken the family car and would meet him in Portland. Peter earlier had become well known in our State as the publisher and editor of the *Maine Times*, a no-holds-barred weekly newspaper that had for years stood staid Maine journalism on its head.

Tragically, though, Peter was waging a losing battle against cancer of the esophagus. I could see from the change in his appearance that the end was now in sight. Thus I wasn't surprised when he told me he was writing an autobiography (which Tilbury House, my publishing company, was later to put out under the title *Journalism Matters*, Gardiner, Maine, 2005).

In the context of our discussion, he naturally brought up his illustrious father, Oscar S. Cox. Born in Portland, Maine, the elder Cox was best known for his Lend-Lease idea that allowed Roosevelt to supply war material to the British before the U.S. entered World War II. A string of top-level jobs held by his dad in the Roosevelt Administration was rattled off by Peter: Assistant to the General Counsel of the U.S. Treasury Department, general counsel to the Lend-Lease Agency, assistant solicitor general of the United States, general counsel and deputy administrator of the Foreign Economic Administration . . . and finally, said Peter, "It's not well known, but he also came up with the idea for and helped implement the War Refugee Board."

"Huh?" I believe I responded.

"You know, the War Refugee Board," Peter repeated.

"What's that? Never heard of it," I blurted.

For the rest of our ride, Peter W. Cox filled me in on details of the U.S. Government-backed effort, in concert with various NGOs, that directly and indirectly saved some two hundred thousand mostly Jewish lives from extermination.

One final piece of information gleaned from our talk was Peter's telling me he had never known until the day of Oscar Cox's funeral in October 1966 that his father was Jewish. I had always taken my friend for a liberal-minded, bow-tie-wearing, fellow Ivy Leaguer, Exeter and Yale, the type I'd gone to school with at Andover and Yale, and an unalloyed WASP. Peter, ever the veteran journalist, cited me evidence he'd discovered at the Roosevelt Library in Hyde Park, New York, that his father "had been instrumental in the formation of the War Refugee Board." Indeed, in the summer of 1943, the elder Cox wrote the first ever proposal for such an agency, which he would have called The War Rescue Committee.

Peter also spoke during the trip of Oscar Cox's efforts to establish a United Nations War Crimes Commission.

Being Jewish myself, I had to reason that Peter wasn't technically Jewish since his mother wasn't Jewish, and Jewish law was definitive on that criterion for acceptance. He clarified this point later in his book: "Even though while growing up I had not known my father was Jewish and I had adapted to the middle-of-the-road Protestantism derived from my mother's Presbyterianism, by 1993 I was proud of my Jewish heritage."

This comment, also made to me in the car, led to a fascinating explication from him of the tortured history of the War Refugee Board and its struggles, not only with the Nazi enemy but also with doubters and enemies even within the Roosevelt Administration, especially at the State Department. Embedded among the Foggy Bottom bureaucrats were a few genuine anti-Semites and a whole coterie of nativists bent on making a mockery of the Statue of Liberty and Emma Lazarus's stirring poem of welcome. Some, like Wilbur J. Carr, the grand old man of the State Department, had been a leader in pushing Congress to establish the Immigration Law of 1924 that grafted strict limits of unwanted entry on not only Jews but Italians, Greeks, Poles, Lithuanians, Slavs, etc. The issue of liberalizing refugee quotas of victims of Nazi persecution was a political "red-hot potato." Roosevelt's choice for secretary of state Cordell Hull, a Tennessee congressman who had dreams of succeeding FDR, saw fit to suppress the fact his wife had an Austrian Jewish father.

Conversely, it has been stated that Franklin Roosevelt had more Jewish members of his administration than any other president *before or since.*

In the middleclass Jewish environs in which I grew up in Brookline, Massachusetts, I heard nothing but praise for President Roosevelt as "a friend of the Jews." My Republican father in his later years once claimed he had never voted for FDR, but I honestly believe Dad was having a senior moment lapse of memory.

Roosevelt, an ultra-astute politician, no doubt had to be concerned about this important bloc of supporters as he looked to 1944, an election year in which he had most likely settled in his mind that he would again be a candidate.

Thus on the wintry second Sunday of January 1944, he agreed to meet at the White House with a group from the Treasury Department, led by Secretary Morgenthau and two of the officials who had been pressing for a meeting with the Chief Executive: Randolph Paul, general counsel to the Secretary and John Pehle, chief of the Foreign Funds Control. A third member of the triumvirate, threatening to go to the press if nothing were done, Josiah DuBois, special assistant to Morgenthau, was not present but had spent his Christmas holiday writing the document handed to the president.

FDR asked to have it summarized for him. John Pehle obliged. It should be noted that the eight-page document's original shocking title, REPORT TO THE SECRETARY ON THE ACQUIESCENCE OF THIS GOVERNMENT TO THE MURDER OF THE JEWS, had been watered down, at Secretary Morgenthau's insistence, to a bland REPORT TO THE PRESIDENT. But a villain was still named: Samuel Miller Breckinridge Long, one of three undersecretaries of state, who dealt with visas and was vigorously keeping out refugees, mostly Jews fleeing the Nazi slaughter. The chief executive, who had a cold but no doubt was taking puffs through his signature cigarette holder, listened with somber intensity.

After Pehle finished, the president made a feeble defense of his old buddy "Breck" Long, whom he had known since they had both served as undersecretaries in Woodrow's 1916–20 administration,

Long at the State Department and Roosevelt at the Navy, and who had politicked and socialized together ever since. But to avoid the blockage that Breckinridge Long was erecting at Congress, the obvious end-around would be an executive order from the president setting up a temporary agency with full authority to rescue potential victims still alive. Since 1942, it was known the Germans had created death camps, and there were indications that "Breck" Long had tried to suppress this information.

The decision in the Oval Office was to create the War Refugee Board. Control of visas was taken away from Breckinridge Long. Although he declared he was glad to be relieved of that responsibility, he did have a hand in the design of the WRB, perhaps trying subtly to condemn it to failure. For one thing, it was to have three bosses, the secretary of state, the secretary of the treasury, and the secretary of war. Fortunately, neither Cordell Hull at State nor Henry Stimson at the War Department wanted much to do with the new entity, and Treasury took up the slack. The initial—and most critical need—was to obtain an effective director.

The search began with the idea of attracting a "name"—some public figure of stature. From an extensive list, two names stood out—Frank Graham, president of the University of North Carolina and Eugene Meyer, publisher of the *Washington Post*. Neither of these men finally won Roosevelt's approval. When Wendell Willkie, FDR's Republican opponent in 1940, was mentioned, that notion was aggressively nixed by the "Skipper" himself.

The alternative was to appoint an acting director. John Pehle's name was brought forward and an active lobbying campaign for him got underway. Besides the backing of his boss, Secretary Morgenthau, he had the support of: Edward Stettinius, the newly appointed number-two man at the State Department; John J. McCloy, number-two man at the War Department; Herbert Lehman, ex-governor of New York and head of UNRRA, the new United Nations Relief Agency; Oscar Cox and his friends; Rabbi Stephen Wise and important Jewish organizations like the World Jewish Congress and the Joint Distribution Committee. But by February 1, a week after the executive order had been issued, there was still no one yet in charge.

However the next day word came from the White House that John Pehle was the pick—at least he was made acting director. One of his supporters consoled him that in these cases "acting" soon would turn into "full time"—as did happen in late March. Randolph Paul joked with Morgenthau that he had "gotten his man not for an *indictment* but *into a job.*"

Literally overnight by D.C. standards, a structure was put in place. The Treasury Department gave Pehle a headquarters within its confines. Fellow agitator Josiah DuBois was appointed general counsel. No doubt Randolph Paul looked in on their operations and offered advice and blessings on what they were doing. It was a ridiculously small bureaucracy, no more than thirty-six staff at full complement, and that was to include their agents abroad in neutral countries, who were attached to U.S. embassies with full power to save intended Nazi victims.

John William Pehle was a Midwesterner, born in Minneapolis, educated there and in Sioux Falls, South Dakota, who matriculated at Creighton University in Omaha, a Jesuit college, where he was a Captain of ROTC cadets and received a bachelor of philosophy degree. Graduating in 1930, he went on to Yale Law School and entered the Treasury Department as general counsel in 1934.

Randolph Paul, exulting ten years later in his friend's promotion to run the WRB, declared, "It gives us reason to hope that the Board isn't going to be another stuffed-shirt ladies' aid society . . ."

Soon, conservative Republican Charles Taft, brother of U.S. Senator Robert Taft, groused that "Pehle was starting out like a bull in a china shop." The future mayor of Cincinnati's sour grapes perhaps stemmed from the fact he had been a rejected candidate.

The British, it might be said, were not "amused" by the divergence in American policy toward the Jews. *Benign neglect and paying lip service* had been their procedure heretofore. Their real *bête noire*, however, was fear that doing anything constructive about the problem would lead to increased floods of Jews seeking to enter Palestine. Now, with straight faces, they insisted the main Anglo concern was the effect the new agency could have on an old ineffective group set up at the Évian Conference in 1938 called the Intergovernmental Conference on Refugees, which had lain essentially moribund since the British Foreign Office was essentially opposed to it. Suddenly, though, in 1944, this rump group's continued existence became His Majesty's Government's excuse to try to stymie the threatening activism of the War Refugee Board.

Even before his appointment, Pehle had already displayed his aptitude for getting things done. Tasked with having to rush a copy of the president's executive order to the Bureau of the Budget for funding plus a draft message to Secretary Hull for transmission to Samuel Rosenman, FDR's speech writer, he had to travel from his home in Bethesda into the city. But the car that Secretary Morgenthau had arranged for him mysteriously failed to arrive. So he hurried by public transportation and met his deadlines.

Prior to Pehle's official installation, liaisons were already being established with other D.C. entities. Most important was the War Department, whose boss Secretary Stimson would be one of Pehle's superiors. A request for cooperation was answered politely but pro forma, with the caveat that only as military operations permitted could they assist.

On February 5, three days legally into his new position, John Pehle might have been more encouraged by a personal letter he received. It contained congratulations from Boy Scout Troop #326 of Washington, D.C., whose correspondent Ben Kohn explained the Troop collected autographs and they wanted his.

By February 8, more than ne hundred letters had been sent to *private* groups, seeking their cooperation and suggestions.

Aware of complications that might ensue with the Intergovernmental Committee on Refugees, Pehle, smart bureaucrat that he was, assigned his closest aide Assistant Director Lawrence Lessing to do a thorough report on the IGC, now that the WRB opponents like the British were saying the IGC should do the job instead.

And with Pehle once ensconced in office, the pace picked up. On February 11, an irate Pehle contacted Undersecretary Stettinius at the State Department to complain that cables had been sent to U.S. diplomatic Missions abroad in neutral countries requesting information about refugees in their locales and recommendations for helping them, and after more than two weeks none had responded. He demanded they be wired again and *answered!* This, of course, was not exactly the way things were done at the leisurely State Department pace.

In fact, foot dragging by State Department officials had already been evident on that same day of February 11, 1944, when State's European Division objected to a note Pehle proposed sending to the British Embassy. They suggested strongly that he rewrite it in diplomatic parlance, to wit that the War Refugee Board "finds itself unable to agree with the British position regarding the issuance of a declamation relating to the murder of Jews." Then, the EUR, as dubbed at State, expressed in hissy-fit tones that they were "unable to understand how the plight of the Jew can be ameliorated through an argument with the British government."

Symptomatic of Pehle's realization of his need for outside help in overcoming such haughty attitudes was a dinner party with prominent national opinion makers held in New York City on February 17. The host was Morris Ernst, an Alabama-born prominent Jewish lawyer in Manhattan and a cofounder of the American Civil Liberties Union. Among the attendees were public luminaries like Helen Reid, whose family owned the *New York Herald Tribune*, Quincy Howe, a director of the ACLU and chief editor of Simon and Schuster, Russell Leffingwell, a banker and the board chairman of the Carnegie Corporation, and J.P. Morgan Investor, who was also head of the Foreign Affairs Council, plus Samuel Grafton, a columnist for *The New York Times*, and George Fielding Eliot, staff writer for the *Herald Tribune*, magazine contributor and well-known broadcaster.

They were joined after dinner by Harriet Pilpel, a partner in Morris Ernst's law firm and her husband Robert, who was representing the Joint Distribution Committee, destined to be the major private financial backer of the new agency. Pehle reported that after dinner "the Ernsts, the Pilpels and I called on Dorothy Thompson . . ." the acerbic but widely read and quoted journalist/broadcaster whom *Time* magazine cited as the *second most influential woman in America next to Eleanor Roosevelt*. Pehle described a conversation they had with her about psychological warfare. "Dorothy said it was very important to make it clear not only that we are watching the Germans who commit atrocities but we are also taking note of the Germans who refrain from engaging in such activities."

The next morning, Pehle was in touch with Louis Dolivet of the Free World Association, who was rumored to have ties to the French Underground.

Two days prior to the official release of FDR's executive order, a document entered in the War Refugee Board's files on January 20, 1944, authorized the new agency to accept private funds under Title XI of the Second War Powers Act. That formality done, the organization was allowed to use the donations for their own activities and not have to deposit them willy-nilly into the general Treasury pot.

Much earlier still, the foremost of their donors, the American-

Jewish Joint Distribution Committee, had been working with refugees. Operating since 1914, when it was inspired by Henry Morgenthau Sr., the Treasury Secretary's father, the "Joint" was estimated to have helped more than eighty thousand Jews to asylum between 1939 and 1944. Already in December 1943, they had agreed to borrow one hundred thousand Swiss francs for relief efforts in Shanghai, China, to which numerous Jews had fled. In her book, *Ghetto Shanghai*, author Evelyn Pike Rubin wrote that the Joint had been "relentlessly pressuring [the U. S. Government] for permission to transfer funds" for the refugees in Shanghai, of which she had been one, but "it was not until the beginning of 1944 that this permission was granted."

Furthermore, on New Year's Day 1944, the Joint made one hundred thousand Swiss francs available to Saly Mayer, the head of its Swiss operations who lived in Saint Gall, to be used for Jewish children trapped in France, and a month later two hundred thousand more Swiss francs were released. Meanwhile, the World Jewish Congress was also communicating to its operatives in France and Romania that the Union of Orthodox Rabbis had likewise entered the picture.

There was some initial handwringing in American-Jewish quarters over this setup whereby the War Refugee Board had been granted a mere one million in government dollars from the President's Emergency Fund. Skimpy as this seemed, it had to be accepted since otherwise any money would have to come from Congress, and getting an appropriation could take months. Still, on February 14, Henry Montor, executive vice president of the United Jewish Appeal, told his superior Moses Leavitt at the Joint, of which UJA was a component, how he worried his group would be blamed for having "urged this reliance on private funds." The UJA was then embarking on a thirty-two-million-dollar campaign for ALL Jewish charity in the U.S. and abroad.

The plot was thickening. The British, possibly chastened by the response to their snootiness, decided a different tack. They released information on February 18, 1944, to Secretary of State Hull, kept under wraps for more than three months, dated September 9, 1943, about their willingness to admit refugees to Palestine who had escaped into Turkey and other neutral countries. The belated news was being sent "in strict confidence" only to Hull, FDR's confidante Myron C. Taylor, and the U.S. ambassador to Turkey, Laurence Steinhardt. Somehow that news also ended up on John Pehle's desk.

Mid February saw the fledgling agency turning out 150 letters a day. The word was spreading. Pehle's romancing of press gurus and high-powered publicists was starting to pay off. Laurence Steinhardt (incidentally one of the few Jews high up in the Diplomatic Corps) was informed that an important private citizen, Ira Hirschmann, a vice president of Bloomingdale's department store, would be arriving in Ankara soon, having left for Turkey on January 25. The War Refugee Board, Steinhardt was informed, had designated this well-known businessman and advertising expert to be the "Acting Special Representative of the War Refugee Board." Concurrently, the State Department had named him a "Special Attaché on War Refugee Matters." It was made clear, however, that Hirschmann would be directly accountable to Ambassador Steinhardt.

Following the obligatory input of titles, a pithier paragraph assured the Ambassador: "So far as the Trading With The Enemy Act is concerned, the Secretary of the Treasury has vested in the War Refugee Board and its Representatives in the field full authority to communicate with enemy territory to carry out the purposes of the Order [Executive Order 9417]."

The story broke in *The New York Times* on February 20, 1944.

Its headline proclaimed:

REFUGEE AID CHIEF AT WORK IN TURKEY

The subhead perfectly fit the image Pehle was trying to project.

HIRSCHMANN CUTS RED TAPE
AS HE MAPS PLAN TO HELP OPPRESSED EUROPEANS

The reporting then started: "Jesse Herzog, Chief Rabbi of Palestine, at present in Ankara, got out a sick bed [influenza] to greet Ira Hirschmann, Bloomingdale Vice President, who has arrived to take up his duties as official representative of the newly formed War Refugee Board. Mr. Hirschmann went to work within half an hour of his arrival in Ankara."

It was commented that "Mr. Hirschmann will be the first and only U.S. citizen in Turkey to disregard the Trading With The Enemy Act."

The story goes on: "Asked if he had an idea of the enormous difficulties he would face, Hirschmann replied: "Certainly no one more than I realize how complex and intricate is the task undertaken by the War Refugee Board. I expect to encounter great obstacles to my work. I expect help not only from individuals and organizations but from the entire civilized world."

With that ringing declaration, the overseas adventure of the War Refugee Board was publicly launched.

One more voice should be added here. It came in the form of a letter from the small city of Piqua, Ohio, north of Dayton. The writer was an elderly gentleman named Arthur Werner and enclosed was a check for ten dollars, plus the explanation that he and his wife were old now and not able to do much work, so this was all they could afford. Also included was the fact that in Germany on *Kristallnacht* in 1938, he had been arrested by the Nazis and interned at Buchenwald, where he'd experienced firsthand the concentration camp's horrors. Released, he and his wife, God be praised, had been able to find refuge in the United States.

It was the War Refugee Board's first donation.

Chapter Two

In 1944, I was twelve years old. It was a year in which I was edging toward teenagehood and like a patriotic young American, doing my small part for the war effort by collecting scrap materials, like paper, fats, and flattened tin cans. Our family, I should add, at 5 Grasmere Road in the section of Brookline, Massachusetts, then called South Brookline and later Putterham, was also growing a lush Victory Garden.

Of my Jewishness, I was well aware. Already, with the advent of my thirteenth birthday looming in the following July, I was preparing for the most momentous event in a young Jewish boy's life—his *Bar Mitzvah*—whereupon he is ceremoniously inducted into recognized membership in the Hebrew community. My parents had arranged for me to have a private Hebrew tutor, and Mr. Korinow patiently taught me the letters of the Hebrew alphabet and drilled me endlessly on the portion of the Torah I would have to recite at the synagogue. Rote was the important thing. I didn't understand a single word of what I was intoning.

The latter half of 1944 was when Burton Bernstein, who would become my best boyhood (and afterward) friend, entered our seventh grade class at the Edith C. Baker School. I had returned after several months of attending school in Miami Beach, and my classmates excitedly informed me: "We have a new kid in school, and he has a famous brother."

"Who's his brother?" I naturally asked.

"Leonard Bernstein," they answered.

"Never heard of him."

But soon I was properly impressed by reading a piece in *Time* magazine about "Lenny's" dramatic emergency conducting of the New York Philharmonic.

The Bernstein family opened a wider perspective on my Jewish heritage than I received at home. The father, Samuel J. Bernstein, had been born and raised in Russia, and his Yiddish-tinged English immediately revealed the fact. My family and their friends were all first generation Americans and spoke like everyone else did in the Greater Boston area—with *Boston accents*. Sam Bernstein, I should add, was such a fiery Zionist that several years later in 1947 he chided fifteen-year-olds Burtie and myself for not leaving high school to go fight for Israeli independence. Yiddish words and expressions like *farblondzhet* and *Rovno Gubernia* were added to my vocabulary.

My brief winter stay in Miami Beach put me in touch with Jewish kids from other parts of the U.S., and I knew others, too, from the Jewish summer camp I went to in Casco, Maine. No memory I have remains of any discussions amongst ourselves of the plight of the Jews in Europe. We knew they were being persecuted, and we were asked to pray for them at our religious services. But as for any connection to those suffering coreligionists, they might as well have been on another planet.

One small exception was the presence in our South Brookline neighborhood of two German Jewish brothers, Peter and Werner Goessels, living with a local family. Since Peter was older than me and Werner younger, I didn't have much to do with them. Years later, I saw a film made by Peter's daughter depicting how the two boys had made it out of Germany, were sheltered in a mountainous Protestant region of France and taken eventually to Massachusetts. All this happened *before* the War Refugee Board was formed.

In those years when I was growing up in the 1930s and even during the war, anti-Semitism was rife in the United States. I was not shielded from it in the prosperous suburb where I lived, populated mostly by lace-curtain Irish and an increasing number of Jews. We in our patch of South Brookline did not really feel its sting—maybe a few nasty words here and there when an angry goy playmate might call you a "dirty Jew." But these guys would also take me to the rectory of the Catholic church, where I would play ping-pong with the priest. It was mainly in sports when we took on other Brookline schools, particularly those in poor areas, where the problems lay. We started competitive baseball teams in the sixth grade. The tough mean kids we hated to play against were from the Lincoln, Pierce, and Heath Schools. Fistfights broke out. Once we Jewish kids had to escape from a mob chasing us hollering for our blood. And it was wartime and America was fighting the Nazis and yet—

Not until the concentration camp photographs penetrated the American public's consciousness did the situation ameliorate, it seemed.

If apathy and lack of curiosity on this juvenile level in Jewish communities was so rife, it had to betoken a vast unstated measure of what John Pehle and the War Refugee Board were up against.

Historians who are not necessarily apologists for FDR have pointed to his early aversion to letting his opponents charge that he was pushing America to war primarily for the sake of the Jews. In fact, Roosevelt *was* pushing America to war after 1939 but keeping his intentions secret. The "cripple in the White House" has been deemed a *political genius*. Wasted time and wasted lives notwithstanding, the president was soon accepting plaudits for his tardy action.

John Pehle had had almost a decade of experience in the D.C. bureaucracy. He effortlessly moved within clearly defined markers of what he needed to do from a policy standpoint. The immediate problem to be addressed was amorphous, rooted in the country's still-lingering ambivalence toward the Jews, despite more than two years of war against the Axis. The big bugaboo had always been to counter the Nazi claims that Americans were dying for the *a-priori* evil Jews. Yet the Jews were *special*. They were being slaughtered wholesale on the grounds of that very reason, that they were Jews, and notwithstanding the U.S. State Department's attempts to keep the news "unconfirmed," the death camps were an established if not widely known fact.

On February 2, 1944, Pehle contacted his WRB Assistant Secretary Lawrence Lesser and assigned him to prepare a written justification for *special* attention focused on the Jews.

Unsurprisingly, its opening sentence was: "Nazi persecution and the threat of extermination is not limited to Jews." Mention was made of Poles, Ukrainians and other Slavs. But then, the text goes on to say: "There are indications, however, that the slaughter of the Slavs is not quite so indiscriminate as that of the Jews." Hitler's killers were targeting the upper levels of non-Jewish leaders—intellectuals, doctors, lawyers, professors, military officers, etc.—but their populations, themselves, were not being killed wholesale like the Jews. The conclusion Lawrence Lesser drew was: "It would seem the Jews constitute a special problem requiring the consideration of the [War Refugee] Board."

Further elucidating, Lesser recommended: "I strongly urge that before going much further, the WRB call a conference of representatives of each and every private organization engaged in relief and rescue work and of each and every one of the fast multiplying self-constituted 'Save the Jews' committees." They would be asked for "specific written statements" of what they would do if they had the WRB's powers. Otherwise, Lesser warned, the WRB "will find itself wrapped up in a maze of intrigue, politics and fault-finding," and that that those groups might be inclined to use the WRB "as a scape-goat for their own ineffectiveness."

Voices were raised against the president's saying anything at all and in such unforgiving language. The branch of the U.S. Office of War Information in London issued a veiled public declaration that: "In regard to the President's SPECIAL REFERENCE to the persecution of the Jews, it does not give the impression that his denunciation was limited to this subject alone or especially aimed at it."

Robert T. Pell, representing the State Department, also objected. He "challenged the wisdom of the [War Refugee] Board's program for a propaganda offensive against the Germans." It should be pointed out, though, that he was connected to the European Division, EUR, a hotbed of reluctance to help the Jews.

On March 5, Morgenthau okayed the proposed proclamation warning the war criminals. The next day, it went to Undersecretary of State Stettinius, and he took it to Steve Early of FDR's staff. On March 7, Morgenthau had an appointment with FDR. He told the chief executive that "Pehle and his boys were doing a great job" and then raised the matter of the declaration. Apparently, he had to ask three times.

FDR's hesitation had several sources. The State Department was still nattering on about the need to clear such a message with the British. Roosevelt, himself, had told Ed Stettinius that "the declaration referred to the atrocities against the Jews in too pointed a manner." He also insisted it be called a "statement" not a "declaration."

Such fine-line dicing always has a definite logic in politics, yet the *statement* or *declaration* or *condemnation* or *threat*, whatever it should be called, did become public on March 24.

The previous November, there had been a Joint Declaration on War Crimes coming out of the Moscow Conference of the Allied Powers that October. Inexcusably, it did not mention Jews at all but did cry over peasants executed on Crete who were victims of the Nazi occupiers of their island. Roosevelt was reminded that "the Germans are half convinced that it is relatively safe to murder Jews."

Essentially, only one paragraph of the new issuance did mention the Jews.

After considerable verbiage about the non-Jews under attack, Franklin Roosevelt launched into the following: "In one of the blackest crimes in all history . . . the wholesale murder of the Jews goes on unabated every hour . . . and hundreds of thousands of Jews who while persecuted have found a haven in Hungary and the Balkans are now threatened with annihilation by Hitler." At the end of the document, the president issued a stern warning: "All who knowingly take part in the deportation of Jews to their death in Poland or Norwegians and French to their deaths in Germany are equally guilty with the executioner."

It wasn't much, but it was something of a breakthrough.

James Byrnes, who became secretary of state under Truman, was said to have referred to "those little bastards at the State Department" after reading a memo initialed by one "Jimmy" Dunn. If so, the coterie on the third floor of the rococo building that housed the European Division would have been apt fodder for anger. The names, now known but then of faceless obstructionists working under Assistant Secretary Breckinridge Long, were James Dunn, R. Borden Reams, Ray Atherton, Howard Travers, Avra Warren, and Wallace May.

Let us take up Dunn first, because he was closest to Secretary Hull as his "political advisor." Not because he had once slipped his diplomat's cool and made the ill-considered crack, on the occasion when Breck Long lost his powers to deal with visas: "That Jew Morgenthau and his Jewish assistants like DuBois are trying to take over this place." Born in Newark, New Jersey, educated privately, Dunn seemed the epitome of the sophisticated socialite WASP, given the long list of exclusive clubs to which he belonged and accented by the site of his final resting place—West Palm Beach. A full-length photo of him in his early thirties shows an impeccably tailored supercilious-looking young man, wearing an elegant black overcoat, black homburg and rep tie, posing on a set of stone steps presumably outside the State Department building.

Incidentally, Eleanor Roosevelt called Dunn "a Fascist." Yet on December 11, 1941, four days after Pearl Harbor, it was Dunn, in effect, who offered the official U.S. Government reaction to Germany's declaration of war against the United States. His comment that the U.S. had "long expected Germany to carry out its threat against the hemisphere and the United States" was carried by newspapers throughout the nation. Also that the Italian declaration of war had been "fully anticipated."

Dunn, in time, was being listed as the "second-ranking member of the State Department," and it was his initialed memo to Secretary of State Byrnes that had elicited the "little bastards" remark.

A James Clement Dunn Award for Excellence is among thirty-two State Department recognitions. It is given for "excellence, intellectual skills, managerial ability and personal qualities" for employees at the midcareer level. The winner not only gets a certificate signed by the secretary of state but he or she also pockets ten thousand dollars.

R. Borden Reams appropriately comes next in this high-level rogue's gallery. The R stands for Robert, but he was universally referred to as Borden Reams. A balding, moon-faced person with a brush moustache and grim mouth, he has been described as "more Grotty" (stuck-up) than any graduate of the ultra-exclusive Groton School in Massachusetts, which was FDR's alma mater.

Borden Reams was born in Luthersburg, Pennsylvania, in farm country, and held various sales and managerial jobs before passing the foreign service exam. In 1942, the State Department assigned him to the European Division (EUR). Tagged a "major force in anti-refugee activities," Reams modestly referred to himself as a mere "master sergeant." However, the unthinkable might well have happened in his case. Among those mentioned as possible leaders for the War Refugee Board, the name of R. Borden Reams had made the list. A witless editorial in *The New York Times* actually made the suggestion. This man has been accused of having watered down the UN War Crimes Declaration and of fighting a proposal to rescue the Jews trapped in Transnistria, a part of Ukraine occupied by Axis ally Romania.

Even after the War Refugee Board had been in operation for almost six months, Reams was still pounding the drum of shielding the American public from news of the Holocaust in progress. The touchstone of his policy was in *withholding* the State Department's confirmation of history's greatest war crime. His qualification for doing this: he bore the technical title of "specialist on Jewish matters at the EUR Division." By the way, it was his name that appeared on the snotty memo about how Jews could not be helped by "an argument with the British government," and most likely he had authored it.

His actually voiced *raison d'être* was against increased pressure to do something more specific to aid these people. He labeled any action, even any mention, to be "a danger."

It was a sure red flag that nothing would be done at the Bermuda Conference in 1943 when Reams was assigned by State to be the secretary to the American delegation.

A year later, in a conversation with Meier Schenkolewski, representing Agudath Israel, a worldwide organization of Orthodox Jews, Reams could not contain his outrage over a visit by three of its member rabbis to him in D.C., asking even at this late date that something concrete be done. One of them, Reams ranted, had actually faked a faint. But his real ire was directed at Rabbi Baruch Korff, from a congregation in the small Massachusetts city of Taunton near the Rhode Island border. Reams, in his temper tantrum, declared he "would not be an anti-Semite," but he would never "lift a finger any more for a Jew in matters of rescue since his experience with Mr. Korff."

A frontal photograph of the terrible Rabbi shows an oval-faced, friendly looking man with a pointed chin and an ineffable sense of strong personality about him. He had been five years old in Ukrainian town of Novohrad-Volynskyi when he saw his mother shot to death during a 1919 pogrom, which as if in a forecast of things to come, the U.S. State Department at the time, abetted by Breckinridge Long, denied had happened. His father, Grand Rabbi Jacob Korff, took the survivors across into nearby Poland, where young Baruch received part of his education at a Yeshiva in the *shtetl* of Korets. By 1926, the family was settled in America, but young Baruch went back to Korets to be ordained. Later, he took an advanced degree in Jerusalem before returning to the U.S.

Outspoken, eloquent, although his English not learned until age fourteen had a distinctive Yiddish intonation, he played an active leadership role in lobbying the State Department for action to save the imperiled Jews still alive overseas. Actually, he was to become better known to history as "Nixon's Rabbi," the sole major Jewish cleric to defend our disgraced president.

It is easy to see how Rabbi Korff had unnerved Borden Reams.

As reported by Rafael Medoff in his 2009 book, *Blowing the Whistle On Genocide* (7), Korff fearlessly took on Reams' top boss, Secretary of State Cordell Hull, in a testy exchange. The courtly, silver-haired, normally affable Tennessean was described as absolutely "frigid" at the outset of the encounter. He began with a slashing attack on the columnist Drew Pearson, who in a radio broadcast had made public the complaints of "certain rabbis" about egregious inaction by the State Department in helping save a group of Orthodox clerics under great threat from the Nazis.

Addressing himself to Korff at a meeting in April 1944, Hull angrily declaimed: "Do you know that I am the nominal head of the War Refugee Board and no one is going to tell me how to run it."

Unfazed, the Rabbi shot back: "I had hoped you would be that in fact and not just nominally."

Hull, still spluttering, barked: "No one is going to intimidate me."

Trying to be respectful, Korff continued: "If I may, Mr. Secretary, I will give you a dozen instances when your subordinates, without cause, have overridden the president's directions and made a mockery of your own good intentions."

At the conclusion of their tense back and forth, Hull softened. He helped clear a matter of telegrams that had been held up for six weeks and asked "What else is there to be done?"

The Rabbi gave him an example of a situation in Spain that needed straightening out and cannily emphasized that Mr. (Breckinridge) Long, Mr. (Adolph) Berle and Mr. (James) Dunn "should be apprised of your interest."

Borden Reams, if he were not present during the confrontation, no doubt heard of it soon enough. Then, as we have seen, he was so asinine as to pontificate that due to Korff he would "not lift a finger" to aid any Jew, whereas he had never lifted a finger theretofore nor would he ever in any event.

In a riposte years later regarding R. Borden Reams in the book *America's Soul in the Balance,* author Gregory J. Wallance opined, "Rarely has an historical non-entity done so much damage to this country's moral stature (5)."

Ray Atherton was Borden Reams' immediate superior at the European Division. He was born in my hometown of Brookline, Massachusetts, went to Harvard, spent time in Paris where he earned the nickname of "Beau of Beaux Arts," joined the Foreign Service, was sent to London and caused a flurry when the king objected to his overly English style of attire. His Majesty thought Atherton's "Bond Street topper, Savile Row cutaway, cream-colored gloves and Malacca stick" more than a bit too much and said he wanted "America represented by an American, not an imitation Englishman."

When FDR entered office, Atherton found himself transferred and sardonically labeled *sotto voce*, "the only American diplomat ever removed for 'excessive foppery.'"

Nevertheless, despite his offending garb and his privately voiced contention that FDR's New Deal had kept America "on the dole" for a decade, he was retained at the State Department, served as minister to Bulgaria and later held the same role in Denmark, where he observed the German occupation on April 9, 1940.

Staying on in the conquered Scandinavian country until the end of 1941, he returned home to replace the aristocratically named Jay Pierrepont Moffat as the acting director of the European Division. In the brief window of time Atherton had in his powerful D.C. post—before succeeding Moffat as U.S. minister to Canada (the first since our northern neighbor received autonomy from the British) and leaving D.C. during that year and a half—he managed to do a good deal of harm to Europe's Jews.

There should be a gasp of horror accompanying the revelation that Ray Atherton was at the helm of the European Division when the *first inkling of the Nazi extermination policy reached D.C.* Here we are speaking of the information relayed by telegram from Bern, Switzerland, by Dr. Gerhart Riegner, a German Jewish refugee representing the Joint Distribution Committee in the neutral Alpine country.

It was in the summer of 1942 that Riegner learned from a German manufacturer Eduard Schulte what was taking place in Auschwitz not far from Breslau, where the secret anti-Nazi lived. The contents of the telegram Dr. Riegner sent after meeting with Schulte in Bern seemed utterly fantastic. *The Nazis were methodically murdering thousands of Jews daily with poison gas!!!*

Whether the pushback campaign to debunk the "rumor" was deliberately (if secretly) elaborated or was simply an instinctive fabrication is anybody's guess. A smart operator like Ray Atherton would be sure not to leave his prints on any incriminating document. Nonetheless he did allow his initials on a cable sent overseas that was to become a *cause célèbre*. True, while certainly no friend of the Jews, Atherton had also been depicted as "lazy" and "gossipy," inured to the slow rhythms of operation in his part of the bureaucracy. Delay, for Ray, was a form of action.

Accompanying his R. A. on the infamous cable wired to Leland Harrison, the U.S. minister in Bern, was the message that would come back to haunt its senders (who included Borden Reams). It would have been prime evidence of intention in a murder trial. It baldly stated: "In the future we would suggest that you do not accept reports submitted to you to be transferred to private persons in the United States unless such action is advisable because of extraordinary circumstances."

It didn't say to investigate further. It plainly said, if not in these exact words: *Sit on the stuff.*

Unbeknown to those who were trying to suppress even the intimation of such a human-inflicted catastrophe, the invisible gestation period of the War Refugee Board had begun.

Once the news reached Rabbi Stephen Wise, the primary Jewish leader in the U.S., Atherton was urged by Borden Reams among others to convince the Jewish cleric to squelch or at least minimize any publicity about mass murders. Thus, the acting director of State's European Division could more easily be frankly dismissive of the alleged news. Responding to his boss, Under Secretary of State Sumner Welles, Atherton baldly stated that the deported "Jews would be put to work for the German war machine just as Poles and Soviets and other prisoners of war were."

On the strength of this prevarication (or maybe Atherton believed what he was saying), Welles signed his name to cablegram 354.

Who knows what further damage Ray Atherton could have wreaked while he headed up the EUR Division? His leaving the post seemingly prematurely could easily be explained, however. It was a promotion. Jay Pierrepont Moffat, the Ambassador to Canada, had died suddenly at the age of forty-seven. Atherton was picked as his replacement for this plum job.

This happened in the summer of 1943. Earlier that year, Ray Atherton had been involved in another bit of scheming that had gained him the opprobrium of "the man who arranged for an anti-Semitic French Nazi to become Governor-General in liberated North Africa where he maintained Nazi laws that discriminated against Jews." The designation may be overstated but in essence involved a French Vichyite named Marcel Peyrouton, who actually had been France's minister of the interior under the Pétain regime.

However the request for Peyrouton to work for the Allies had come from Robert Murphy, the U.S. representative in North Africa. At the time, the erstwhile Vichyite was serving as the French ambassador to Argentina. Atherton may well have worked on his transfer to Algeria where General Henri Giraud, the archly conservative but anti-Nazi military figure had been installed by the Americans and British. Working for him, Peyrouton did not immediately repeal the anti-Jewish laws installed under Vichy. Shamefully many Jews remained in the camps where they had been interned.

A famous French law, the nineteenth century Crémieux Decree, had long ago given Jews in North Africa the status of French citizens. Ironically, it was Peyrouton as Vichy's minister of the interior who had abrogated it in 1940.

Back in the seat of power in Algiers by the beginning of 1943, Peyrouton made no immediate move to reinstate the Crémieux Decree. Thus, the North African Jews, although eventually released from the camps, were still juridically considered *stateless* persons. Their Kafka-like existence continued in this fashion until De Gaulle's people moved in and Peyrouton was arrested. Considered an ultimate *opportuniste* by the French, he spent five years in prison.

The ruse used by "the little bastards" had been diabolical, to say the least. It was made to seem that Peyrouton had been requested to run Algeria by General Dwight Eisenhower, himself. Later Ike said he'd never heard of the guy. What role Ray Atherton had played in this flimflam has never been unearthed. True to form, he left no fingerprints.

Neither as notorious as Borden Reams and Ray Atherton yet equally iniquitous was Howard K. Travers.

An upstate New Yorker, Travers had worked himself through the State Department ranks to head of the Visa Division when, in 1943, he admitted the consulates in Madrid and Barcelona were holding up visas for refugees who had been approved. Promising to look into the matter, he could only blithely report six weeks later that he had no response from his inquiry. Nor did he have any news two weeks later. A suspicion that the Visa Division under Travers was a party to this disgrace would not have been amiss.

But State Department officials were nothing if not circumspect.

A consular official who had served with Travers in Hungary, named James Bonbright, aptly demonstrated this characteristic when later discussing Travers during an interview (9). In Budapest in 1941 before Hungary declared war on the U.S., Travers was first secretary and consul, the number-two man, and Bonbright stated "the office ran smoothly under him." Nevertheless, referring to the fact that Travers for some reason had acquired the nickname of "Purse," he could not forbear slipping in a "catty remark," i.e. that Travers "reminded me of the old adage that you can't make a silk *purse* out of a sow's ear," and after a cautionary tale about a colleague's career ruined by insulting a superior, he added: "We kept that very quiet."

There were occasional exceptions to this consular ironfistedness. Bonbright mentioned a woman named Agi Jambor, half Jewish, for whom "we were able to get visas and she got out finally through Sweden and got over to the States." His postscript was that she married the movie actor Claude Rains, "who beat her," he claimed. This marriage, in any event, one of six for Rains, lasted no more than a year.

Prior to Travers as head of the Visa Division, the post was held by the oddly named Avra Milvin Warren, a Virginian born in Maryland. He acted as Breckinridge Long's right-hand man in the task of denying U.S. entrance visas to European refugees, of whom Jews were the majority and the most desperate.

A Rabbi Max Nussbaum, an escapee from Berlin, characterized Avra Warren's role in the Visa Division as "the greatest misfortune for the Jews in Berlin. Warren sabotaged the procedure . . . was responsible for the deaths of hundreds of Jews . . . delayed giving already granted visas until the person was taken off to a concentration camp."

These State Department types were good at what we now call catch-22. For example, giving an okay to the erection of a refugee camp in liberated French North Africa but refusing to allow refugees to go to it. They claimed there was no marine transportation available for carrying refugees to the U.S., while American vessels going to Europe were sailing home empty. Nor could the refugees take advantage of transport unless they had assurances from the military, which they knew the military couldn't give. Potential emigrants were asked: "Are you Jewish by race or faith? Have you read Tolstoy? Would you call yourself a Socialist?" The crowning example of their malignity might have been achieved with a Czech soldier in the English Army, evacuated from Dunkirk, who sought help to get his wife and children out of his German-occupied homeland. "Why didn't you go back to get them?" his inquisitors demanded.

Statistics show the influence of these policies as practiced by the State Department. The immigrants reaching the U.S. and the percentages of quotas they filled under the 1924 law were:

1941: 28,927—47.6%
1942: 11,702—19.2%
1943: 5,944—9.8%
1944: 5,606—9.2%
1945: 4,793—7.9%

Admittedly, the war was a factor in keeping the numbers down. The problem of saving Jews and other Nazi enemies might have been thrust on the back burner in any case, even had it not received the complicit and eager support it did from State Department personnel. In this regard, lesser players not already mentioned like Paul Culbertson and Elbridge Durbrow and Robert Brandin can be cited. But the actual statistics of two hundred thousand saved attributed to the War Refugee Board in its short existence offers proof of what could have been done if the will were there.

After a year at the Visa Division, Avra Warren was made minister to dictator Trujillo's Dominican Republic and replaced by Howard Travers. It took two more years before the War Refugee Board could break the logjam that had been created.

As soon as the WRB was established, letters began pouring into John Pehle's office, mainly but not all congratulatory. One from a Miss Rose Bardack of Camden, New Jersey, reached him on January 27, 1944, only five days after the issuance of FDR's executive order.

"It is especially gratifying," she wrote, without any acknowledgment of the lateness of the act, "that the American government has been the first to hear the cry of these tortured human beings . . . I know that for all time my people will remember the name of Franklin Roosevelt with gladness and thanksgiving."

The American Jewish Congress called the action "an act of great historic significance."

Peter Bergson (Hillel Kook) the prime agitator for something to be done, told Pehle in a letter: "You now head civilization's battle against massacre."

Aage Birn of the Royal Norwegian Ministry of Foreign Affairs, with whom Pehle had previously worked at Foreign Funds Control, wrote to him from London of his delight and received a "Dear Aage" letter in return.

Congressman Manny Celler sent congratulations.

Another Foreign Funds veteran, Verne B. Lewis, chimed in as well.

The Jewish Labor Committee, representing five hundred thousand Jewish trade unionists, offered their support.

Pehle's Creighton University classmate Louis M. Shauck, executive director of the Yale Jewish Center, was heard from and an extended communication went on with another friend from his past, Ensign J. R. Johnston, Fleet Air Wing 4, San Francisco, Fleet Post Office, whom Pehle called "Dick." The first letter reached him from overseas on March 19, 1944, and Dick Johnston told him he originally heard of his appointment from his wife and then ran across the story in the *New Republic* of February 11. "It seems to me," Ensign Johnston told his old buddy, "this country, which should be taking a position of leadership in helping war refugees has done criminally little so far in this field." Then in a more gossipy collegial fashion, he added: "Elizabeth and Roger are in Los Angeles, living with Elizabeth's folks and unable to find an apartment."

Pehle had sent him copies of the press release and FDR's statement, and in Dick's return letter were his thanks and that he had heard from Buzz and "he tells me that you have many of the old gang working with you."

Another friend of Pehle's, also in the Service, Irwin Seibel, sent greetings to him and also best wishes to Florence Hodel, the indispensable secretary whom Pehle had brought from Foreign Funds Control.

Roger Spencer was yet another of the gang who contacted John Pehle. He was with the American Friends Service Committee, the Quaker organization that would play such a strong part in the efforts that the War Refugee Board was about to unleash.

No time had been wasted by Pehle in gearing up, and the news was spreading.

On February 4, 1944, *The Jewish Comment*, the magazine of the World Jewish Congress, another group soon to play a major role supporting Pehle, ran an extensive article on the new agency. It printed the full text of FDR's executive order issued less than two weeks earlier and editorialized on it as "an historic act of statesmanship which marks a turning point in the attitude of Western democracies to the problems created by Hitler's extermination policy."

"The WRB," the article continued, "will surpass the previous policy of only dealing with Jews who have escaped to neutral countries but also to participate in assisting such escapes, as well as to extend relief to persons in danger of death." Continuing on this note, the article emphasizes: "Of particular importance is the clause (in the Order) instructing the State Department to appoint on the recommendation of the Board 'Special Attachés' with diplomatic status to be stationed abroad in places where it is likely that assistance can be rendered to war refugees."

The blueprint had been set.

Chapter Three

And, moreover, within less than two weeks, Ira Hirschmann, the vice-president of Bloomingdale's department store, the first of those *special attachés*, was en route to Ankara, Turkey, to take up his not very specified duties.

Ingenuity, ability to improvise, tenacity and sheer grit were to mark the work of all of the War Refugee Board representatives. Ira Hirschmann was an example of what in Hollywood they would call "off-beat casting." He was no dashing cloak-and-dagger type steeped in overseas adventure but rather a successful imaginative business executive, an accomplished pianist, indefatigable music lover, and dabbler in New York City politics as a supporter of Fiorello La Guardia.

In fact, his first hurdle in taking on the assignment of the WRB's first envoy abroad was to convince his boss at Bloomingdale's to allow him a six weeks leave of absence to go to Ankara, Turkey. When Walter Rothschild, the acting president of the department store said he couldn't be spared, Hirschmann decided to go "whatever the consequences." Later, he was to praise Rothschild and the Federated Department Stores, the overall owner, for their fairness in paying his salary, even as the six weeks stretched into months.

Getting to his destination was decidedly not half the fun. From the time he left the U.S. on February 4, 1944, it took practically a whole month before he stepped off his train in Ankara to be greeted by U.S. Ambassador Laurence Steinhardt and Joseph Levy of *The New York Times*. Meanwhile, he had stopped in Natal, Brazil, Ascension Island, Accra on the Gold Coast of Africa, spending an entire week before getting to Cairo. Welcome to the Middle East. He discovered the Turks had not even issued him an entrance visa. While cooling his heels in Egypt, he learned to ride on a camel but more importantly bummed a ride on an RAF plane to Palestine. Gazing down at the Egyptian "land of Goshen," the Sinai, which "looked barren and abandoned," he was soon cheered by the sight of green, "an exciting reminder of the Land of Promise." Once in the future state of Israel, he met the president of Hebrew University, Dr. Judah Magnes, to whom he had a letter of introduction given him by his friend Arthur Sulzberger, publisher of *The New York Times*, and met other prominent Jews in the Holy Land, such as David Ben-Gurion, Moshe Shertok, and Henrietta Szold, the founder of the Hadassah Women's group, whose family he had known in his hometown of Baltimore. He learned he was the first U.S. representative in the area "with the funds and authorization to effectuate rescue operations from enemy territory."

In point of fact, he barely had time to catch his breath once he'd arrived in Ankara. No sooner had he settled into his quarters than two young Palestinian Jews appeared at his door. "Quick!" they said. "You must come with us. We can save some Jewish children, but we must act immediately."

The hot bath he was about to take had to be left for the future, and he hurried with the two of them to a house nearby. "Some of the players, obviously Turks, looked like characters from the pirate stories of my childhood," he reported.

There was a spate of Middle-Eastern-style haggling and finally an agreement was reached. The price was set at three hundred dollars per child.

Hirschmann was to comment that in his department store career he had bought and sold everything, "but how do you set a price on a child . . . let alone a Jewish child marked for death?"

Over the next eight months, he and "The Boys," as he called his supporters, were to buy fifteen thousand men, women and children.

During a moment of reflection following his first *purchase* of Jewish children, Hirschmann may well have looked back in wonder at how he'd landed where he had.

First his mind might have flashed back to a trip he took to Germany in August 1932. In the city of Weimar, he came upon a crowd outside a meeting hall and went inside where a political gathering was being held. The speaker he saw was, in his own words, "a wild-eyed moustached man with an inappropriate resemblance to Charlie Chaplin." Yet there was nothing comical about this figure. "His appeal was magnetic and maniacal eyes fixed on each individual in the audience, gripped and held them."

The strange but dynamic person was, of course, Adolf Hitler.

Hirschmann must have paled when he heard the demagogue rant that he would liquidate the Jews—"Not only in Germany but all over the world" and realized, as he put it, "He was talking about me."

Hirschmann later would write: "Hitler had forced another realization on me, an awareness of myself as a Jew." When he wrote a piece in *The New York Times* saying, "the little man with the moustache must be stopped," he was upbraided by Adolph Ochs, the distinguished newspaper's publisher, for holding "intemperate and extreme views."

But his attitude was only reinforced by a subsequent trip he took to Austria in 1938, shortly after the country had been joined to Germany in an infamous *Anschluss* vote. "I saw Austrian Nazis in a frenzy of animal enthusiasm," which reminded him of "a bloodthirsty posse as a prelude to a Negro lynching in our own South." This "isolated excess" in the U.S. represented something he was witnessing "wholesale" in Europe. The futile Évian Conference of 1938 that he attended as an observer simply added a new milestone on his ultimate voyage to a War Refugee Board assignment.

Once America entered the war, Ira Hirschmann gained direct experience in refugee matters through his involvement in setting up the University in Exile in New York City to employ renowned European academics who had found haven in the U.S. He also was on the War Labor Board and the War Plants Board. On top of all that, he strongly and vocally supported efforts in Congress for a presidential commission "to effectuate plans of immediate action to save the surviving Jewish people of Europe from extinction at the hands of Nazi Germany."

Regarding Turkey, the eventual pipeline to it for him may have been sparked at a meeting he attended of the Emergency Committee to save the Jewish People of Europe. There he encountered Mrs. John Gunther and Peter Bergson, who told him: "Turkey would be an ideal base for rescue operations." Their group wanted to go there but had been blocked by the State Department.

As a take-charge guy, Hirschmann went to confront the major person who was standing in the way, Assistant Secretary of State Breckinridge Long. This hard-nosed Missourian asked him skeptically how he thought he could do anything for refugees, as he was at the time a single private person acting on his own. Hirschmann retorted that once he was on the scene seeing the actual problems, he would devise a plan. Somehow this logic convinced Long to cable Ambassador Steinhardt that a well-known New York businessman would be travelling to Ankara at his own expense. However, the creation of the War Refugee Board intervened, and the solo trip was canceled. But before long, Hirschmann received a phone call from Oscar Cox telling him he'd been chosen the War Refugee Board's initial representative overseas covering Turkey and the Middle East. He then went to Washington and met John Pehle, who impressed him greatly as "a handsome, intelligent man of about 36" and "a key figure in a collection of young energetic aides" at the Treasury Department. Hirschmann called Pehle "a brilliant choice for one of the toughest of wartime assignments."

In a preview of the enormous obstacles he would face, Pehle showed a large wall map and pointed to Transnistria, a sliver of territory once belonging to Ukraine but which the Nazis had given to Romania, and described it as "Death Valley," where of 170,000 Romanian Jews interned there, only 70,000 still remained alive.

Before his hurried departure, Hirschmann also had time to confer with Secretary Morgenthau, Felix Frankfurter, Ben Cohen, Isador Lubin, and Harry Hopkins, all advisors to Franklin Roosevelt. Warning Hirschmann he might encounter resistance from the British, Lubin, who was head of the Bureau of Labor Statistics—special statistical advisor to the president with an office in the West Wing and a prominent member of FDR's "Brain Trust"—handed him a slip of paper on which a single word was written. "If you get in a jam," he told the neophyte WRB agent, "cable that word to me at the White House."

This bit of spy mystery stuff was to prove invaluable.

Hirschmann likewise managed prior to his departure to meet the top leaders of the country's American-Jewish community at the home of Judge Joseph Proskauer, yet another of FDR's intimates. Collectively, these men would prove to be crucial to the funding of his mission.

One ghost haunting the rescue operation scene in Ankara was that of the *SS Struma*, a chartered Greek vessel that in December 1941 left Constanţa, Romania, with 769 Palestine-bound refugees aboard. She was actually an old river barge that had previously carried cattle. The plan was to anchor in nearby Turkey and await their Palestine certificates. Once in Turkey, however, the authorities would not let them disembark and they were kept on board in squalid conditions for seventy days.

It has been claimed that the trouble was not enough money paid in bribes. To make matters worse, the British refused to give them certificates to Palestine on the grounds these fleers of persecution were Romanians and thus enemy nationals. Then on February 23, 1942, the Turks forced the ship to leave port. A day later, out on the Black Sea, the *Struma* was ripped apart by an explosion, either that of a mine or torpedo. All but a dozen of the would-be salvation seekers perished.

Hirschmann's own maiden experience with a ship of this nature was the *SS Milka*, also out of Constanţa. Once more, the Turks had refused to let passengers go ashore.

With Hirschmann having enlisted the help of Ambassador Steinhardt, the two Americans pressured Numan Menemencioğlu, the Turkish foreign minister, to make an exception for the *Milka*. In this high-tense drama, some headway was finally achieved. The foreign minister allowed the *Milka* to tie up and the Jews to disembark, but with conditions. They would have to be put in sealed railroad cars and taken to Syria and from there presumably to Palestine. Along with Dr. Joseph Schwartz of the Joint Distribution Committee and *New York Times* correspondent Joe Levy, Hirschmann watched the transfer at Haydarpaşa, a port on the Asiatic side of Istanbul. The latter, more flowery than usual, would comment: "This was a new pilgrimage, the march of people redeemed to new homes, new hopes and the promise of a bright future."

Other ships followed successfully: the *SS Maritza*, the *SS Ballacitta* and the *SS Kazbek*.

Soon afterward, a trio of new ships headed from Constanţa for Istanbul: the *SS Marina*, the *SS Bulbil*, and the *SS Mefküre*. Once more, Hirschmann awaited them, watching with satisfaction as the *Marina* docked and disgorged its human cargo, then worrying about the *Bulbil*, which was struggling amid rough seas. Wise now to the ways of the area, he paid a bribe to the Red Crescent (Muslim equivalent of the Red Cross) to send a message to the captain of the *Bulbil*, telling him to head for the nearest shore and not try to make it to Istanbul. He next dispatched a convoy of ox carts to pick up the passengers. Hirschmann, himself, was not allowed to greet them, but one of The Boys was allowed to do so.

Yet what of the *Mefküre*? With the arrival of the *Bulbil* came the awful news that the *Mefküre* had been sunk on the Black Sea by a submarine, possibly German but possibly also Russian. On board the *Bilbul* were a handful of the few survivors of the doomed vessel.

Badly shaken by this experience, Hirschmann cabled Secretary of

State Cordell Hull, asking to be replaced as the WRB representative. Send someone stronger, less emotional, he urged. Hull wired back for him to stay where he was and continue the work of his "little Dunkirk," evacuating those in peril of their lives.

The Turkish rules once the ships landed were that no one, including Hirschmann, could talk to the passengers as they moved directly into trains bound out of the Ottoman country.

Sarcastically, Hirschmann later wrote: "We would violate Turkish security to learn more of the hardships suffered by these people as well as their aspirations."

He was particularly "struck" by one of the young refugees he encountered, thirteen-year-old Polish-Jewish Motek, whose story was epic in its proportions. "I shall never forget the first boy who was brought to me in a small apartment in Istanbul by Chaim Barlas of the (Palestine-based) Jewish agency," he wrote. The lad had been walking for five years across Europe, having started from his native village when he was eight years old, after he saw his mother and father murdered. He ran off with his little sister who was caught by the SS and brutally killed. He, alone, escaped, hiding in a barrel of cold water, standing upright all night, his head sticking out just enough so he could breathe. Then, discovering the Nazis had gone, he fled the devastated *shtetl* and headed he knew not where.

During his flight, he had among other things the incredible adventure of taking refuge inside a concentration camp. Since the German authorities had no record of him, Motek was able to slip out as easily as he'd slipped in. Reaching the Slovakian border, he met members of the underground who helped him reach Hungary, where he joined a group of children led by a beautiful nineteen-year-old girl. Alas, in leading her charges to safety, she was caught by the Germans and hanged. Motek carried a picture of her he kept close to his heart, as did the other kids she'd saved.

Hirschmann thought of attempting to adopt the boy, bring him to America and give him a new life. But the complications and red tape he would incur seemed too daunting. Motek left for Palestine with his companions.

Much of the success stories like that of Motek could be credited to The Boys, Hirschmann insisted. These were Haganah (Jewish Secret Army) volunteers, who specialized in working behind enemy lines. They were not only fearless but fluent in various languages and had established contacts with Germans, Hungarians, Bulgarians, and Poles. They were parachuted into Nazi-occupied territories to facilitate the escape of intended victims of the Hitlerians. Their work was the most dangerous imaginable, and they suffered numerous casualties.

Nor were they exclusively "The Boys." There were "The Girls" among them. Two became noted martyrs. Hannah Szenes, Hungarian, caught in Hungary on June 7, 1944, after having returned, who was shot by a firing squad on November 7, 1944. Refusing a blindfold, she faced her killers unflinchingly. Also losing her life was Haviva Reik who'd been sent into Slovakia to help Jewish children escape to Hungary, which was then a sanctuary until occupied by the Nazis in mid-March, 1944. Run by British Intelligence, the parachutist outfit similarly had as its mission locating Allied airmen forced down and assisting them to get away and return to the fight. Out of the one unit that had twelve of its thirty-plus members captured, seven were executed. Male names like Rafael Reiss, Zvi Ben-Yaacov, and Abba Berdiczew were added to the fatalities. An Italian Jew, the Zionist Enzo Sereni, whose father was the king of Italy's doctor, had helped organize the group and at the age of almost forty, also jumped, was captured and died at Dachau in November 1944.

In Ankara, which had displaced Istanbul as the capital of Turkey in 1923, Hirschmann's work went smoothly—but only for a while.

The first six shiploads of refugees that managed to land safely were dispatched to Palestine without difficulty. The key to the operation was the visas for entry into the Holy Land that the British provided.

Then, without warning, the pipeline mysteriously clogged. Arriving at the British Embassy in Ankara to pick up the certificates for the seventh ship's passengers, Hirschmann was informed that the visas had been lost, presumably in the mails. But the British minister in charge, one Sterndale Bennett and his man in charge of refugees, named Knox Helm, seemed utterly unconcerned if not pleased about the matter and blithely disregarded the American's consternation.

So infuriated was Hirschmann by the two Britons' smugness that he rushed back to his own embassy and sent a cable to Isador Lubin at the White House. It contained merely a single word—the word that Lubin had penned on the sheet of paper he'd given him. It was, indeed, a magical word!

Overnight, the British attitude changed. Knox Helm informed him the visas had been found and he would cooperate with Hirschmann's work. Then, reluctantly, it still seemed, he handed over the package of missing visas. Upon receiving it, the WRB representative archly remarked how the British must have such wonderful eyes to spot it in the immensity of the Middle East.

The word that Hirschmann sent has never been identified but the immediate action it spurred was that Lubin rushed to see FDR, who contacted Prime Minister Churchill and got "Winnie" to intervene.

The key word in Turkey for opening doors, needless to say, was *baksheesh*, actually in the local language meaning "extra," but in plain language *outright bribery*. It posed problems for government accountants in Washington trying to keep track of Hirschmann's expenditures. So when D.C. sent Hirschmann five million dollars worth of gold sovereigns, he was told he didn't have to keep an account of it.

Ambassador Steinhardt wisecracked they should use it to start a poker game. But having such a sum in coinage did present a real problem, especially considering the shakiness of Turkish banks. Thus, they buried the hoard. As it turned out, Hirschmann never had to use the hidden treasure. For far less than five million dollars he was able to rely on private donations, mostly from Jewish organizations, to continue his work.

This can-do attitude of his followed into other arenas. When he had trouble placing Jewish kids to get them out of Turkey, he hopped a plane to Palestine, met with Henrietta Szold, and she said, "Bring them all here," and pledged to oversee the effort. Finding Ankara a cultural wasteland, he set about organizing a quartet to play Mozart and Beethoven. In addition, this was upstaging the German ambassador in Ankara, the wily Austrian Franz Von Papen, who had brought in Walter Gieseking, "the Nazi pianist."

The next item on Hirschmann's plate involved what was happening to Jews in Romania. More than 170,000 of them had been shipped across the Dniester River to the narrow land strip of Transnistria. Three large concentration camps had been built there by the Romanians after the territory was taken from Ukraine and given to them by their Nazi allies. The names of Bogdanovka, Domanovka and Acmecetca do not immediately invoke the horror of Auschwitz, Treblinka and Bergen-Belsen, but they were just as deadly and thousands of Jews—some transported from the nearby Odessa region of Russia but the majority of Romanian citizenship—died within their confines of hunger, disease and bullets. When told he could do nothing about this, Ira Hirschmann acted characteristically. He jumped into the fray.

Before leaving America, he had on his own contacted Carol Davila, the prewar Romanian minister to the U.S., then in exile, who gave him a letter of introduction to Romania's minister to Turkey at the time, Alexander Cretzianu. Obtaining a waiver from the Trading with the Enemy Act, since Romania was currently at war with the United States, Hirschmann employed a Swiss citizen, Gilbert Simond of the Red Cross, to act as intermediary. A meeting at Simond's home was arranged for an appropriate neutral setting in which Hirschmann and Cretzianu could privately confer.

The bargaining was swift and personal.

The American offered visas for Cretzianu and his family to enter the U.S., if in exchange the doors would be opened to the Jews left in Transnistria to go back to Romania. The bargain was accepted.

Hirschmann had spoken of "kids fed on bullets, not butter," and on a return visit to Palestine, he was eager to see "kids I had put on the train in Istanbul."

When his swap was successful, Hirschmann called it his best business deal ever—trading four visas to rescue one hundred thousand people. But here is where a confusion of numbers occurs.

Were there that many Jews left in Transnistria? One figure published was that 75,000 Jews had perished in Transnistria; another that the number of their deaths was 130,000. Or another set of figures quoted a wide spread between 115,000 and 180,000 liquidated. At the start of World War II, Transnistria allegedly held 311,000 Jews. All of Romania had 756,000, of which about half survived the war. Transnistria was described as a "killing field for Jews." For Gypsies, too. Also, in particular, Transnistria was home to a large number of *Volksdeutsche*, Germans who had emigrated to the region, and they formed killer bands to supplement the SS and Romanian fascists in their massacres.

The Holocaust author Raul Hilberg called Transnistria "a prolonged disaster." Other figures spoke of 50,744 Jews alive in 1943 before departing from Transnistria and of 65,000 Jews being shifted from place to place within that territory. The Red Army reached Transnistria in mid-March 1944, a month after Hirschmann's arrival in Ankara.

The handwriting on the wall as the Russians advanced had no doubt aided Hirschmann in his dealings with his Romanian counterpart in Ankara.

The WRB especially focused on assisting Romanian Jewish children who had remained alive.

A photo exists showing Jewish kids of both sexes but mostly girls leaving their orphanage at Domanovka on their way to Romania proper. Pictured surrounding the orphanage director, a Mr. Felstein, some of them identified: Klara Sandman, Malka Burstein, Henia Mogilenski and two known only as Raaya and Llya. The date was February 28, 1944. A human face was put on innocents who had been condemned to death but hopefully were among the lucky few who outlasted their tormentors.

Testimonies exist, too, of those caught in the giant deathtrap of Transnistria and, unsurprisingly make for grim reading.

"We came to Obodovka," wrote Goldiak Wolf, one of the survivors. "There we met Levis Zamia and his wife and many people from Kishinevski Street . . . They pushed us into a stable instead of the animals where we suffered from the terrible cold . . . to this Hell the wretched and miserable of Giurgiu, Romania also arrived."

It was in stables like these that many Jews were burned alive when the buildings were set on fire and they were kept locked in.

Bella Rot, another survivor, described Yom Kippur in Scazinets, another of the Axis holding pens in the giant killing field of Transnistria: "Throughout the camp, the silence of a graveyard and a stifling feeling prevailed . . . in the building were distorted people, some of them completely naked, some covered with rags . . . we entered the long, clean hall in which the stench of death also lingered . . . in the depths of the hall stood a holy ark made of four planks of wood . . . we sat down among the worshippers, some of them so bloated we could not recognize them, almost dying." A touch of Jewish gallows humor was interspersed. The victims said they were all fasting that day. "Suddenly a tall, desiccated male figure appeared with the face of a skeleton . . . it was the rabbi. The entire congregation gathered there prayed and cried with him."

When the Hirschmann-Cretzianu negotiations were nearing an end, the Romanian touched a sore spot for the American. "Why didn't you come sooner?" he asked. "You could have saved more lives."

Although in no way responsible for the American government's delay in accepting a rescue mission, the pioneer American abroad for the War Refugee Board felt guilt. "Then and there I resolved never again to indulge in hesitant mercy," Hirschmann wrote in his memoirs. "All who said it was a hopeless mission were wrong, pessimistically and unimaginatively wrong." He somehow blamed himself for the tardiness.

He still had unfinished business in Romania. There were five thousand Romanian Jewish children awaiting transportation to Palestine and ships were needed to carry them across the Black Sea.

Pressuring the Turks, Hirschmann was able to charter the *SS Tari*, a French-built 4,050 ton passenger ship, for $175,000. Helping him to negotiate for its lease was a maritime expert, Myron Black, sent by the U.S. War Shipping Board. The *Tari* normally carried nine hundred passengers. Hurried carpentry added five hundred additional spaces.

However, the key sticking point was to be able to obtain safe-conduct flags for the revamped vessel. All belligerent nations agreed to honor them, except the Germans. Hirschmann enlisted his Swiss friend Gilbert Simond who was a Roman Catholic to approach the German Minister Franz Von Papen, also of the same faith, to see if he could get the Third Reich to agree. Before leaving on a trip to the U.S., Hirschmann received word that Von Papen had promised to help.

Also there had been a mess in Bulgaria he had attended to through the assistance of another American whose last name was Black—Dr. Floyd H. Black, the president of Roberts College in Istanbul. The problem was that since Bulgaria had joined the Axis, the forty-five thousand native Bulgarian Jews had been subjected to Nazi-type Nuremberg laws that deprived them of everything except their lives and were left destitute. The refugee ship *Maritza* on its return from Istanbul had been sunk, and the Bulgarians refused to release any further vessels to carry refugees.

Dr. Black had earlier been president of the American College in Sofia, Bulgaria, for eighteen years and, in Istanbul, served as a specialist in Bulgarian matters for the U.S. consul general. With his help contact was made with Nicholas Balabanoff, the Bulgarian minister to Turkey, and once again the home of Gilbert Simond furnished a meeting place.

The encounter was not a slam-dunk for Hirschmann. Balabanoff was tough. His goal was an end to Allied air raids on his country. His attitude was not friendly since his government was now run by the pro-Nazis. Nevertheless, the two men scheduled another meeting.

In the meantime, the government in Sofia changed to "one more temperate than its predecessor." Hirschmann's demand was for a letter from the regime promising to repeal its anti-Jewish laws. The American, though, had to settle for half a loaf. The new Bulgarian administration declared it regretted those Nuremberg-type laws and at *the opportune moment* would repeal them. Meanwhile, although the regulations remained in force, they would do away with "all arbitrary methods in the application of these laws and other restrictions."

Dissatisfied, Hirschmann decided he would now push for "saving the entire persecuted population inside Bulgaria."

By then, he had received an assistant from the WRB office in D.C. His name was Herbert Katzki, and he had previously worked for the Joint Distribution Committee. Together they focused on prodding the Bulgarian Government to call its puppet parliament into special session and wipe those laws off the books. Once done, there would be no need for the Bulgarian Jews to leave their homeland. Hirschmann's conduit in this case was Dr. Black's wife. Her father had been a Bulgarian general.

Despite a rebuke from, where else, the State Department, for seeming to meddle in what might be postwar problems such as seeking action from the Bulgarian parliament, Ira Hirschmann received a warm welcome in Washington from his chiefs, "who were overjoyed by his progress." Morgenthau and Pehle wanted him to return to Turkey immediately.

Since they likewise wanted him to remain on staff, they arranged to obviate the leave of absence problem by *drafting* him into service.

Unfortunately, bad news from abroad reached Hirschmann in D.C. The *SS Tari* hadn't sailed. Von Papen had reneged in a fit of anger because Turkey, seeing how the war was going, had stopped shipping chrome to the Nazis to be used in the manufacture of hard steel.

There was bad news from Hungary, as well. The Germans had overthrown the government of Admiral Nicholas Horthy and installed a puppet of their own, Ferenc Szálasi, the leader of the violently anti-Semitic Arrow Cross party.

Two loose threads were thus left hanging on Hirschmann's watch. But here we will leave him until his return to Istanbul, since now his counterparts had been established in other neutral countries and were having adventures and frustrations as dramatic as his own.

Chapter Four

So far, the War Refugee Board had gotten off to a good start. It still had to dodge and weave amid the pitfalls of Washington and remain ever vigilant. Turf battles occurred then behind the scenes inside the Beltway, just as they do now. Myron C. Taylor, close pal of FDR's that he was, had been put in charge of the Intergovernmental Committee on Refugees, resurrected after the 1943 Bermuda Conference fiasco. In the name of *collaboration*, Taylor proposed to Pehle that all communications of his new agency be routed through his intergovernmental committee—an age-old political power play that ensures control. Pehle, easily dodging the bullet, said only he would keep the IGC informed.

It was the ineffectuality of the IGC that initially tainted the WRB. "Oh, no, not another bunch of bureaucrats to waster our tax money!" was an obvious cry. The *Chicago Daily News*, although not as right wing and isolationist as the *Chicago Tribune*, editorialized against it. True haters were also heard from. A letter brim full of anger was sent by a W. D. Fuller of Philadelphia. He was upset about "hordes" of refugees flooding into the U.S. In fact, he was opposed to any and all immigrants and raved: "To dilute our population any more is apt to bring about serious consequences."

However, offsetting Mr. Fuller and his ilk were letters like one from Miss Belle Fenstock of Washington D.C., which enclosed the sheet music of *Song of the Refugees* that she called a "song of hope . . . a song of appropriateness with the work of the War Refugee Board."

The lyrics were by Otto Harbach, the Utah-born son of Danish immigrants, who is considered one of America's great lyricists, working with composers of equal stature such as Jerome Kern, Vincent Yeomans, George Gershwin, and Sigmund Romberg. His lyrics began:

I heard a refugee's prayer as he lay weeping alone,
God of my fathers, oh where are the days and the ways I have known?
Where are the works of my hand?
And the fruits of our dear, dear land?
What foreign soul must I sow?
That my daily bread might grow.

. . .

Refugees rise in your might

. . .

Free men will answer your call.

Or from Louis Fisch of Brooklyn, offering a tract of 550 acres near Pocono Summit, Pennsylvania, as a haven for refugees.

Or from the Federation of Bessarabian societies of America: Explaining that there are one hundred thousand citizens from Bessarabia (a portion of the USSR presently annexed by Romania) and in their name wished to express "our profound appreciation for the creation of the War Refugee Board" and predicted its results "will undoubtedly be recorded as one of the Humanitarian chapters in the history of the United States." The two signers were Sol Serwitz, president, and H. Silverman, secretary.

It has been stated that 850,000 letters in support of the WRB were addressed to President Roosevelt and transmitted to Pehle et al.

There was even a letter from Howard K. Travers, the hard-bitten State Department nativist formerly in control of visas, saying, "Whereas I am no longer charged with any responsibilities concerning refugees, I am, of course, interested to assist the Intergovernmental Committee, the War Refugee Board and other organizations to save the lives of persons living under the threat of death by Hitler." No hint of sour grapes, no mention of Jews, but a show of diplomatic acumen by its total implied inclusion.

The rest of *the little band of brothers,* so to speak, in addition to Ira Hirschmann, had been assembled as rapidly as possible in bureaucratic Washington. Roswell McClelland for Switzerland, Robert C. Dexter for Portugal, Leonard Ackerman for North Africa, Iver Olsen for Sweden, James Mann, an assistant executive director of the WRB, later sent to Spain . . . these were all men with experience overseas, strong personalities, mostly non-Jews. Like John Pehle and his crew in D.C., they were *take-charge* guys used to acting on their own.

As always in politics, a few intentions were thwarted. A special attaché for the Soviet Union had been contemplated, but this never worked. The hope was to mobilize Russian influence in Bulgaria to help safeguard that fellow Slavic nation's native Jewish population and even down the line possibly use the Soviet's policy of deporting Germans from territory occupied by the Red Army as a counterweight to stop the death camp deportations of Jews by the Nazis.

Schlomo Aronson in his book, *Hitler, the Allies and the Jews*, perceptively pointed out that the "very birth of the War Refugee Board in January 1944" could have been viewed by the Nazis "as a challenge to the Final Solution itself." Yet on the opposite side, Jewish expectations might have been raised too high. The author pointed out that "the War Refugee Board was born into circumstances and attitudes that were not essentially changed from those of several years before."

We will follow those overseas special attachés as we have with the starting adventures of Ira Hirschmann in the Balkans and Middle East and witness their triumphs and failures counterposed to the enormous obstacles they faced. That they accomplished anything at all with the odds so heavily stacked against them is not a miracle but a testimony to their devotion to a humanistic task of unthinkable magnitude.

Were this fiction, the story could be deemed a *passion play* of sorts— half a dozen battlers who personified Good against monumental Evil, backed up by little more than two dozen support personnel in the home office on the Potomac.

Even before the official release of FDR's executive order, the news had travelled around. The Jewish Labor Committee founded in New York in 1933 to rescue Jewish leaders and scholars from Germany's new Chancellor Hitler had been getting Swiss visas through close contacts in Switzerland, Dr. B. Tchemlov of the International Red Cross in Geneva and Dr. L. Hersch, a professor at the University of Geneva.

A meeting in Geneva to help the Jewish Labor Committee, whose top officers were Adolph Held of the Amalgamated Clothing Workers Union Bank and David Dubinsky of the International Ladies Garment Workers Union, was reported to Pehle in a letter dated February 16, 1944, from Held. It contained a paragraph that read: "It is our firm conviction that with the aid of the President's War Refugee Board, the rescue of people from France into Switzerland may be greatly expanded and thousands more Jews and anti-Nazis rescued."

The Jewish Labor Committee had also been working with Dr. A. Freudenberg, a representative of the Protestant Churches and with the Hungarian Social Democratic Party to evacuate people in danger from Poland into Hungary. The letter continued: "Here, too, with the help of the President's Refugee Board and the Hungarian anti-Nazi underground, the evacuation process can be accelerated and thousands more refugees rescued."

It might seem a bit odd that removing Polish Jews from Poland to Hungary would constitute a rescue, but at that moment in time, Hungary had not yet come under the Nazi thumb. Prime Minister Miklós Kállay supported Hungary's joining the German assault on the Soviet Union, but as that war was turning sour, he secretly signed an agreement with the British that if Hungary surrendered, it would be to the Western Allies, not to the Soviets. Word of this putative deal was leaked and Germany invaded Hungary early in March 1944, setting up a puppet regime headed by the Arrow Cross Party, as viciously an anti-Semitic movement as the Nazis, possibly even worse though not as well organized in their mass murdering. An underground resistance, particularly against the Arrow Cross, had been slowly building and was soon battling the homegrown fascists and the German occupiers, causing them to keep several divisions of troops in Hungary that should have been spared for Russia. One of the underground's leaders was János Kádár, who after the German defeat became prime minister.

The WRB's net kept spreading. Leon Dennen of the American Jewish Labor Committee suggested the WRB contact the International Rescue and Relief Committee (IRRC) on West 43rd Street in Manhattan. It's chair was Frank Kingdon, a prominent New Jersey clergyman and president of the University of Newark and his members included Dorothy Thompson and another nationally known journalist William Allen White of Kansas. The nonsectarian organization was a member of the National War Fund (which the American Jewish Labor Committee was not) and had "considerable money available for rescue work."

On February 23, 1944, a notice went out from Pehle overseas to "Dear Mike"—Michael J. Hoffman, Allied Forces Headquarters Civil Affairs Office—that the War Refugee Board "was planning to designate Leonard Ackerman as their North African representative."

Two days later, Pehle (still acting director) told the State Department that David Blickenstaff would be the WRB's man in Spain. However, cooperation on the matter was not forthcoming from the State

Department's top official in Madrid, U.S. Ambassador Carleton Hayes. This lengthy dispute would end with James Mann leaving his post in Washington at the WRB and taking over in Spain on a trial basis. James J. Saxon, later to be U.S. controller of currency, but then a "roving problem solver" overseas for the Treasury was originally offered to Hayes but turned down by the ambassador, the only one at the designated postings to give the War Refugee Board a hard time.

While appointments for overseas agents (technically special attachés to embassies) were continuing, the World Jewish Congress on March 3, 1944, responded to Pehle's request for ideas with a proposed "Program of General Measures of Relief and Rescue of Jews Threatened with Extermination by the Enemy." Among other things the text stated: "On the way to the rescue of the remnants of European Jewry, many a Gordian Knot will have to be cut" and that the situation had "immensely changed for the worse," since the World Jewish Congress representatives in Geneva first acquainted the U.S. minister in Bern with the facts relating to the extermination of the Jews of Europe.

Attention was drawn in the WJC's communication to the fact that "steady contact" had been established with Congress and the headquarters of the War Refugee Board in Washington with the WRB's representatives in Geneva, Lisbon, and Stockholm. Gratitude was expressed for the "frequent, sometimes daily" consultations with WRB employees, and they named Lawrence Lesser, Dr. Benjamin Akzin, Paul McCormack, and I. M. Weinstein.

Originally, an official special representative from the WRB had been contemplated for the London embassy. The person under consideration was an American, a recent Harvard graduate and freelance journalist, Varian Fry, who had made a reputation for helping anti-Nazi refugees escape through Vichy-controlled southern France. These were prominent figures in European public life, in the arts, the sciences, and political affairs. They were writers like Hannah Arendt, Arthur Koestler, and Franz Werfel, painters such as Marc Chagall, Max Ernst, and Marcel Duchamp, the sculptor Jacques Lipchitz, the renowned Polish Jewish pianist Wanda Landowska, the film director Max Ophüls, the Nobel Prize winning scientist Otto Meyerhof, and lesser-known leaders in their fields. It has been estimated that 2,200 persons were helped to escape, primarily via Marseille and also with aid of visas provided by the sympathetic American vice-consul in that

French port, Hiram Bingham IV, whose father was a powerful U.S. senator from Connecticut.

After Fry was expelled from France by the Vichyites, the State Department sought his services but he turned them down and eventually threw his support behind the scenes to the War Refugee Board. (The London post was never established.) His frank analysis of the situation was, as he put it, "We can offer asylum now, without delay or red tape, to those few fortunate enough to escape from the Aryan Paradise. There have been bureaucratic delays in visa procedures, which have literally condemned to death many stalwart democrats."

In other words, as he declared, "The War Refugee Board meant business."

It should be noted that in the postwar period, Fry was the first American to be named "Righteous Among the Nations," at Yad Vashem, Israel's national Holocaust Museum, and he was also awarded France's highest decoration, the *Légion d'honneur*, as well as the Eisenhower Liberation Medal from the U.S. Holocaust Museum. There is even a street, *Varian-Fry-Straße*, in today's Berlin.

Despite his valor and dedication, Fry was also a controversial figure, in part because of those very qualities. Another outspoken, tenacious person to welcome the War Refugee Board, Peter Bergson, has already been mentioned. His real name was Hillel Kook, and he used an alias so that his uncle, the Chief Rabbi of Palestine, would not be embarrassed by the activities of a member of the prestigious Kook family. Kook was not a U.S. citizen and in the United States from Palestine on a visa. His hard-hitting style of agitating for his coreligionists offended a number of American Jewish activists, and attempts were even made by them (including the top leader Rabbi Stephen Wise) to have him deported and in the end successfully so, but only after the war in Europe had ended.

On February 22, 1944, Peter Bergson gave a dinner for John Pehle. It was held in D.C. at the home of Mr. and Mrs. Ernest Lindley on Massachusetts Avenue and, as reported in the *Washington Post*, attended by many "diplomats and friends from Congress." Lindley, who was *Newsweek*'s D.C. bureau chief, had earlier written a column in the same newspaper on February 4, in which he stated: "For the first time the United States government has an operating agency under specific orders to do everything . . . to rescue victims of enemy oppression who are in imminent danger of death."

For several years, Peter Bergson had been a devoted—and pesty—
gadfly in the campaign to open America's consciousness about the
Nazis' deadly extermination plan for all Jews worldwide. This stepped-
up effort included a mass rally at Madison Square Garden attended by
forty thousand people. The pageant staged there, written by Ben Hecht
and starring film celebrities like Paul Muni and Edward G. Robinson,
then went on to play in five other major American cities—all of which
attracted a good deal of attention but no real action until after the War
Refugee Board was born.

Once the new agency was up and running, Bergson did not lessen
his crusade. Barely more than a month since the War Refugee Board's
inception, we find him on a business basis in John Pehle's office. The
report of their discussion began: "Mr. Bergson stated that his group
believed the stateless Jews of Europe and Asia and the Jews in Palestine
composed a 'Hebrew Nation' . . . and that Jews in the U.S. can be
descendants of this Hebrew Nation, but not members of it [because
they are not stateless]." After having worked as a statistician for the
Hadassah medical group in Palestine, Bergson had had his eyes opened
to Zionism at a 1937 conference of theirs in Warsaw. Staying in Poland
for several months afterward, he witnessed firsthand the plight of his
coreligionists in that increasingly anti-Semitic country. Accompanying
him at his 1944 meeting with Pehle was Eri (or Ari) Jabotinsky, the son
of Vladimir Ze'ev Jabotinsky, the famed militant founder of the group
Irgun Zvai Leumi, whose adopted Hebrew name appropriately means
wolf. Originally dedicated to the creating of a Jewish army, the fledgling
Irgun turned its attention to saving Jews from slaughter in Europe
and bringing them, legally or illegally, to Palestine. Both Bergson and
Jabotinsky were leading figures in the organization in America called
the Free Palestine Committee.

From my own experiences in State government, I know how
complicated matters can become in trying to stay on top of issues and
bring some order to ever-incipient chaos. John Pehle appears to have
been a cool customer, not easily given to anger nor even irritation. He
also knew that he, personally, not only his fledgling operation, would be
the target of verbal brickbats and misinformation. One such instance
of the latter two annoyances must have gotten his goat, yet he had a
forceful but politic response, not without its twinge of counterattack.

His comment concerned an article in the *Day Jewish Journal*, a
Yiddish-English publication by Dr. Samuel Margoshes on March

1, 1944. Pehle stated: "Based on a purported conversation between representatives of an anonymous organization and myself, which appeared in the *Forward* [the leading Yiddish newspaper's English edition] for February 26, 1944 . . . Since no such conversation ever took place," he went on, "there is no occasion for me to comment on the inferences, deductions and arguments that Dr. Margoshes makes on the wholly erroneous assumption that it did."

Dr. Margoshes wrote a column called *News and Views* for the *Day Jewish Journal.*

Brushing off such pinpricks as a necessary annoyance, the WRB forged ahead. Leonard Ackerman *did get* the assignment proposed for him to follow Ira Hirschmann into the roster of WRB's special attachés, and North Africa was a natural for him. He had already been working for the Treasury Department in the Maghreb (Algeria, Tunisia, Morocco). Plus Lawrence Lesser, John Pehle's chief assistant, was a friend of his, and in a letter to him, Ackerman wrote: "Mike Hoffman [another Treasury man] also asked me whether I was interested in the problem you are working on and of course I responded in the affirmative." He naturally added he would have to check with his superiors, "the boys upstairs." He also asked Lesser for suggestions informally for the part he might play "as official communications sometimes fail to convey the real feel of a subject." Apparently even before Lesser received his missive, Ackerman was given word that he had the job.

His correspondence, reports, etc. are the most voluminous of his fellow special attachés in the files of the War Refugee Board. They deserve a chapter unto themselves. Ackerman, in effect, covered a wide geographical extent of responsibility, not only the three North African countries-to-be but essentially the entire Mediterranean and, in particular, southern Italy and southern France.

A new addition to the WRB's presence overseas was Roswell McClelland, who after working for the American Friends Service Committee out of Geneva since 1942, moved with his wife Marjorie to nearby Bern, the Swiss capital. This was in early 1944 and, like Ira Hirschmann, he hit the ground running. Switzerland was in a pivotal spot, a neutral neighbor of Germany's, the scene of many negotiations and tolerated by the Nazis. Hitler knew that the Swiss, although speaking four different languages, would put up a ferocious, unified front should he order the Wehrmacht to invade, and so he left them alone.

The Switzerland in which the McClellands had been living for the past two years was not a *tabula rasa* for rescue activities. Since 1938, a Belgian Jewish businessman Isaac Sternbuch and his wife, Recha, had been living in Montreux and assiduously smuggling in Jews from Germany and occupied Austria next door. Isaac's brother Eli Sternbuch was also involved in their activities. Recha's role was so outstanding that she inspired not one but two books about her heroics. With the advent of the War Refugee Board, they "could receive donations from the U.S. and form closer ties to the American Embassy," where McClelland was stationed, and that resulted in increased rescue attempts.

Switzerland, because of its location, if nothing else, was a beehive of refugee activity, particularly as the war advanced inexorably toward its end. It was also a center for American intelligence's spying and cloak-and-dagger OSS work (Office of Strategic Services). Roswell McClelland found himself a very busy man, and his story will be told in detail as our chronology progresses.

Seemingly Sweden, on the periphery of Europe, would be a much quieter spot. That Iver C. Olsen whom the WRB dispatched there seemed equally as busy as McClellan was due less to the WRB workload than to the fact he was handling three jobs at one time. Sent by the Treasury Department to Stockholm as a finance attaché to study the economic conditions of the Scandinavian countries, he was to report his findings monthly to his superior Harry Dexter White in D.C. White was a special assistant to Secretary Morgenthau. His arrival in the Swedish capital shortly prior to Christmas 1943 occurred around the same time the War Refugee Board was being gestated. Soon Olsen, wearing his three hats—Treasury, U.S. Intelligence, and War Refugee Board representative—had to conduct economic surveys, arrange for Baltic refugee rescue, negotiate ransom offers from the Nazis, and anything else that came his way.

His reports home make for lively reading. He had a way with words that was not stiff and diplomatic but even verged on the sarcastic, except softened by his witty pen.

A pungent example was: "Heretofore, Sweden has been faced by a pointed gun from one direction and an extended lollypop from the other."

Or calling Sweden "Germany's most potent satellite," attacking their shipments to the Nazis of millions of tons of iron ore and railing at a fuss made of "shipping 20 tandem bicycles to blind veterans in

Finland but with nothing said about shipments of ball bearings to Germany."

There was light skewering of the Enskilda Bank, run by the Wallenberg brothers Marcus and Jacob (not cousin Raoul). The former of the two was considered strongly pro-Allied, while the latter was "entrenched with the Germans." Olsen's wry conclusion: "I note the Enskilda bank has its position well hedged."

Nevertheless, Olsen had faith enough in the Enskilda Bank to deposit two million dollars in the Enskilda for the WRB's use. Mostly provided by Jewish organizations in the U.S., the money was earmarked for a last-ditch effort to save what remained of Latvia's dwindling population. The addition of Latvia extended Olsen's responsibility to all of the Baltic area—Lithuania, Estonia, Finland—and even included Ukraine.

Next on the list of WRB's frontline warriors was Robert C. Dexter. Although he is basically connected with Portugal, where he became the WRB's representative in 1944, his work with refugees began well before that assignment. In an interesting book, *Rescue and Flight* by Susan Subak (15), the author credits Dexter and his wife, Elizabeth Anthony Dexter, with having saved her Jewish father's life by signing an affidavit for him to enter the United States. This was in 1938, following the Nazi takeover of Austria and a year before the outbreak of World War II.

Susan Subak writes that it was at the urging of their daughter Harriet that "the Dexters wrote the affidavit . . . the first they ever wrote. If their daughter had not pressed them to help my father come to the United States, the Dexters may never have had an interest in directly helping refugees (16)."

Harriet Dexter and Susan's father had met at a summer camp in England in August 1937. The following year, Hans Subak, after viewing a park bench sign in Vienna stating no Jews could sit on it, fled to Riga, Latvia, then as yet not under German occupation.

The Dexters, on a fact-finding trip to Europe, met with Hans and learned firsthand what was happening in Austria, and Robert sent a report back to the American Unitarians, with whom he and his wife were very active. It began: "The lot of the Jew in Austria is far worse than it ever was or is at present in Germany. Many go daily to Dachau the worst of the concentration camps, their families knowing in all probability their next word will be a brief form letter. 'Please come get the ashes.'"

Robert Dexter also detailed documented knowledge of the frustration of Jewish applicants who were unlikely to fit into the U.S. quota system, which the Unitarians viewed to be overly restrictive. From Vienna, alone, there were 65,000 applications, and all of Germany, now including Austria, had only 27,000 slots. Since émigrés were allowed only to take out ten or twenty marks, each applicant had to be guaranteed by an American that he or she would not become a public charge. He ended: "This is the problem the Friends are trying to solve" (through their American Friends Service Committee) and he signaled his hope that the Unitarians could also assist.

Back in Boston, the Unitarian international headquarters, Robert Dexter eloquently argued for the American Unitarian Association to set up a similar overseas operation. It would be patterned on the American Friends Service Committee, even to its name of Unitarian Service Committee, and work with the Quakers. His proposal was accepted after some discussion.

Thus, he and Susan entered their WRB position in Lisbon, Portugal, with a good deal of refugee handling experience behind them and also—secretly—a tie to the intelligence gathering of the OSS.

Although born in Nova Scotia, Robert Dexter was raised in Boston and formed part of its liberal-minded clergy. Susan Dexter came by her liberal predilections ancestrally. She was a great-niece of Susan B. Anthony, the famed women's suffrage leader and abolitionist.

When they took their post in Lisbon in the spring of 1944, the most immediate problem facing them was to free Jews who had come to Portugal without visas and been jailed. Some—those with money—had already been released and allowed to live in the upscale seaside resorts of Ericeira and Caldas da Rainha. But others were kept confined for long periods. There were six hundred Jewish refugees at the time in Portugal, eighty anti-Nazi Catholics, a smaller number of Quakers, and perhaps surprisingly, three hundred Unitarians, half of whom were Spanish.

These figures were contained in Robert's first report to James Mann back at the WRB headquarters in D.C. Later Mann would come to Spain and serve belatedly as the WRB representative, once the resistance to such a move by Ambassador Carleton Hayes was overcome.

No matter how noble the cause, it seems personal peccadilloes and egos enter the scene. The Carlton Hayes episode was a striking instance, and before we leave Robert Cloutman Dexter, in his Lisbon surroundings, there was another such flare-up between himself and a fellow Unitarian (and Bostonian) named Charles R. Joy. If the latter's name is recognizable, it is because this same Charles R. Joy was vetoed by the U.S. State Department for a role as one of the WRB's special representatives abroad.

Lisbon would have been an ideal site for Joy. Thanks to Dexter, he had done rescue work in the Portuguese capital beginning in 1940 and also paid visits to a Marseille office that he had had staffed. Both the Lisbon office and the Marseille office had been set up by fellow Unitarians the Reverend Waitstill Sharp and his wife, Martha, whose life-risking efforts to save stateless Jews won them recognition in Israel as Righteous Among the Nations (to date the only other Americans along with Varian Fry).

An unspoken power struggle may have been brewing between Dexter and Joy for several years. It burst into the open in June 1944, when Dexter and his wife accused Joy of "incompetence and dishonesty" and demanded the Unitarians fire him. Once these charges proved baseless, the tables were turned. The Dexters were fired and Joy became the executive director of the entire Unitarian Service Committee.

Notwithstanding which, Dexter *was* picked by the War Refugee Board to be one of their special attachés overseas and sent to Lisbon, where in the early days of the Unitarian Service Committee, he had worked for six months.

An ancillary addition to these WRB elite representatives was James J. Saxon, an Ohioan who joined the Treasury Department in 1937. His name has been mentioned earlier as having been rebuffed from coming to Spain by Ambassador Carlton Hayes, who wanted nothing to do with the War Refugee Board.

It is interesting to consider that if the derring-do of the WRB operatives in the field had been contemplated ahead of time, many folks would picture swashbuckling movie-type heroes outwitting the Gestapo and other Nazi thugs. The closest to filling that romanticized bill in reality, I can say with no hesitation, was James J. Saxon.

Prior to World War II, he had been sent by Treasury to the Philippines. As soon as Pearl Harbor happened, his assignment was to confiscate all Japanese holdings on those islands. They included six tons of gold and millions in cash and securities. With the Japanese breathing down his neck on Luzon, he burnt the cash and securities but was able to flee with the gold to Corregidor.

Once Corregidor was under siege, Saxon managed to transfer the hoard of gold into a U.S. Navy submarine and escape in an accompanying submarine.

From then on, his duties at the Treasury were to continue his swashbuckling (he was a handsome man and always fastidiously dressed, the perfect model for a future 007) as a "roving problem solver" in Hawaii, the Caribbean, Spain (finally), North Africa and Scandinavia. His final stop was Paris after its liberation, from whence he went tracing hidden Nazi wealth.

Toward the end of the war, Jim Saxon replaced Iver Olsen in Sweden, serving WRB—and OSS—in the guise of a financial attaché.

The tussle between the new War Refugee Board and the existing Intergovernmental Committee on Refugees was brief and, as we have seen, the WRB was able to free the handcuffs that Myron C. Taylor, FDR's pal, had wanted to clasp on him.

But there were some dicey moments. It is therefore instructive to hark back to an attack in a major big city newspaper only four days after the first announcement of the WRB's existence. It puts in perspective the final happy denouement that allowed the new kid on the block to proceed without a nasty territorial battle.

Helen Kirkpatrick was the hard-bitten foreign correspondent of the *Chicago Daily News*, stationed in London in World War II. In a piece dated January 26, 1944, she began not exactly tamely:

"American, British and Allied relief officials here [in London] appear to have been surprised and confused by President Roosevelt's announcement of the appointment of a War Refugee Board. Relief officials here saw the President's Board as cutting across both the Intergovernmental Committee [IGC] and United Nations Relief and Rehabilitation Agency [UNRRA]."

Then, she unloaded: "To date, IGC has not been able to accomplish a great deal—blaming non-European countries who won't take refugees. There is a belief that the new committee can convince South Americans, Canadians and Americans to take more."

A jab: "But if in addition to cutting relief appropriations more and larger bureaucracies established, Europeans are likely to be still further disillusioned about American efficiency."

And the final punch: "The setting up of another organization to overlap the IGC, UNRRA and the Army will be a positive guarantee that money will be wasted in Europe in the view of experts."

Well, the agency was set up and the prediction proved wrong. At a White House meeting on October 17, 1939, shortly after the Nazis had conquered Poland, FDR entertained the Anglo-American leadership of the International Committee comprised of Lord Winterton, chair, Sir Herbert Emerson, soon-to-be chair and Myron C. Taylor, vice-chair. Indeed, at the time, the IGC *was* a "new" agency, created at the Évian Conference a year earlier. Roosevelt finished his speech to the assembled IGC leaders by injecting the word "new" into the immortal poem of Emma Lazarus on the base of the Statue of Liberty: "A *new* golden door, a *new* refuge for huddled masses yearning to be free."

At the Bermuda Conference in 1943, the IGC was resuscitated. Sir Herbert Emerson was now its chairman, and Patrick Malin became its executive director. Following which, the essentially Anglo-American operation did nothing very much.

Malin, it must be said, already had proved his dedication to rescue and refuge, in 1940 in the incident of the *SS Quanza*, a ship loaded with mainly Jewish refugees destined for Cuba and not allowed to land its passengers. A similar incident three years earlier with the *SS Saint Louis* had stirred worldwide outrage and harsh criticism of President Roosevelt for not allowing it to dock and thus sending these refugees fleeing for the lives back to Europe.

This time, with the *Quanza*, Roosevelt pushed by Eleanor, said he would not send the fugitives back and allowed them to enter the United States. Patrick Malin, who had gone down to Norfolk, Virginia, when the refugees came ashore, had played a strong part in the effort, which may have led to his being hired to run the IGC. The only one vehemently outraged by this act of mercy was Breckinridge Long, and he kept his tantrum on paper in his diary, unfortunately without a visualization of him stomping, holding his breath and turning blue.

Once John Pehle had put his foot down against kowtowing to the IGC, Sir Herbert and Patrick Malin journeyed at their bequest from London to speak to him in D.C. The discussion was not recorded. It has to be noted, incidentally, that Sir Herbert was definitely naïve about what was entailed in rescue operations. Not that he was a stranger to politics. Most of his life he'd spent in India, employed by the Imperial Civil Service and had been knighted because of his role as governor of the Punjab. But he let it be known he was shocked to learn that escapees often used false names. "That isn't cricket!" he declared. "Not playing the game fairly." Yet their parley in Washington with Pehle proved both amiable and fruitful. They would act together independently only still keeping in touch.

Thus, an "amiable and fruitful" footnote: On the exact same day, January 26, 1944, that Helen Kirkpatrick's piece appeared in the *Chicago Daily News*, the *Jewish Morning Journal* printed the report of a meeting at 132 Nassau Street in downtown Manhattan of a major organization of Orthodox Jews, the Vaad Hatsalah, that voted to donate $154,000 for the rescue effort.

In the notice of their action to the War Refugee Board, they ended: "The Vaad Hatsalah has already given its answer."

Chapter Five

An obvious segue is to present word pictures of the many organizations that rallied to the assistance of the War Refugee Board.

First among them has to be—to give it its full official title—the Jewish American Joint Distribution Committee—the Joint—as it has been universally nicknamed. Its founding was the work on November 27, 1914, of extremely American wealthy Jews—mostly of German Jewish families who'd moved to the United States. It also had merged with an Orthodox group established less than two months earlier with the tongue-wearying title of Central Committee for the Relief of Jews Suffering Through the War The Joint's major donors and officers were already recognized countrywide for their wealth, success in business and charitable activities. They were men such as Felix Warburg of the banking family, Louis Marshall, one of the nation's outstanding lawyers, and Henry Morgenthau Sr., both lawyer and businessman and U.S. ambassador to the Ottoman Empire. The head of this Orthodox organization, one Leon Kamaiky, seemingly has been lost to history.

Felix Warburg was the first chairman of the Joint. The initial target for their largesse was an Eastern Europe already enveloped in warfare. By the end of 1917, the Joint had transferred $2.5 million to Russia, $1 million to German-occupied Poland and Lithuania, $1.5 million to Galicia, a province under Austro-Hungarian control, and $76,000 to Romania. With the Great War's termination on November 11, 1918, they opened an office in Warsaw, now the capital of an independent Poland. During 1919–20, their expenditure increased to $20 million, and by April 1923, the Joint had helped 300,000 refugees in Poland, Lithuania and Hungary. Two of their personnel were killed by the Red Army in fighting between Poland and Soviet Russia in the brief 1919–1920 war those two entities contested.

The men who assembled these expenditures had deep pockets. They were all Jews obviously, although their Yiddish-speaking coreligionists in Eastern Europe hadn't been targeted as they were to be in World War II. Suffice it to say, they suffered a great deal and experienced transient pogroms but faced no effectively organized slaughter and for the most part their *shtetls* (small towns) weren't utterly destroyed. While there was a significant gap between German-speaking Jews and Yiddish-speaking eastern Jews, the heavy lifters at the Joint were following the age-old admonishment of the religion that "every Jew is responsible for every other Jew."

The Joint's work continued during peacetime. During 1928, for example, the American Society for Jewish Farm Settlement was formed in Soviet Russia with their help. The lead backer was Julius Rosenwald of Chicago, co-owner of Sears, Roebuck, who at his death in 1932 had a net worth of $80 million ($1.4 billion today). He had a long-standing interest in agriculture, having given grants to the first one hundred counties in the U.S. to hire county directors for the Agriculture Department's Farm Extension Service that essentially began in 1914. Also helping backstop this endeavor was James N. Rosenberg, a high-powered New York defense attorney and patron of the arts, who himself was a painter and poet.

As a postscript, the experiment in Russia had to end in 1938, after two of its employees were arrested by the Soviets.

In 1939, Felix Warburg's son, Edward M. M. Warburg, another philanthropist and patron of the arts, stepped into the role of co-chair and treasurer of the Joint. With time out for service in World War II, winning a Bronze Star at the Normandy beaches, he took over the Joint's full chairmanship in 1946. His first public announcement was that the Joint would need more than $58 million to continue its work with displaced refugees. The year before, the Joint had spent $28 million. Paul Baerwald, its retiring chair, was an American partner in the French investment firm of Lazard-Frères and had been among the founders of the Joint in 1914. Baerwald also served on FDR's President's Advisory Board on Refugees.

Employees of the Joint whose names are prominent in its operational work with the War Refugee Board were Moses Leavitt, executive director essentially from 1940 to 1965, and Dr. Joseph Schwartz, an ordained rabbi, chairman of the European Executive Council from 1942 to 1950. Located in Switzerland, Schwartz worked closely with the director of Joint's Swiss branch, Saly Mayer. Their activities, as may be imagined, were manifold. For example, the two men assisted Isaac Gitterman, director of the Polish branch, to get $300,000 to the Polish Jewish underground in 1943–1944, the same year they snuck funds into Transnistria. In 1944, Saly Mayer helped ransom three trainloads of Hungarian Jews (13,344 persons) from the Nazis. Mayer was a colorful—and highly controversial—figure, and we will come across him as we proceed.

Joseph Schwartz must have been a feisty individual. He had been born in Ukraine but educated in the U.S. and received a PhD in Oriental history from Yale. He was not above defying his superiors in accomplishing needed work. Despite the Joint's policy of no assistance to armed Jewish resistance groups, he defied the order and sent them money. He endorsed illegal immigration to Palestine in 1940 and 1941. He set up the Joint office in Istanbul that supported Ira Hirschmann's WRB efforts. He sent aid packages to starving Jews in Soviet Russia. He spent to sustain Jewish religious institutions in Palestine. He established a Joint office in Lisbon.

Most of these efforts by Joe Schwartz have gone unheralded. Not so for his aid to the War Refugee Board in its sending of Raoul Wallenberg to Hungary and worldwide lasting fame.

The range of Joint activities was indeed global and too voluminous to detail, apart from two more examples with historic connotations. One was helping Polish Jews expelled from Germany in 1939 but left in limbo on the border at Zb□szy□ , when Poland refused to let them enter. Out of this incident arose the killing in Paris by Herschel Grynszpan, whose parents were thus maltreated, of a German embassy employee, from which sprang the excuse for *Kristallnacht*, world history's greatest pogrom. The other was the tragic saga of the Jewish refugees aboard the *SS Saint Louis*, turned back from Cuba and the United States in prewar 1939, and who received aid from the Joint to be resettled in Europe.

Next on the list has to be a similarly powerful Jewish group, the American Jewish Congress. It was formed under that name in 1918 for the purpose of preparing a Jewish presentation to the upcoming Paris Peace Conference the following year. Among its founders were outstanding Jewish American leaders such as Rabbi Steven Wise, Felix Frankfurter, and U.S. Supreme Court Justice Louis Brandeis.

Although financially the AJC's contribution to the War Refugee was a pittance compared to the Joint's—$330,000 as against $15,000,000—

the organization derived much of its prominence from the persona of its longtime leader Rabbi Wise, who took command as president and chief spokesperson in 1928. In the 1930s, the AJC used rallies to alert the American public to the growing dangers of Nazism, and in 1936 it went worldwide and spun off the World Jewish Congress, to which Rabbi Wise was also elected president.

Thus coordinated, the AJC and WJC focused on refugee matters and were able to bring some five thousand German Jews to America prior to the War Refugee Board's entrance on the scene.

In August, 1942, Rabbi Wise was the recipient of the fateful telegram from Gerhart Riegner, the WJC's representative in Geneva, Switzerland. It told of the installation of the Nazi plan for a "Final Solution of the Jewish Problem"—mass mechanized murder of all Jewish men, women and children they could get their hands on. The source of the information, the non-Jewish businessman Eduard Schulte, of Breslau, a city close to Auschwitz-Birkenau, was an unimpeachable eyewitness risking his life to reveal the horrific secret.

However, the initial reaction to this shocker in the U.S. was general disbelief. The bewilderment is epitomized in the case of Jan Karski, a non-Jewish Polish Resistance fighter, who came to the U.S. at a later date on a speaking tour and told his story first to President Roosevelt at a private White House meeting, then to other important Americans, including Felix Frankfurter, who was now a U.S. Supreme Court Justice. Frankfurter's verdict on Karski's message is famously reported to have been: "I did not say he was lying. I said I could not believe him. That is different."

Rabbi Wise was an imposing man, physically commanding, extremely tall, broad-shouldered, jut-jawed, born in Budapest, then part of the Austro-Hungarian Empire, and brought to the U.S. as an infant. His grandfather and father both were rabbis, the latter of a congregation in Brooklyn followed by a posh Manhattan synagogue founded by wealthy German Jews. Ordained himself, Stephen Wise showed strong support for Zionism, which put him at odds with many of his Reform Jewish colleagues. Incidentally, he was also a cofounder of the NAACP (National Association for the Advancement of Colored People).

An adviser on Jewish matters to President Woodrow Wilson, Wise also performed the same service for FDR and became a close personal friend. It was on November 24, 1942, that the rabbi held a dramatic news conference to reveal the German extermination plan and announce that two million Jews had already been slaughtered. But the newspapers of the time kept the story on the back pages.

Pushed by the "radical" activism of Peter Bergson and others, Wise apparently pushed back, even advocating that the fiery Palestinian Jew be deported.

But during the war, Wise's group did support the rescue effort of the War Refugee Board and teamed up with the Joint when the two weren't feuding.

A third Jewish organization that came into play, the Vaad Hatzalah, has already been identified at the first significant outside donor to the War Refugee Board. Their gift of more than $100,000 became more than one million before the end of the war. Yet they had no nationally known leaders like the Joint and the AJC. These were Orthodox Jews who had transferred their Ashkenazic devotion to ritualized living from Eastern Europe across the Atlantic to the New World.

The Vaad Hatzalah (in Hebrew literally, Rescue Committee) was created in November 1939 by the overarching Union of Orthodox Rabbis of the United States and Canada at an emergency meeting. World War II had started two months earlier in September 1939, when the Germans overran Poland in no more than a month. Its initial thrust was to funnel its Polish members from Poland into Lithuania, which was still then an independent country. The leader of this effort was Lithuania-born Rabbi Eliezer Silver of Cincinnati who had come to the U.S. in 1907 and by 1939 was president of the Orthodox rabbis group. Silver convened the meeting where the Vaad Hatzalah was born. The specified goal was to save Torah scholars from the Nazis, and to that end five million dollars was raised. Rabbi Silver also helped put together an umbrella organization for all of the Orthodox, calling it Agudath Israel, which could take advantage of an exemption in U.S. immigration law to allow in ordained clerics and religious students outside the quota system. Eventually the Vaad was able to obtain two thousand emergency visas for its people.

By 1940, after receiving criticism for its exclusivity, the Vaad agreed to try to save all Jews. Their change of policy helped to ease tensions they'd had with both the Joint and the American Jewish Congress. It has been claimed that another of the Vaad's members, Rabbi Aharon Kotler, who came to the U.S. in 1940, helped enlist Henry Morgenthau Jr.'s aid for forming a rescue committee that became the War Refugee

Board. After having fulfilled its wartime mission and participated postwar in the resettlement of the displaced Orthodox Jews, the Vaad Hatzalah dissolved in the 1950s.

Meanwhile, an offshoot Jewish action group known by its acronym HIJEFS (Hilfsverein für Jüdische Flüechtlinge am Shanghai) had been set up by Recha Sternbuch and her family at their Montreux, Switzerland, residence. The Asian reference in the title reflected its earliest goal of transporting Jews out of Europe to the safety of that cosmopolitan Chinese port city. Two years after its naming, HIJEFS hooked up with the War Refugee Board, bringing to it a wealth of rescue experience. The Sternbuchs had already formed clandestine contacts with Jewish community activists in Slovakia, Romania, Hungary, Poland, Belgium, France, and even neutral Turkey. Upon the establishment of the WRB in 1944, HIJEFS became the Swiss representative of Vaad Hatzalah of America. Actually, they could conduct work under three rubrics, depending on the need and preference for whatever mission they undertook: HIJEFS, Vaad Hatzalah, or the Orthodox Rabbis of the United States. On occasion, due to disagreements with WRB's station chief in Switzerland, Roswell McClelland, who was adamantly opposed to paying ransoms to the Nazis, subterfuge had to be used, like using the Polish Government-in-Exile's cables to bypass the Americans.

The list of *non-Jewish* organizations that collaborated with the War Refugee Board has to be headed by the Unitarian Service Committee and the American Friends Service Committee. Both contributed former employees of theirs to the pool of special attachés the WRB hired and kept posted overseas: Robert Dexter in the case of the Unitarians and Roswell McClelland for the Quakers.

It was in May 1940 that the rescue action organization Robert Dexter had pleaded for began its operations. Consequently as France was falling to the Nazis, the strikingly named Reverend Waitstill Hastings Sharp and his wife, Martha, moved into the Marseille office they had organized and agreed to run. Sharp was a Boston-born graduate of Harvard and Harvard Law School before his ordination, officiating at a Unitarian church in Wellesley Hills, Massachusetts, until called overseas with his wife. Three months ahead of the German takeover of Czechoslovakia, the couple went to Prague. When the Gestapo shut them down in the summer of 1939, they stayed until August and fled arrest. The following May they were back in France, ostensibly to establish a USC branch in Paris. But that possibility failed as soon as the Nazis marched into the City of Lights. So, after setting up an office in Lisbon, they retreated back to Marseille in the zone controlled by the Vichy Government.

Under Vichy, they helped Czech servicemen trapped in France escape to fight another day and, as the Pétain government grew more and more anti-Semitic, funneled Jewish children to safety. Martha founded a group called Children to Palestine and raised money for these kids, many of them orphans, to start new lives in the Holy Land. She and Waitstill also assisted Jewish intellectuals, in one case personally escorting the noted author Lion Feuchtwanger from Marseilles to the U.S. One year later, she went back to neutral Lisbon to become the associate European director of the Unitarian Service Committee. On another trip to the U.S., she took twenty-seven Jewish children and ten adults with her, and in Lisbon she ferried intended Nazi victims out of harm's way.

The strain of these dangerous activities eventually affected the marriage of Waitstill and Martha, and they divorced. Martha married again and took her husband's last name of Cogan. He was a wealthy Jewish businessman, and she kept up her charitable humanitarian work, serving on the boards of Hadassah, the national Jewish women's group, and the nonsectarian Girls Club of America. Waitstill also remarried and spent most of the rest of his life in Flint, Michigan, and Greenfield, Massachusetts. In 2006, they received their honors of inclusion among the Righteous Gentiles who risked death to save the hunted Jews of Europe.

The Unitarians were actually the older of these two organizations, founded in 1825, although its Service Committee, organized in 1940, trailed the American Friends Service Committee's creation by twenty-three years. The AFSC was founded in April 1917, just as the U.S. was entering World War I. Its initial intention was to protect conscientious objectors from having to serve in the military and potentially take lives, substituting noncombat activities for them, like driving ambulances, caring for the wounded, and feeding civilian victims, particularly children, in Germany, Russia, and Poland. Thirty years later, in 1947, this American Quaker branch shared the Nobel Peace Prize with its British equivalent.

Kristallnacht in Nazi Germany, the November 1938 government-sponsored super-pogrom of the Hitlerites against their fellow Jewish citizens, spurred the American Quakers to become involved. Three of them, Rufus Jones, George Walton, and Robert Yarnell, officially were sent to Berlin. Goebbels was to mock them snidely as "the three wise men." Nevertheless, they were allowed to meet with the Gestapo, an interview arranged by the American consul in the Third Reich's capital.

They presented a statement, translated into German, to the two "hard-faced men" provided by the secret police. It said, among other things: "Our task is to support and save life and to suffer with those who are suffering." Their written words were then delivered to Reinhard Heydrich, the ruthless youthful head of the Gestapo. While left alone in the Gestapo headquarters, the three Quakers held an impromptu Quaker meeting, no doubt the only one ever conducted in such surroundings. It was mostly silent prayer, which was a good thing, since they later learned their whole interview was being surreptitiously taped. Upon the return of the Nazis, they were told they could bring relief to sufferers. Indeed, they were informed that every police station in Germany would be alerted that the Quakers had full permission to investigate the suffering of the Jews and to bring relief as they saw necessary.

The memory of Quaker solicitude in Germany right after World War I was given credit for this ostensible softening of the Gestapo's attitude. "They shook our hands with good-bye wishes and a touch of gentleness," the delegation reported.

It was fitting therefore that a Quaker, California-born Roswell McClelland, should have played a key rescue-and-relief role in Europe after war did break out in 1939.

During the summer of 1940, McClelland and his wife, Marjorie, traveled to Rome first, then France and ultimately Switzerland, under the auspices of the Friends Service Committee. In these early years, he often worked with the Joint Distribution Committee on Jewish refugee issues.

By 1942, two years before he was to go to work for the War Refugee Board, McClelland's concerns about the deportation of non-French Jews in France led him to interactions with the Nazi puppet Vichy administration.

In the office of Doctor Bernard Ménétrel, a physician and close confidante of Marshall Philippe Pétain, the head of that rump government, McClelland encountered Pierre Laval, its premier. He reported the latter as utterly dismissive of foreign-born Jews, even those with French citizenship, and supportive of "their movement to an ethnic reservation in Poland." But when McClelland countered that the Jews sent there were being exterminated, Laval vehemently denied the fact. The Vichy leader (who would be executed for treason postwar) did almost all the talking at this meeting and insisted that only French Jews were his responsibility.

Today we would call the hiring of Roswell McClelland by the War Refugee Board for its Swiss post a no-brainer. With his experience, contacts and competence, he could step right into the job, as he did, and be a vital cog in negotiations with Nazis at the highest levels.

The American Roman Catholic input on refugee matters was in the hands of the National Catholic Welfare Conference. This organization had been in existence since 1919, created by Pope Benedict XV originally to promote the labor reforms of one of his predecessors, Pope Leo XIII, as expressed in his encyclical *Rerum Novarum*, which supported the forming of unions and rejected communism and unbridled capitalism. A meeting at Catholic University in Washington, D.C. had brought together ninety-five prelates from American dioceses, who chose Archbishop Joseph Hanna of San Francisco to lead the effort.

Within three years, however, political infighting among the U.S. church hierarchy nearly sank the fledgling operation. Changes were finally made that reflected the intention of certain top Catholic clergy, such as William Cardinal O'Connell of Boston, to curb the organization's powers and make it mainly advisory. Its original title of *Council* was switched to *Conference* to reflect this emphasis.

Having survived the threat to its existence, the NCWC in 1936 established the Catholic Committee for Refugees (including children). By January 1937, it was operational with offices in New York City.

Be that as it may, after the advent of World War II, the Bishops conference created a War Relief Services unit that took full shape in 1943. They had already been assisting Catholic war victims in Poland, working in tandem with Jewish groups like HIAS (Hebrew Immigrant Aid Society), the American Jewish Congress, and other appropriate entities on a nonsectarian basis.

Their interaction with the War Refugee Board may be characterized in a series of letters back and forth between the Right Reverend Monsignor Patrick M. O'Boyle of the National Catholic Welfare Center and John Pehle.

Given the ways of bureaucracy, we see that these communications didn't always go from sender to recipient but perforce had to be vetted by a third party as a matter of protocol.

For example, on May 24, 1944, the report of Dr. J. Henry Amiel, the American Catholics' man in Lisbon was sent first to the State Department by Foreign Service Officer Edward S. Crocker, the counselor of the U.S. Embassy in Portugal. Crocker wrote: "It is believed the War Refugee Board would be interested to see this report and if the Department sees no objection, we request it be transmitted to the War Refugee Board."

All properly done but time consuming.

Amiel's report covered the present refugee situation then in the Portuguese capital, starting with a bit of history, i.e.: that in 1940–1941 "when thousands were arriving in Lisbon, the Joint had 2,800 refugees dependent on aid, the Unitarians between 260 and 300, and the Quakers 180–200. Four years later, the figures were 600 for the Joint, 250 for the Unitarians, 70 for the Quakers, and 80 Catholics—about 1,000 in all.

Shortly after FDR's executive order created the WRB, the Catholics in a letter dated February 17, 1944, informed John Pehle that Dr. Amiel would arrive in Lisbon to supervise the refugee work there. A Miss Eileen Egan, also with the NCWC, would go to Madrid unofficially and work among the refugees in Spain at the U.S. Embassy directly with Mr. David Blickenstaff.

Pehle was assured that the "National Catholic Welfare Conference is most anxious to lend its whole cooperation to the [War Refugee] Board" and that anytime "one of the representatives of Mr. Pehle's office wishes to call upon us, we could discuss the best manner in which we could be of service to this Board."

Further information furnished was that the Catholic group had projects going for Polish refugees in Palestine, Egypt, Iran, Kenya, Tanganyika, Uganda, India, and Nyasaland . . . also Spain, Portugal, and Mexico.

It was added that although "we can't state specific actions at this point, we can, however, acquaint Mr. Pehle with the activities of this office as regards relief and rehabilitation of refugees."

It was stated they had close to 5,700 cases and that their function was "the granting of material and spiritual aid to Catholics who on account of racial, political or religious reasons have been victims of persecution and involuntary exile from their homelands."

In mid August 1944, there was a clear-cut illustration of how the War Refugee Board could buttress the Catholics' rescue operations. The assistant executive director of their war relief effort, Father Edward E. Swanstrom reported that an effort by them to send funds for Polish Catholic refugees in Hungary and France had been thwarted by the U.S. Office of Censorship. A cable to their operatives in Geneva was *rejected* basically on the grounds "that any message concerning refugees in occupied countries had to be cleared by the War Refugee Board."

Even with an organization as efficient (albeit swamped) as the WRB, it took more than a week for an answer to be sent back.

They had learned that the censors had objected to a single sentence in the telegram. When it had been deleted, the letter had to be resubmitted, and Pehle told them to send the original to his office "and we will arrange to secure the desired data by transmitting the message through the WRB facilities."

Ponderous and picayune as this bit of red-tape haggling might seem, the usual State Department inaction might have delayed such an exchange of communication far, far longer.

About the same period, the Catholics' representative in Lisbon Henry Amiel was reporting to his boss Monsignor O'Boyle that he expected the imminent arrival of Mother Mauricia of the White Sisters but had checked with the Portuguese Patriarchate, which had no word about her. He also detailed what Miss Egan had confided to him about her experiences with Blickenstaff in Barcelona, where they'd discovered that many of those seeking money for passage and repatriation were not refugees.

"It is very likely," he continued, "that in the near future, I may have requests from the Joint, who assume responsibility for all cases regardless of whether or not they will be reimbursed," and he would like to tell them that if the cases concern Catholics, "we will reimburse them for the passage of all Catholic refugees."

Then, he shifted focus to refugees in Tangier, now part of Morocco but at the time an international city. "Of the seventy-three Catholic cases referred to me," he stated, "five were not Catholics, sixty-three are self-dependent residents . . which leaves two. I have requested the Joint to have their correspondent in Tangier give aid to one, while the other may leave soon for Canada."

Amid these almost formalistic utterances on paper, Amiel, a native of New Orleans and fluent in French, offered a human touch. He was an American still and his personal needs familiar to Americans. If persons were traveling to Italy (since liberated from the Fascists) and passing through Lisbon, would they be kind enough to bring him "some first-aid bands (no mercurochrome), some Ungentine (unobtainable here), some Pepsodent tooth powder, a few recent books in English or in French, a dozen golf balls, any brand."

Dr. Amiel must have felt more than a touch of homesickness when, sitting in his Rua Castilho office in Lisbon on September 23, 1944, he penned a letter to Miss Eileen Egan.

"Dear Eileen, I have no doubt that you reached New York safely . . . When I saw that clipper rise, there was a lump on my throat as I realized that very shortly you would be home and to say the truth I envied you and wondered when it would be my turn.

"Make clear to Monsignor O'Boyle that the very delicate matter of passage and repatriation money is of the greatest importance . . . half the people here will be left stranded when we close (if we are to close within a few months) and the other half will need financial aid in order to be able to leave . . . I understand that I am to use up the money until it is exhausted and then stop operating . . . What will happen to all these people here? . . . Could we ask for a special fund for transportation? . . . Did you get your luggage and what about the camera? . . . I am told that the entry of a camera is extremely difficult . . . Cordially, Henry Amiel."

Doctor Amiel, by the way, was not a physician, but the recipient of a doctorate from the Catholic Loyola University of New Orleans where, in its 1943 yearbook, *The Wolf*, he was listed as an associate professor of modern languages and chairman of that department.

A question naturally put to him while serving the National Catholic Welfare Conference in wartime Lisbon was: Do you think the number of refugees in Portugal will remain constant? His answer—yes— differed from the attitude of his War Refugee Board counterpart Robert Dexter, who predicted an influx.

Reported Amiel: "He [Dexter] called me recently to the Embassy to meet Mr. James H. Mann, who arrived recently and went back to Washington last week . . . Mr. Mann asked me, among other things, if I thought refugees would flood to Spain and Portugal," and also "What would I do if French collaborationists would come to me for help."

Amiel's opinion was: "Not a single French person would leave France now, that the refugees would go from town to town ahead of the armies, that possibly a few Jews and some non-French if freed might come to Spain." In the end, Amiel admitted he didn't know what he would do about French collaborationists and besides he didn't think that if new refugees came to Spain and Portugal, there would be many Catholics among them.

A further conundrum for him was: "Shall we continue the Catholic Poles through the Polish committee or should we deal with them ourselves?"

A final call for advice in this instance concerned the fact he was thinking of bringing his wife and "my baby" to Lisbon. Should he?

In another of his communications, we encounter the aviso that he is taking better care of himself, pruning his intensive work time down to six hours a day and spending a long period encamped at the famous beach resort of Estoril but moving his residence back to Lisbon, having become wearied of the commute from the suburbs. We also have a quick glimpse of actual recipients of his effort or at least learn their names:

"At the request of Mr. Blickenstaff, I paid one repatriation to Argentina and I am about to pay now two passages to Canada for Mr. and Mrs. Khmelevsky, who are very fine and deserving people. I will pay also one passage to Canada for Mrs. Scheinberger . . . as per your authorization." He tells his boss he sees seven more obligations in the near future.

Moving on to others associated with the War Refugee Board's activities, we find the President's Advisory Committee on Political Refugees. Advisory committees in general are mere window dressing, essentially toothless in exerting real influence but creating the illusion of an accomplishment. This committee arrangement here, first concocted during 1938 in conjunction with FDR's attempt to show leadership by convening the Évian Conference, even advertised—by the "Political" component of its title—that Americans should fear no hordes of Nazi victims overloading our shores. Their one relatively positive accomplishment in those early years was that the full quota of twenty-seven thousand Germans and Austrians allowed into the U.S.—usually underfilled—could be used to its maximum, and ninety percent of those lucky ones accepted were Jews, like my own in-laws and wife.

The original membership of FDR's advisors on this thorniest of issues included some names we have encountered before such as Rabbi

Stephen Wise and the investment banker and Joint cofounder Paul Baerwald, plus Hamilton Fish Armstrong, Editor of *Foreign Affairs*, Basil Harris, vice-president of U.S. Lines shipping company and prominent in the National Council of Catholic Men, Isaiah Bowman, president of Johns Hopkins University and Joseph Chamberlain, professor of law at Columbia Law School. The Chairman was James G. McDonald, a mild-mannered Indiana Hoosier, of whom one book reviewer wrote: "Despite his earnest desire to help European Jewish refugees . . . achieved precious little. His diaries make for sad reading, displaying a well-meaning type dashing to endless conferences, meetings, negotiations, cocktail parties, dinners, chasing his tail fruitlessly, so to speak."

Advocate for the Doomed, the title given to McDonald's collection of memoirs, letters and documents indeed does carry an overhang of *doom* for which his flailing accomplished little.

McDonald's credentials for head of the President's Advisory Board most likely were based on the fact that he had been the High Commissioner of Refugees for the League of Nations in the mid-1930s. His American post had been created in conjunction with the Évian Conference of 1938. One reviewer of his two-volume publication summed up: "McDonald soon realized he was facing the same obstacles that had stumped him as a High Commissioner." He was constantly fighting with the State Department over *special visas* for outstanding Europeans, Jewish and otherwise. When invited to lead the U.S. delegation to the Bermuda Conference, anticipating it would be as useless in wartime as Évian had been in peacetime, which it was, he declined. Post war, McDonald was appointed the first U.S. ambassador to Israel.

The type of rigmarole McDonald continually faced may well be illustrated by his experience at the League of Nations, when he encountered the obstinacy of the State Department's Avra Warren, who in 1935 sabotaged his efforts to convince the Argentinean Government to let in German-Jewish refugees.

In 1940, Avra Warren was in a key role as chief of the Visa Division at State. During the presidential election that year, James McDonald initially had planned to vote for the Republican candidate Wendell Wilkie, who had been his student at Indiana University. However, it has since been claimed by McDonald's family that in the end he did support FDR for a third term. Meanwhile, Avra Warren was on a tour of American consulates in Europe, explaining the new brutal U.S. policy on immigrants.

A statement from the American Consulate in Basel, Switzerland, starts: "Mr. Avra M. Warren, Chief of the Visa Division . . . recently inspected this office and stated that the instructions under reference had been correctly interpreted here as being highly restrictive."

A Margaret Jones, then working for the American Friends Service Committee in Vienna indignantly commented: "I had a conference with [Avra] Warren a few weeks ago—there is absolutely no chance for anyone, except in most unusual cases. FDR doesn't want more aliens from Europe—refugees have been implicated in espionage—and so forth. All part of the spy hysteria. (What kind of U.S.A. am I coming back to??? I am almost afraid to ask) . . . The strain of the past month has been something. Day after day, men and women just sat at my desk and sobbed. They are caught and crushed and they know it."

When the President's Advisory Committee decided it had to involve itself, its secretary, a *George* Warren, met with the State Department's Robert Pell, who explained the need for action because groups were forming, each having its own high priority list of persons for rescue and they "were beginning to fight among themselves." In short, Pell warned, "there will soon be a highly chaotic condition which may give rise to political embarrassment if the situation is not taken in hand."

Such handwringing did not produce much in the way of results.

For example, in August 1940 McDonald contacted the State Department's Breckinridge Long about "the plight of a number of Jewish Orthodox rabbis," who were being taken into Russia from Soviet occupied parts of Estonia, Lithuania and other places recently absorbed by the USSR. Long responded that each rabbi had to be approved first by McDonald's committee before they could be considered collectively for the entry list.

More runaround. More delay.

Ironically, at this same juncture, the *Quanza* incident occurred. This Portuguese steamship had docked in Norfolk, Virginia, with a boatload of refugees turned away from Mexico, although they all had Mexicans visas for which they'd paid. FDR, having been stung by the strong criticism of his inaction in the *Saint Louis* episode, and with Eleanor urging him on, let it be known he was not sending these refugees back to the horrors of Europe. Breckinridge Long was silently apoplectic but helpless.

Nevertheless, in his diary, Long swore: "And now it remains for the President's Committee to be curbed in its activities so that the laws can operate in their normal course."

As Rabbi Wise remarked of the rescue, this was "one of the things that could only be done because Eleanor and Marshall Field appealed to the Skipper for the liberation of the refugees on the *Quanza*. All of them were released."

The wrangle between the State Department and the President's Advisory Committee continued with McDonald's response to Secretary Hull concerning State's suggestion that "no additional names of refugees be accepted by the Advisory Committee for transmittal to the Departments of State and Justice, "except those refugees in imminent danger who are intellectual leaders of the liberal movement in Europe."

Pointed out afterward was that of 561 names recommended by the Advisory Committee, less than 15 visas had been issued.

Politely albeit pointedly it was implied that "this failure to ease the tragedy of those refugees in imminent danger" could be laid to State's changing an agreement "without previous notice to the Department of Justice or to the President's Advisory Committee on Political Refugees."

Wartime had made no difference in the situation although news of the Final Solution had become ever more verifiable. In January 16, 1944, the famous high-level meeting was held at the White House where the WRB's creation was decided upon and later described by John Pehle in a lengthy memorandum. Attending were President Roosevelt, Secretary Morgenthau, Randolph Paul and Pehle. Morgenthau had requested the gathering to "discuss the problem of saving the remaining Jews in Europe."

This conference lasted about twenty minutes.

Morgenthau began it by stating he was "deeply disturbed about the failure of the State Department to take any effective action" and worse, that "people in the State Department were not only inefficient but were actively taking actions to prevent the saving of the Jews." However, the focus soon turned to the composition of the War Refugee Board, itself. FDR wondered why Leo Crowley's name had been included as one of the Board's members. Crowley was then head of the Federal Economic Administration and apparently was having trouble with that assignment. Besides, Roosevelt wanted Henry

Stimson, the secretary of war, to complete the trio of department heads he was contemplating, the others being Hull at State and Morgenthau at Treasury. He similarly made it clear he wished to involve Edward Stettinius, second in command at the State Department and Judge Samuel Rosenman, his key speechwriter.

When Morgenthau spoke of how his father, as ambassador to Turkey, had been able to save many Armenians threatened by massacre, FDR agreed that in the present situation "some effective action" could be taken, and he referred specifically to the movement of Jews through Romania and Bulgaria. The president also talked about getting people "over the Spanish and Swiss borders." There was seemingly no discussion of using the President's Advisory Committee on Political Refugees.

The following day, Morgenthau called an afterhours work meeting at his home with the same folks plus Judge Rosenman, and final details were hammered out for the executive order to put the War Refugee Board in place.

The President's Advisory Committee continued its existence until 1945 and then quietly faded away.

Aside from the Joint, the American Jewish Congress and the Vaad Hatzalah, on a lesser scale, there was a host of groups among whom, not surprisingly, smaller Jewish organizations were prominent.

The Comunidade Israelita de Lisboa was an example. It had been around since 1913, connected with the Sinagoga Tikva a Sephardic Temple and later in Portugal a Sinagoga Ohel Yaacov (an Ashkenazi Shul). In the World War II era, there were only 380 native Portuguese Jews in the country but also 700 Jewish refugees from the Nazis who had "residence status." During World War II, once France capitulated, the government of the archconservative dictator, António de Oliveira Salazar, liberalized its visa policy, allowing "thousands of Jews" to enter but only for transit elsewhere, and those of Russian (i.e. Soviet Communist) provenance were excluded. Late in the war, special efforts were made to save Hungarian Jews. More than one hundred thousand Jews in all were estimated to have escaped through Lisbon, and the entire native Portuguese Jewish population and resident Jews did survive.

HIAS—the Hebrew Sheltering and Immigrant Aid Society has previously been mentioned. So, too, the Jewish Labor Committee. Add the Underground Jewish National Council in Warsaw, the Immigration

Department of the Jewish Agency (located in Palestine as a shadow Jewish Government), also the Jewish Agency's Committee for the Rescue of Jews in Nazi occupied Europe, the National Council for Palestine Jews (Va'ad Leumi), the New Zionist Organization, Poale Zion, the Jewish Anti-Fascist Committee in Russia, the Free Palestine Committee, the Hebrew Committee of National Liberation organized by Peter Bergson (not recognized by the State Department), ICA (Jewish Colonization Association), OSE (Œuvre de Secours aux Enfants, helping children, a French Jewish organization), and ARIF (Association for Restoration of Jewish Works, Edward de Rothschild chairman, started by French refugees in New York).

On the non-Jewish side, needless to say, the International Red Cross was involved through its Commission Mixte de Secours. The Federation of Bessarabian Societies of America has been cited. The International Free World Association, MERRA (the Middle East Relief and Rehabilitation Association), the International Government Committee. The United Palestine Appeal, Office of Representation in Spain of American Relief Organizations, the Forest Hills (New York) Civic Association, the International Rescue and Relief Committee (New York), the National Conference on Palestine, the Polish National Council in London, the Yugoslav Mission in D.C., Milan (Italy) Liberation Committee, the Relief Sub-Committee of the Blockade Committee, the AFL Labor League for Human Rights, Workmen's Circle, United Trades of New York, American Relief for Norway.

As opposed to all of these, in a special category of its own, was the Yiddish Unterstützungsstelle, a Nazi front organization set up by them in Kraków after their Conquest of Poland.

This welter of players, quite probably underrepresented here, may be dizzying and by no means were entanglements between some of them prevented from snarling matters on occasion. Yet what they avoided was the inertia that had existed for so long vis-à-vis Nazi victims, and certainly they managed some unification of efforts. I have listed as many of the outfits as I could for the sheer purpose of showing the length and breadth of the reach John Pehle and his cohorts were able to achieve against the nearly impossible odds they faced during the small amount of time they had to act.

Chapter Six

L et us quickly return to Ira Hirschmann in Ankara and Istanbul, Turkey. One might label him a "pioneer" in that he had been the first of the "special attachés" to go into action. His title, which all of the other representatives of the War Refugee Board on the front lines bore, was a bit of bureaucratic artistry. All of these WRB guys were placed in U.S. embassies, masquerading as bona fide State Department officials, and they needed credibility. The term "special attaché" conveyed no meaning, really. It was merely cover, cleverly vague as to its holders' duties, yet definitely sounding official.

Left undone when we last left Ira Hirschmann, the on-leave department-store executive in Istanbul, was the problem of the Jews of Romania, Hungary, and Bulgaria. These were Axis countries where the rightist governments had gone to war against the Allies alongside the Germans, primarily against the Communist Soviet Union. In and of themselves, the leaders of the satellites were not essentially murderously anti-Semitic. But the Nazis were pressing them hard to deliver up their Jews to them.

It was getting late in the day. By 1944 only the most diehard Hitlerites had faith in the Third Reich's victory. The vaunted Wehrmacht and Waffen SS were on the defensive and often in retreat. Still, the Nazi fanatics were so dedicated to their Holocaust policy that they sacrificed military personnel to it that could better have been used on the battlefield.

The Goebbels propaganda machine never let up on its use of the pejorative word *Jew*, apparently believing, as in the past, the power of a holy banner to arouse the German troops.

Thus we find a June 1944 tirade in the primary Nazi newspaper, the *Völkischer Beobachter* that stated: "A Jew named Ira Hirschmann was appointed representative in Turkey and he has already departed for Washington in order to make a personal report on the situation with regard to the Jewish refugees in the Balkans." This notation was included in a broader diatribe against Franklin D. Roosevelt and the War Refugee Board.

To wit, there were statements like: "In reality, the War Refugee Board was set up to look after Jewish interests" and "that Roosevelt has once again demonstrated through the establishment of the War Refugee Board to what great extent he stands in the service of World Jewry that he really deserves the homage rendered him by the Jews."

In total, Hirschmann spent only six months in Turkey, his stay punctuated by a visit back to New York and then a return to his post.

Hirschmann's work there with the Roman Catholic nuncio (i.e. ambassador of the Vatican) Angelo Giuseppe Roncalli was highlighted postwar by the fact that the portly, convivial, much-loved Italian prelate was elected Pope as John XXIII and after his death *canonized*, made a saint.

Roncalli, who actually had been the Vatican's man in that eastern Mediterranean region of the world since 1935, resisted the command from Rome not to assist the Jews. Furthermore, he used his friendship with King Boris of Bulgaria to persuade the monarch and his parliament to resist Nazi demands that Bulgarian Jews be deported to the death camps.

The priest and Hirschmann worked closely together. An amalgam of papal aides and diplomatic couriers combined with agents of the Aliyah Bet Jewish underground in Palestine were employed to save Hungarian Jews especially threatened by the Germans' occupation of their one-time ally in March 1944 and their installation of a virulently anti-Semitic Arrow Cross government.

Roncalli, for example, relied on Catholic groups like the Sisters of Notre Dame de Sion (Zion), whose order had been in Turkey since 1858 and had a convent on the Bosporus and also one in Budapest and were assigned "to send 1000 Turkish visas and Palestinian immigration certificates . . . some genuine, most forged" to Hungarian Jews.

On the delicate issue of Jews receiving proof of Christian baptism, Hirschmann has written that Roncalli very diplomatically if slyly asked him: "Do you think Jews would be willing to undergo baptism ceremonies?"

"I said if it meant saving their lives, I'm sure they would. I know what I would do."

"Roncalli said: 'It would be up to them to decide later whether to remain in the Church or go their way.'"

Hirschmann later wrote: "I saw that Roncalli was testing me. I had no doubt the wheels would soon be set in motion in Hungary for Operation Baptism under the auspices and mercy of the Catholic Church."

The spring of 1944 brought a heightened sense of crisis. For one thing, the Nazis invaded Hungary. The nuncio learned that Jews allowed to depart would need Palestine certificates. Since they couldn't leave their occupied country, the papers had to be snuck in to them. The documents therefore were sent to Roncalli in Turkey and then forwarded to Jewish communities in Hungary through Catholic networks. Physical transportation was needed next. Once more, a ship was brought into play. Early in July 1944, the *SS Kazet* sailed with 756 refugees crammed into space accommodating only 300, many of these escapees being from Transnistria. When the vessel pulled into her Turkish port, passengers were hanging from the riggings. Some Jews now safely installed in Istanbul had come down to see if the newcomers might have any news of their relatives. The new arrivals, stuffed by the Turkish police into second- and third-class train compartments at Haydarpa□ a Terminal and provided with food—bread, cucumbers, tomatoes, almost forgotten luxuries—and lots of cigarettes, were hustled off to the Promised Land.

But not before one woman went berserk, smashing windows and shouting madly. Hirschmann was told she had been like that ever since seeing her mother and three children shot before her eyes.

The train pulled out after sunset.

In vain, Hirschmann tried to convince the Turkish authorities to allow him to charter larger and more seaworthy vessels. However close to 1,400 Jewish refugees were able to go by train from Romania, bearing Turkish transit visas, and allowed to continue on to Palestine. The apparent total number—ship and train—of Jews saved on Hirschmann's watch was 7,000 by boat, in addition to the train riders.

The money for this admittedly disappointing result had come through the Jewish Agency in Palestine via War Refugee Board funds. A sum of 12,064.51 Turkish pounds had gone to the firm of W. F. Henry Vandersee for the seaborne transportation with twenty-five thousand American dollars held in reserve.

But a cheering-up letter was received by the New Yorker from

President Roosevelt in June 1944, saying he was following Hirschmann's work with great interest.

Early on, Chaim Barlas of the Jewish Agency in Palestine had written to explain why news of the WRB's creation had been greeted with high hopes. It had been seen as an opening to put pressure on the Germans "even in influential circles, even in the ranks of the Gestapo . . . to establish for themselves some sort of personal alibi by disassociating themselves from the slaughter . . . even conceivably helping Jews to escape."

This was an astute prognostication well before cracks began to appear on the Third Reich's surface. It dovetailed neatly into Hirschmann's work before he ended his tour of duty. The "Blood for Goods" episode has been thoroughly documented. *Obersturmbannführer* (Lieutenant Colonel) Adolf Eichmann, the SS officer in charge in German-occupied Hungary, summoned Joel Brand, an official of the Relief and Rescue Committee of Budapest (the Va'ad) to the city's Majestic Hotel. Plainly and simply, the arrogant Nazi leader announced his willingness to sell the lives of one million Jews in return for ten thousand military trucks and emphasized these vehicles would only be used on the Eastern Front against the Communist Russians. It was a proposal, he declared, that had been approved by his boss, *Reichsführer* Heinrich Himmler.

What was behind this seemingly quixotic proposal in May 1944, when it was still by no means certain Germany would be defeated?

The non-provable but most plausible surmise was that SS commander-in-chief Himmler was plotting to save his skin by presenting an offer to the Western Allies for a negotiated peace.

Or, others have argued, it was a Machiavellian maneuver that would split the Allies, since Russia would be excluded if the Americans, British, Free French, etc. accepted.

Joel Brand, whose work for the Budapest Va'ad was mainly in border crossing operations, was thus camouflage for the man who would accompany him to talks with Allied intelligence officers in Istanbul. He was a fellow Hungarian Jew, Andor Grosz, nicknamed Bandi, who would present the real motivation of peace talks. Given a German passport under the name of Eugen Brand, Joel, the one-time prewar man about Budapest, travelled to Vienna with a high-ranking SS officer and caught up with Grosz. The pair subsequently left for Istanbul, where they both met with officials of the Jewish Agency and others, including Ira Hirschmann. On June 10, the WRB special attaché and Moshe Sharett (née Shertok, later to be the second president of Israel) interviewed Brand and pronounce themselves impressed by him.

Grosz and Brand were thus to proceed to Palestine. Grosz left first, and the British arrested him, and Brand who followed almost a week later was also taken into custody.

The British were determined to end this initiative, certain of them decrying what would they do with a million saved Jews. Yet the Americans wanted to continue the negotiations, so that the mass murdering would be kept in abeyance, while bringing the Allied victory day-by-day closer in time.

All this happened in June 1944. Brand was taken to Cairo and kept a prisoner until October 14, when he was at long last allowed to proceed to Palestine.

Moshe Sharett would charge that he had been "tricked by the British promise that Brand, after meeting him in Aleppo, would be allowed to return to Budapest."

In any event, by that October date, Ira A. Hirschman was back in New York, announcing his retirement from the WRB and his return to Bloomingdale's.

Years later in 1980, a snapshot assessment of Hirschmann's work was included in a lecture at Tel Aviv University by historian Dr. Herbert Rosenbloom. His title was *The U.S. Government, the Jewish Organizations and the War Refugee Board During the Holocaust*. Rosenbloom, touching upon the work of the WRB operatives, stated: "In Istanbul, Ira Hirschmann was only temporary. He was on leave from Bloomingdale's, and did some very important work in a critical period, but since he came and went, he was not able to lend structure to the agency the way McClelland did in Berne."

But perhaps the best epitaph for this first of the special attachés is a drumroll of names, such as this excerpt from one published by the Zionist Organization of America on November 14, 1944:

Jacob Horowitz, 53 years old
Mali (wife), 53 years old
Alfred (son), 24 years old
Rudi (daughter), 19 years old
From Strozinetz, Bucovina (Romania)

Comment: "It is not unlikely that Jacob Horowitz has been deported somewhere long ago and he may not even be alive," but his wife and children were able to use certificates for Palestine.

Also: The Paechter family, Wilhelm and wife Feige, daughter Chana Riesel, son Berthold.

And: Mr. Izaak Holdengraber, wife Mentzia, no children; the applicant for them was Mr. Jacob Safier, 36 Clarkson Avenue, Brooklyn, New York.

They, too, are elements of the War Refugee Board history.

At the other end of the Mediterranean from Asia Minor and the Balkans, Leonard Ackerman had been settled in French North Africa.

The position there of special attaché was a natural for him since he had already been working for the Treasury Department in the Maghreb (Algeria, Tunisia and Morocco). In addition, Lawrence Lesser, John Pehle's number-two man, was a friend of his, and in a letter to Lesser, Ackerman wrote: "Mike Hoffman [another Treasury employee] also asked me whether I was interested in the problem on which you are working and of course I responded in the affirmative." Ackerman naturally added that he would have to check with "the boys upstairs" at Treasury for their okay. He also asked his future superior, Lesser, for suggestions informally of the role he might play, "as official communications sometimes fail to convey the real feel of a subject." Apparently even before Lesser received his letter, Ackerman was told he had the job.

His correspondence, reports, memorandums, etc. are the most voluminous of his fellow special attachés contained in the papers of the War Refugee Board. Ackerman, in effect, covered a wide area of responsibility, not only the three North African countries-to-be but Italy and most of the rest of the western Mediterranean, including southern France and Yugoslavia.

It should be added that there was a qualitative difference between the circumstances in which Ackerman found himself as compared to Hirschman's sphere of activity. For starters, Ackerman was never in a neutral country. French North Africa, by the time he arrived there, had already been liberated—*twice!* The Germans had been driven out after being finally defeated in Tunisia, and the Vichy French slowly but surely afterward by De Gaulle's forces. Among the bureaucracies with which Ackerman had to interact were not only the Free French but also the Allied Command in the captured portions of the Mediterranean.

The first document in Ackerman's files at the War Refugee Board was from one C. Offie, the deputy political advisor to the Allied commander in chief—someone he knew.

Ackerman was told that his files would be sent to him, "except for classified telegrams," and that his "luggage will go forward as soon as transportation is available."

An added P.S. included: "I see your brother every now and then. He is looking well."

Ackerman's appointment to be the special attaché for the North African region was sent to him by a cable dated February 26, 1944. On April 12, 1944, it was amended to include the "Whole Mediterranean area." His first assignment was to act in cooperation with the American representative to the French Committee of National Liberation.

In May, he was authorized to work outside of French North Africa and attached to the staff of the U.S. ambassador, Robert D. Murphy, who until September 1944 was the U.S. political advisor to the Supreme Allied Command in the Mediterranean.

While Hirschmann had had to battle Turkish cupidity and indifference to time, Ackerman was forced to fight a French mindset of indifference, if not outright hostility, no less prevalent in De Gaulle's ranks than among the Vichy personnel. Complicating matters was Roosevelt's necessarily secret anti-De Gaulle attitude, expressed in his famous *bon mot*: "The worst cross I had to bear was the Cross of Lorraine" (the Gaullist symbol, also standing for De Gaulle, himself).

Initially, the Gaullists were bypassed after the "liberation" of the Maghreb. The man the Allies had first installed in power was the French naval officer François Louis Xavier Darlan. Previously, he had been in charge of all of France's property north of the Sahara. Four young patriotic French youths planned his assassination, drawing straws to see who would be the triggerman. The twenty-year-old resistance member Fernand Bonnier de La Chapelle was thus designated via this old-fashioned style and proved successful in his point-blank aim. Captured on the spot, *le jeune* Bonnier was imprisoned, tried and executed in short order, turning into an immediate martyr, *mort pour la France.*

This drama had occurred several months shy of two years before Leonard Ackerman took up his duties.

The first assignment the American received was to familiarize himself "with the program involving the refugee holding facility located at Fedhala in Morocco, 15 miles northeast of Casablanca." The

French had named it Camp Lyautey after Maréchal Hubert Lyautey, the hero of their imperialist prewar expansion into the region. From an aristocratic family in Lorraine, Lyautey had made his name by successfully pacifying perennially turbulent Morocco.

Lyautey had died in 1934. This future holding pen for refugees named after him had long been closed. When Ackerman started his job in early 1944, his immediate assignment was to reopen it, which he did, negotiating with the French Committee of National Liberation and agreeing the Allies would assume all the costs. Soon the ex-Vichy facility was filled to the brim. In June, alone, six hundred refugees had been transferred from Spain, complying with the insistence of the Franco government that the present population of asylum seekers in Spain promptly exit before any new ones were accepted. A second and four-times-larger camp at Philippeville in Algeria was created to take the overflow from Morocco.

Ackerman's orders also directed him to work with the Joint Distribution Committee, the American Friends Service Committee, the Military Government of Allied Force Headquarters, and the UN Relief and Rehabilitation Committee (UNRRA). He was, as he wrote: "Told there were no parts of the official or non-official agency programs that required his immediate assistance." So he set about learning "what was going on, so he could help in the future." The most pressing concern was occurring geographically far from the Maghreb, the need to aid the clandestine flow of refugees from France into Spain across the Pyrenees. He found this first endeavor discouraging, to say the least. Touching base with the G-2 Military Intelligence Unit within the U.S. Army, the local "detachment" of the OSS, and the French Secret Service, he received uniformly negative responses. Passage over the Pyrenees was "extremely dangerous," he was informed. In the matter of triage, the number-one priority was getting out Allied airmen behind enemy lines who'd been downed but not captured. Facilities for refugees were overflowing. There was talk of a route only by sea into Corsica. In June, Ackerman left for Italy, admitting disconsolately that "no substantial results were accomplished."

More pressure was asserted when plans for additional reception centers in Australia, Cyprus, and Cyrenaica and Tripolitania in Libya were cancelled. Also, newly liberated Italy was insisting the refugees in their midst be sent elsewhere. Following the Spaniards, they would not accept new arrivals until the existing escapees, or most of them, had left.

Fedhala was a port on the Atlantic side of Morocco, and its name in Arabic derived from the words *fadl Allah*—"favor of God." By the fourteenth and fifteenth centuries, it was handling merchant ships from Europe, and in the eighteenth century the reigning Moroccan sultan turned it into a giant grain warehouse and created a kasbah. Post World War II, it became the most modern oil port in North Africa, and a decade later the city was renamed Mohammédia, in honor of King Mohammed V.

On his new job in 1944, Leonard Ackerman soon made contact with Camp Lyautey's director, a Monsieur M. Beckleman. Among others he quickly reached was Selden Chapin, the American representative to the French Comité départemental de libération and together they went to see René Massigli, the Free French foreign minister to relay the concern expressed in the statement presented by them: "The highly technical, obstructionist tactics of the lower ranking French officials has already unduly delayed the movement of the refugees. They cannot be permitted to continue if the refugee center is to be opened in time to be of some value."

Promised by Massigli that these "dilatory tactics" would be investigated, the American duo also called on Pierre Mendès France, the Jewish French politician who was then finance minister and later prime minister. They also met with Paul Bonnet, the minister of propaganda. Both top officials promised help. "These calls produced results," Ackerman reported. The technical delays were dropped. Soon, he could also report: "Approximately 400 refugees were approved for movement."

But not all hurdles had been overcome. There was the problem of transporting refugees out of Spain. The U.S. promised to pay the costs with WRB money. The British were to provide ships. But the Brits reneged. That left the Americans to rely on the French who had a ship finishing her repairs at Casablanca. A deal was made to move those refugees, thus freeing up room for more of them to leave France. Unfortunately, the French ship was called away for "an urgent French voyage." It was promised, though, that after the voyage was done, she could be used.

Beckleman expressed his worry that with the closing of the American air base in Casablanca, he would not have enough supplies or personnel. Ackerman took him to Allied Headquarters in Algiers and received assurance of U.S. military help.

Again the British proved non-cooperative if not outright obstructionist. They finally did supply a ship but with only two days notice of its sailing date. To round up scattered refugees within the time limit was obviously impossible. Nor would they agree to offer a new date. Consequently, Ackerman hurried to Algiers, talked to the U.S. War Shipping Administration and also to Ambassador Robert Murphy, who immediately wrote a letter to Admiral Hewitt, head of the North African Naval Forces. His intervention brought results. A ship with seven hundred refugees left from Spain in the third week of June 1944.

The complications, it seemed, never ceased. The problem of a group of Sephardic Jews was a case in point. These Sephardics were descendants of Jews that Spain had expelled in 1492 and Portugal did sometime later. They were quite distinct from the far more numerous Jews in Western and Eastern Europe. Their language, Ladino, was Spanish in origin in contrast to the Ashkenazim, whose tongue Yiddish was mainly a form of German with Slavic additions.

In Greece especially, the Sephardics had suffered greatly. At first the Nazis, who had occupied their heartland in Northern Macedonia and its capital Salonica in April 1941, gave them a year's grace. But in July 1942, all Greek Jews between the ages of eighteen and thirty-five were order to register for forced labor. In effect, this was a form of blackmail in which the Germans milked the community for an ever higher ransom that was to reach *1.5 billion drachmas*.

Sephardic Jews from neutral countries also contributed, including a colony from Spain and another from Axis member Italy. Having collected this shakedown money, the Germans seven months later nullified their part of the implied bargain by imposing their draconian racial laws: yellow stars, concentration in ghettoes, etc. Deportations soon commenced. They started in a camp set up in a section of Salonica for refugees in World War I, which had been named for Baron Maurice de Hirsch, a famed German-Jewish philanthropist of the last century, who had established agricultural enclaves of his coreligionists in Russia and Argentina. Seventeen transports departing for Poland led the way. In all, in 1943, 48,000 Greek Sephardics were carted off to the death camps and never heard from again.

The Sephardics in Greece from neutral countries—Spain,

Switzerland, Turkey, Portugal, and even formerly non-neutral Italy—
were also expelled. With the exception of Spain, they were all taken
back in. But the government of Generalissimo Francisco Franco made
difficulties, going back on their promise to repatriate these actual one-
time citizens of theirs.

Madrid insisted the Sephardics could not come in *en bloc* as a single
group. They had to be reviewed individually on a case-by-case basis.
Meanwhile, they would remain in German concentration camps for
two-to-three months. From the homegrown ghetto set up in the
"Baron Hirsch" section of Salonica, these Jews had been sent to
Bergen-Belsen, where the Nazis kept subjects of neutral countries.
Then, the first week of January 1944, the Germans said the Spaniards
among them could leave for Spain.

On the 23rd of March, 1944, an interoffice memo from John Pehle
to one of his assistant executive directors, Joseph Bivens Friedman,
Pehle stated he had talked to "Monet (sic)" (Jean Monnet, the postwar
sparkplug for the European Union) about better cooperation with
the Comité, and Monnet said he would "cable Algiers promptly."
Also he stated that Henri Frenay, who was a member of the Comité
"would handle the problem in Algiers and will probably get in touch
with Ackerman." Pehle said to contact Ackerman and "tell him of
my talking with Monet and advise us of the results. The two points I
stressed with Monet were the security problems and the problem of
the Sephardic Jews."

A letter from the Joint representative in Lisbon dated March 25,
1944, to his superiors in New York City detailed the continued perils
plaguing the Spanish Sephardic group. It spoke of the recent arrival
in Barcelona of 365 Sephardics from Salonica, whom the Franco
government authorities had allowed to enter but stipulated must leave
in short order and be hustled off to Morocco.

Here, too, another beaut of a bureaucratic Catch-22 came into play.
The Moroccan Government initially had been cooperative but now
set a March 1, 1944, deadline for compliance. The ripple effect of this
was that Spain pulled back from receiving a number of Sephardic Jews
still in France until Madrid received assurances they would be shipped
"shortly after their arrival to Camp Lyautey."

It was Ackerman's task to inform the Moroccans no such deadline
could stand, and would violate the agreement on the matter between
the French Committee of Liberation, the British, and the Americans.

The flak came at Ackerman from all sides. For example, when his own American authorities said there were not enough medical personnel on hand and wanted to reduce the number of refugees allowed in by ten thousand, Ackerman had to set about rounding up doctors in the U.S. He was able also to have a restrictive order rescinded cutting the number of refugees to five hundred a week by offering more space and medical staff.

Dropped into the WRB's special attaché's lap was the thorny conundrum of what to do about Spanish Republican refugees in French North Africa, since they had no government of their own to issue visas. Certainly the Franco government whom they had fought in the Spanish Civil War wouldn't lift a finger for them. Nor was there a Mexican representative from the country where many wished to go. Others who needed Ackerman to intervene for them were illegals still hiding in Spain and Italy.

Ackerman's reach was soon well beyond North Africa. He became involved with the evacuation to southern Italy of 1,100 Yugoslav children facing malnutrition. There were refugees on the Yugoslav Croatian island of Rab off the Adriatic coast and in July 1944, Ackerman wrote: "I was visited by a Croatian Jew connected with a partisan relief organization and told of more than 1000 Jews in Croatia whom he thought should be evacuated." Before the Germans reoccupied Rab, the partisans had removed the Jews there to the more distant island of Vis, and some of them were later to come to the U.S. Other such groups attempted to leave Yugoslavia via Slovenia, Serbia and Montenegro, but only twenty-nine succeeded. Also, Josip Broz Tito, the top Yugoslav partisan leader, was imposing restrictions.

During a trip to Bari, Italy, on the other side of the Adriatic, the American agent met with a Max Perlman, a representative of the Joint and they were to continue their discussions after Ackerman left the immediate area.

Refugee camps had sprung up in Italy once the Allies occupied its south and central regions. Located at Bari, Santa Maria di Bagni, Ferramente, Salerno, Campagna, Taranto, Naples and Rome, these were eventually consolidated in a single camp at Aversa, ten miles north of Naples. Efforts were likewise attempted to aid refugees still in northern Italy, principally with the help of the OSS. At Lucca above Pisa, the Allies freed a large number of Jews and political refugees and when Florence was captured, Jews in hiding there were "liberated." No efforts by the Germans to massacre the Jews at Lucca and Florence had taken place.

OSS efforts to enlist the Italian partisans in these efforts ran into the problem of the partisans' own need for support, themselves— food and military equipment especially. Planes dropped them supplies, but there were not enough planes to include supplies for refugees. Ackerman was asked to have the WRB plead for more planes.

In war-torn Yugoslavia, the biggest problem, too, was the lack of relief supplies, not German atrocities.

The German invasion of Hungary on March 19, 1944, added a new dimension to Ackerman's work. Although Jim Saxon, the WRB's "roaming problem solver" was brought in to assist, Leonard Ackerman would end up incorporated into dealing with this latest Nazi aggression.

His contacts in Yugoslavia may have been a reason. Tito had promised to aid the Hungarian Jews, and his partisan forces controlled the Drava River close to Hungary. As many as seven thousand Hungarians were able to escape to safety through this area.

Ackerman was sent to Rome to try to get Pope Pius XII to intervene, not only in Yugoslavia with its large Catholic populations in Croatia and Slovenia but in Slovakia as well, a very Catholic component of Czechoslovakia. In Rome, Ackerman met with Myron C. Taylor, FDR's close friend and emissary to the Vatican, who sent a message to the Holy Father. A plea urging persecutions of Jews to cease went from Rome to Slovakia, whose government was actually headed by a Catholic priest, Father Jozef Tiso, and also in time the same word went to Hungary.

The cable facilities provided by the WRB in this effort proved to be of great help. Ackerman afterward stated: "It can be concluded . . . that if the Board had not operated in the area, much harm might have resulted to the refugee rescue movement."

High-ranking British officers were not known for their sympathies to the refugee problem, but one of them was honest enough to concede publicly that the removal of refugees did aid the war effort. It improved partisan morale in Yugoslavia, made more food available for troops, and got civilians out of the way who might otherwise have impeded military action.

Early in September 1944, the International Committee of the Red Cross had contacted a Monsieur Raymond Courvoisier, newly arrived in Budapest that August, regarding "the urgent emigration of Hungarian

Jews who had emigration certificates." It had been learned that the Nazis intended to deport all three hundred thousand Hungarian Jews to Germany. As they had with Romanian Jews, the Allies summoned a meeting of the Advisory Committee on Refugees and Displaced Persons, Mediterranean Theater, at the American Forces headquarters, during which Ackerman participated along with twenty-four others, both from military and nonmilitary organizations.

It has been estimated that 45,000 displaced persons (DP) received care in Italy, among whom were 28,120 Yugoslavs sent off to camps in Egypt. Of Jews allowed into Palestine, there were only 571 and another 986 stateless survivors eventually evacuated to the United States. That left some 8,500 in DP camps. When the suggestion was offered that Fedhala should be closed, since Philippeville was now in service, Ackerman vigorously opposed such a move.

In doing so, he was supported by Sir Clifford Heathcote-Smith, a British leader of the Intergovernmental Committee on Refugees and also by G-5, the U.S. Intelligence agency. It was the folks at UNRRA who had proposed its closing. An agreement was finally reached on moving Yugoslavs "in and out" of Italy. This flare-up concluded with a decision that Italy could take in four thousand more Yugoslavs and that Philippeville would be put in play if additional space were necessary.

As always, Ackerman faced nitpicky but very real complications. The political and ethnic splits in Yugoslav society decreed, for instance, that the heavily Serbian Royal Yugoslav Red Cross would receive recognition and the all-inclusive Serbian, Croatian, Slovenian, Macedonian, Montenegrin, Bosnian, partisan Red Cross would not. Someone also had the bright idea that stockpiles of relief supplies in the Middle East could not be utilized in any country until the *entire country* was liberated.

Ackerman had to make a personal visit to Siena, Italy, in order to ascertain the real facts about refugees in Nazi-occupied northern Italy. The Italian concentration camp at the walled Tuscan city of Lucca had just been liberated and one thousand prisoners, mainly Jews, set free. Allegedly such camps were awaiting similar salvation at Verona and Padua.

Money to recompense Yugoslav boatmen for evacuating refugees from Rab was likewise needed. The island had been recaptured by the Nazis in February 1944, and thus Ackerman's plan to remove the remaining refugees in March had to be aborted. Prior to then, during the last weeks of 1943 and the first weeks of 1944, approximately 1,500 Yugoslavs escaped their country into Italy, primarily on small native schooners manned by partisans but directed by a few American Army Intelligence officers.

Because of the interference of a British major, there was an attempt in May 1944 to shut down this Yugoslav operation. Again Ackerman loudly protested this new shortsightedness, and he took his case to the commanding officer of the military government and to Ambassador Robert Murphy. His argument was that the number of refugees was far less than the "misinformed" British officer had calculated. The available unused facilities could accommodate one thousand more refugees. The disputed matter went all the way to D.C. and was brought to FDR's attention. One upshot was the adding of Philippeville to the WRB's domain, with its capacity of ten thousand to forty thousand souls. As if he were swatting mosquitoes, Ackerman then had to deal with a proposal, based on an alleged lack of medical personnel, to reduce their forty thousand patients to thirty thousand. The WRB special attaché went straight to work rounding up doctors in the U.S. If these parried assaults weren't enough of a headache, a restrictive order was given from above to reduce the number of allowable refugees to five hundred a week. Ackerman was able to have it rescinded in July 1944.

No doubt it was wearying to cope with all this bureaucratic foolishness, but how could he do otherwise? That same July, the problem landed on his plate of the one thousand Jews in Croatia, who had to be evacuated ahead the resurgent Germans as well as 1,100 Yugoslav children facing death from malnutrition.

At this point, an experiment was tied to clear away some of these roadblocks. It was nothing less than the shipping of refugees into the United States. Roosevelt was aware of the criticism, actually begun at the Évian Conference in 1938, that the American government was pushing other governments to take in German Jews fleeing the Third Reich but wasn't willing to accept many of them except through normal immigration channels. That complaint, if anything, had grown louder as the war progressed in spite of or even because of the exertions of the War Refugee Board. FDR was running for reelection in November 1944. Consequently, the decision was reached to accommodate a sample body of nine hundred-plus mainly Jewish refugees and house them at a deactivated military base in Upstate New York.

The *Oswego* affair will be examined in depth later on. Had it worked and expanded the available catchment area, Leonard Ackerman's tour of duty might have been less frantic than it was.

In the spring of 1944, the question of German war crimes was coming under discussion. A particular atrocity in France was aired on U.S. radio, in which the town of Ascq near Lille in northern France witnessed the massacre of the entire male population in reprisal for an act of sabotage nearby. Particularly striking was the description of the local Catholic priest hearing the confessions of those about to be shot and then, once finished, being himself shot in the back.

That June, a Waffen SS unit containing drafted Alsatians obliterated the town of Oradour-sur-Glane in the Limousin, killing all but two of its six hundred-plus inhabitants.

Stars and Stripes, the U.S. military publication, reported how the Germans, before leaving Lyon, shot one hundred Jews and a few Catholic priests.

Ackerman's British counterpart, Sir Clifford Heathcote-Smith, chimed in while discussing deportations in Italy: "My suggestion is to back up Roosevelt and Churchill's statements of punishment with action. I know that a list of war criminals will be submitted to Washington." To which Ackerman added: "If any are captured, we should go right after them. Try them as soon as possible."

One suggestion that no doubt never passed the *straight-face test* was whether or not to talk directly to the Germans "to permit a mass evacuation of Jewish refugees." However, negotiations to that end, albeit seen as unproductive, "should be continued and the Nazis prompted to treat their Jewish captives like any other civilian internees." This wasn't simply naïve. The idea was to string out the discussions, since every day delayed might in the end save lives. The Americans were to inform their Nazi counterparts that they would accept "exchanges" (of prisoners) because "even if no exchanges materialized, the re-opening of exchange negotiations may help stay the executioner's hand."

On April 17, 1944, *Les Dernières Nouvelles d'Algérie*, the Free French newspaper, gave play to a speech by *Le Grand Rabbin Neuman*, apparently the chief rabbi with the American forces. He was giving a message of hope to the Jews of the entire world on the occasion of *Les Pâques Juives*—literally the "Jewish Easter"—i.e. the holiday of Passover. Neuman was assuring all Jews of the "sympathy of all

Americans and urging them to believe, as expressed by President Franklin D. Roosevelt, that the torturers of the people of Israel will not escape punishment."

About a week later, John Pehle communicated to Ackerman that Ira Hirschmann, back in D.C. from Ankara, "had given a very favorable account of what you and Saxon are trying to do . . . as well as your difficulties."

Around the same time, pressure to take in more Yugoslav civilians was coming from General Vladimir "Vlatko" Velebit of Tito's partisan army. His goal, after completing the agreed-upon 25,500, was to add another four to five thousand persons each month. After expressing concern over some Yugoslav women and children sent to the Canal Zone and their problems with the tropical climate, Velebit provided figures showing that 19,700 of his countrymen had already been evacuated and that 5,800 would need to enter just to complete the originally decided total—3,300 of them destined for Italy. He also pointed out that in the last six weeks, 1,850 per week had been arriving.

A notation on Velebit's plea to *increase the quota* was that it had been made due to the Nazis' recent indiscriminate policy of massacre, herein described.

In point of fact, the quota number of 25,500 had only been reluctantly accepted. Asking for more raised a hornets nest. Also, the partisan-Royalist split among the Yugoslavs already escaped reared its head again and caused a segregating of arrivals between Tito supporters and the Royal Yugoslav Labor companies in Algeria connected to Draža Mihailović, a Serbian foe of Tito in the home country.

When Syria was proposed for additional space, the objection arose that the Arabs would resist accommodating non-Muslims. The suggestion of Libya as a substitution triggered the same response.

General Velebit, nevertheless, kept pushing for Tunisia and Algeria.

Finally, a policy decision was made to bring additional refugees to Tunisia and Algeria and, if rebuffed there, ship them to Egypt.

Robert Murphy was adamant in his opposition to more Yugoslavs, declaring: "Allied personnel operating landing craft used to carry provisions across the Adriatic should be instructed not to provide transportation to Yugoslav refugees when returning to Italy except in such cases where it is impossible to do so."

Strong wills could be anonymous, too. Unnamed Blockade authorities, flourishing their authority, "refused to change their policies with respect to use of Red Cross food parcels for Jews in internment concentration camps and labor camps." The glaring example cited was that there were 1,200 Jews in concentration camps in Croatia and large stocks of Red Cross parcels stored and unused in Switzerland. The entreaties of the War Refugee Board and the International Red Cross to distribute them were to no avail. Dr. Soubbotitch (sic), the Red Cross delegate of the Yugoslav Government-in-Exile, tried to intervene. A Mr. Ryan of the American Red Cross told him he would "not authorize the use of Red Cross parcels for this purpose. These food parcels are earmarked," he said, "for the exclusive use of such internees as are officially recognized as civilian internees. Should the Blockade authorities learn that they have been distributed to people who do not fall within this category, the entire Red Cross food parcel service for POW's and civilian internees would be jeopardized."

The folks negotiating for a change complained they had been at it for more than a year and a half "without making the slightest progress . . . have come up against a blank wall of stubbornness and bad will . . . suggest that the President be respectfully requested to cut the Gordian knot by personally taking up this matter with the Blockade authorities in London."

Aside from policy disputes like these, personnel questions are never far from surfacing during government operations. A protracted one for Leonard Ackerman concerned a certain David Zagha and, as if to assert the global reach of the War Refugee Board, originated in—of all places—Uruguay.

That is to say, this David Zagha was in Montevideo when he wrote to John Pehle on March 30, 1944: "I shall be in Buenos Aires tomorrow and expect to leave for North Africa in ten days time."

Nine days earlier, Ackerman in Algiers had heard from Pehle that the WRB had decided to use "the services of one David Zagha for increasing the flow of refugees from France to Spain. Zagha is a Syrian Jew who has lived for many years in Algiers. He is known to Colonel Bernstein," Colonel Bernard Bernstein, assistant director of Fiscal and Financial Section, Supreme Headquarters, American Expeditionary Force.

Parenthetically, Colonel Bernstein had been asked for his opinion about hiring Zagha and all the reports that came back were "highly favorable." Zagha, it was said, "had been a great aid to the war effort in that area [Algeria], risking his life in connection with this work."

So on March 4, 1944, Pehle wrote Zagha: "You have been appointed special agent of the War Refugee Board." Added was that the authorization expired in three months.

While still in Uruguay, Zagha informed the WRB of a talk he had had with the Uruguayan sub-secretary of foreign relations, Dr. Arbanell-MacColl, about having refugees accepted by Uruguay.

In a subsequent communication from Pehle to Ackerman, it was stressed that the greatest benefit of employing Zagha would be getting him into Spain. "Try to obtain a Spanish visa for him and consider his mission highly confidential." It would be judged on its success in increasing the entry of refugees into Spain.

Government, as everyone knows, works in mysterious ways. By the beginning of June 1944, something had gone wrong concerning the Zagha mission. Pehle wrote Ackerman: "Certain reports I have received give me some doubt as to Zagha's discretion." On June 5, Ackerman in Algiers replied that he had carried out the order to inform David Zagha that "his services could not be used for the WRB in Spain."

Zagha's plaintive response was that if he wasn't a WRB representative, he could end up in a (French?) concentration camp. Claiming that other U.S. agencies wanted his services so, would Ackerman procure him a U.S. visa? He also asked for his original appointment to be renewed. Ackerman's cold response was that he saw "no need for it unless circumstances change." And there, presumably, the puzzling matter stood.

Prickly personalities emerged within the ranks. One of special note was Captain Paul Warburg of the American branch of the famous banking family. On Ambassador Murphy's staff at Algiers, his "nominal duties" were described as dealing with "the so-called Jewish problems arising in French North Africa." Initially, it seemed, even after the *liberation* of the French colonies, anti-Semitic Vichyites had been kept in office and Jews kept in degrading confinement. A memo from Mike Hoffman at the Treasury Department to Pehle stated: "As far as I know, Warburg has never contributed anything to the alleviation of the conditions of Jews in North Africa," and he was likely to be a hindrance to Ackerman's operations. So Ackerman began to bypass Warburg. It was further stated in Hoffman's memo that the "unanimous opinion of the Treasury representatives in the area" that the work of the War Refugee Board "would be furthered by the removal of Warburg from the area."

Paul Warburg's nickname was "Piggy." In the prewar era, he had been described as a "trust fund baby, college dropout, binge drinker, philanderer." One statement about him was that "If God was bent on punishing non-Orthodox Jews, he might have started with Paul 'Piggy' Warburg."

Even his own Father Felix took umbrage with his scapegrace son. He stopped him from undertaking an investment one of his friends wanted to make, stating: "If you are so careless with money, I'm going to put you on an allowance." The friend was William S. Paley and the investment was a radio station called CBS.

Another black mark against Captain Paul Warburg was his going around spreading the *rumor* that "the War Refugee Board was purely a political move on the part of the President for the purpose of getting votes."

The State Department's man in North Africa was Pennsylvania-born Selden Chapin, a graduate of the Naval Academy who had been temporarily put in charge of the embassy, which was accredited to the French National Committee of Liberation, the embryonic Free French Government.

Ackerman's take on Chapin was expressed quite candidly. "I have no great hopes that Chapin will succeed in aiding the program very much. While he morally agrees to adopt some of my suggestions, I do not think that he feels strongly enough on the subject to take any action except the most routine. I have hopes that when Ambassador Wilson [career diplomat Edwin C. Wilson] returns, the greater prestige of the Ambassador's title will be of more assistance."

Thus, less than two weeks into his new job, Ackerman would have been delighted to receive the letter he did from D.C. that might be deemed *anti-bureaucratic* in terms of U.S. Government procedure.

In it, the War Refugee Board's relationship to the still-extant Intergovernmental Committee on Political Refugees was officially spelled out in four points:

The War Refugee Board is an American organization. The Intergovernmental Committee represents more than thirty nations. Therefore, the Intergovernmental Committee "is in no position effectively and promptly to carry out the policy of any one individual nation."

The War Refugee Board will lend help to the Intergovernmental Committee for any or all of its projects "designed to bring about a speedy rescue of victims of enemy oppression."

The War Refugee Board will not clear any project with the Intergovernmental Committee unless it will speed things up. "In the less than two months it has been in existence, the Board [WRB] has already taken many steps designed to save people from death . . . The War Refugee Board is in a better position to take more expeditious action than is the Intergovernmental Committee."

Tucked in among these three was an obvious enjoinder to the WRB that "if the Intergovernmental Committee can do it better, the War Refugee Board will defer to them and help them."

In a matter of weeks, Leonard Ackerman had settled nicely into his job and like all the other WRB special attachés, was working his tail off.

Chapter Seven

Switzerland! The epitome of the country's many assets still is, of course—its *neutrality*. The Helvetic Confederation, which today encompasses twenty-six cantons, holding some eight million citizens, dates its earliest organizing as a country back to 1291. During its modern-day iteration, it has long been a prime venue for peace efforts in a never-ending quest for international cooperation. Its citizens have coexisted effortlessly, despite speaking three major languages—German, French, Italian—and a fourth, Romansh, an archaic argot used in remote areas by approximately forty thousand persons.

In World War II, especially, Switzerland was a beehive of activity—spying, negotiating, providing safe haven, a temporary home to refugees and go-betweens, a funnel for supplies, cradle of fanciful plots, etc. It was a *no-brainer* that the War Refugee Board would place one of its special attachés there, housed in the embassy at Bern, the capital city.

The man they chose, the Quaker Roswell D. McClelland, had been working for the American Friends Service Committee in Vichy France and Switzerland since 1942. Essentially, by going to the War Refugee Board, he simply went on doing what he'd already been doing—dealing with the refugee problem.

It might well be wondered, though, if McClelland's connection with Allen Dulles, head of the OSS in Europe, preceded his recruitment by the WRB. Quaker pacifism apparently was not a barrier to his assisting the superspy and derring-do agency of the American military in combat.

McClelland even formed a working relationship with the bellicose chief of the Swiss Division of Justice and Police, Heinrich Rothmund, who was remembered for his anti-Semitic outburst at the 1938 Évian Conference. His shocking words then were: "Switzerland, which has as little use for the Jews as Nazi Germany will herself take measures to protect Switzerland from being swamped by Jews with the connivance of the Viennese police."

In September of that same prewar year, Rothmund visited the German concentration camp at Orienburg and told the SS officers he met: "The people and government of Switzerland [have] long since become fully cognizant of the danger of Judaization and have consistently defended themselves against it."

Rothmund has also been tagged with having offered a proposal, later dubbed "notorious," that before the Nazis let people leave Germany, the passports of Jews be stamped with a J in scarlet red ink. Or maybe it wasn't original artifice of his and he was reviving an anti-Semitic harassment from the past.

The U.S. State Department—at least certain of its high-level members—might secretly have been applauding Rothmund's obstructionism.

"Jews with false papers" was the pejorative term that no doubt was only uttered among themselves. They went hard at it, "weeding out imposters," as they put it. Their outrage obviously was focused on those they called riffraff frantic to save their lives. How dare they strive to pull down the barriers that so painstakingly had been erected against them? Why couldn't they just quietly accept their fate as murder victims?

Even in March 1944, with the War Refugee Board off and running, the State Department circulated an internal report in D.C. that sets your teeth on edge reading it more than half a century later.

"It is oversimplification to say hundreds or thousands of Jewish refugees will be killed if South American passports are not supplied to them . . . We should not be forced, and we shall not willingly accept, a proposal which is essentially fraudulent and improper . . .

"There have been instances where persons holding such passports later traveled to or through the United States and, once having arrived in this country, have remained here creating a problem for our immigration people . . .

"As a result of this our Government took a definite stand against the practice. We prevailed upon some of the other American republics to stop it, to prevent its recurrence, and to take steps to invalidate documents already issued."

"Heedless persons" were blamed by this vicious State Department report for "pushing" them into "embarrassment and misunderstanding with the other American republics."

When it was made clear to the stuffed shirts at State that they would have to change positions and urge the Latin Americans to honor their documents, including forged ones, the indignation rose to the heavens. Every official called to a meeting to discuss a telegram to their Latin American counterparts about the new policy, loudly protested. Their only excuse afterward was that they didn't know about the Nazis' Final intentions.

Any "war crime" of knowingly or unknowingly committing these people to unjust execution had to be matched against a plethora of what they considered horrific actions, like "fraud, deceit, bribery, counterfeiting, double-crossing, debasing the whole problem of saving refugees and placing this government in an untenable and malodorous position."

The case of the illustrious Yiddish poet and playwright Itzhak Katzenelson and his son Zvi tragically shows the human content of this conflict and the horrifying result of the State Department's alleged unintended consequences.

Katzenelson and the boy had been in Poland for the Warsaw Ghetto Uprising but safely hidden in a non-Jewish section of the city. The papers they carried, making them citizens of Honduras, had been given out (no doubt at a cost) by the Gestapo, who had obtained them and were willing to employ them in a subterfuge wherein the holders of these documents would be exchanged for Germans held as enemy aliens in Central and South America.

Earlier, Katzenelson had lost his wife and two younger sons at the Treblinka death camp and escaped to France where he and Zvi had been interned in a detention camp at the watering spot of Vittel. There he composed the *Vittel Diary* and completed his most famous work, *The Song of the Murdered Jewish Nation*.

As a Jew, it is hard to read it now almost three quarters of a century later without welling up. Sample:

> I saw children brought in from the street.
> I hid in a corner.
> And saw a two-year-old girl in the lap of a teacher.
> Thin, deathly pale, with such grave eyes.
> I watched the two-year-old grandmother.
> The tiny Jewish girl, a hundred years old in her seriousness and grief.

It was not only the loss of his people that Katzenelson mourned. It was his personal tragedy, as well, the murders of his wife and two sons.

"Oh, Chanah, my exalted one! My muse! Oh, my Benzikel and my Benyaminiker . . ."

In April 1944, Katzenelson and Zvi were transported in France to Drancy, a way station, and then on to Auschwitz where they were put to death, no doubt writing untimely finis to a literary talent who might have provided who knows what masterpieces.

Their obviously *un-bona-fide* Honduran papers, in this instance, did not protect them. Nor would *genuine* ones have done so, either.

Since Roswell McClelland had been in Switzerland before he became active with the War Refugee Board, he was sometimes asked— or chided—why he hadn't made any noise about the wholesale murders taking place just across the border in Germany. "You had intimations," he responded weakly. "But then you were swept on and there was a lot of work to do." The allegations, he admitted, "sort of faded to the background."

Not that voices hadn't been raised. Like Gerhart Riegner's, whose 1942 revelation from Switzerland of the Final Solution was shunted aside notwithstanding the American vice-consul in Geneva's vouching for him as "a serious and balanced individual." Or like Jan Karski, the Polish underground fighter whose story was *un-believed* by Felix Frankfurter, who didn't say Karski was lying (maybe just fantasizing). Or Alfred Wetzler and Rudolf Vrba, two Slovakians, the first actual escapees from Auschwitz and eyewitnesses to its horrors.

An *unnamed* State Department official in Washington was quoted as saying apropos of Riegner: "Stuff like this has been coming out of Bern since 1942 . . . This is a Jew talking about other Jews."

McClelland defended his pre-WRB inaction by recalling having "a gut knowledge that the Jews in France would be killed." He had been living in unoccupied France before his move to Bern. Nevertheless, confessions of his fears on an official level were apparently confined to a ten-minute chat he had with Pierre Laval, the Vichy prime minister. Laval, eventually executed for treason by the postwar French Government, told the American he was "a victim of atrocity propaganda . . . Such killings were not taking place."

It was *unwritten* State Department policy to deny and deny. When Herschel Johnson, the U.S. ambassador to Sweden, heard a story from a German eyewitness how of 450,000 Jews in prewar Warsaw only

50,000 remained alive, he pooh-poohed it as "fantastic" in his report to D.C.

Even late in the day, in April 1944, the State Department was still stonewalling. On April 10, Wetzler and Vrba escaped from Auschwitz. A report from them was sent to Western Intelligence officers, along with "an urgent request to bomb" the rail lines leading into the sprawling human abattoir.

That idea was in the air. A rabbi from Slovakia in Palestine, Michael Dov Ber Weissmandl, pushed the suggestion forward to the Jewish Agency, the de facto government for Jews in the Holy Land. So did the future president of Israel, Moshe Shertok (Sharett), and a future Israeli minister of the interior, and Yitzhak Gruenbaum, leader of the Jewish Agency's Rescue Committee. But on June 1, as it was said, the Jewish Agency "promptly squashed the notion."

McClelland forwarded the parts of this report he had received to his superiors in D.C., where they arrived on July 8 and July 16. The entire report came only in October.

The debate raged behind the scenes. David Ben-Gurion, the top Jewish leader in the Holy Land, said absolutely No to bombing—not in places where there were Jews.

At the WRB, a lower-level official, Bernard Akzin, also recommended no bombing. His higher-up Lawrence Lesser on the WRB staff discussed the issue with A. Leon Kubowitzski of the World Jewish Congress's rescue committee. In a letter to John Pehle, Kubowitzski argued that "Jews would be killed and the Nazis would blame the Allies."

There have been endless debates about the dilemma over bombing the rail lines leading to Auschwitz-Birkenau and also hitting the actual camps themselves. Today, we know that no action was ever taken, despite vociferous and high-placed pleas for this to happen.

One of their converts was Benjamin Akzin, himself.

The present-day book, *1944, FDR and the Year that Changed History* by Jay Winnik (New York, Simon and Schuster, 2015), offers a fully-fleshed-out depiction of what happened in this much-bruited wartime instance.

Author Winnick has called the bomb-or-not-to-bomb conundrum "one of the most momentous decisions of Roosevelt's presidency."

While this may have been a bit of hyperbole, the issue remains with us not in relation to its military effect, if any, but as a moral quandary in which the Allied leaders did not exactly shine. Perhaps one hundred thousand more Jews might have survived, even if there would have been casualties among prisoners who had already been marked for death. We will never know the sum total if the *if* had taken place.

For a time, the WRB was forwarding suggestions for bombing but not endorsing them. Finally, on November 8, 1944, Pehle reluctantly did ask John J. McCloy, number-two man at the War Department to authorize a bombing campaign after Benjamin Akzin now drafted a memo that called not only for bombing the rail lines but additionally the camps themselves.

McClelland's contacts with Recha Sternbuch, her husband Yitzhak and his brother Eli have been touched upon already. These three, with Recha seemingly in the lead, had been operating their own "Rescue Committee" long before their hook-up with the War Refugee Board. These were Orthodox Jews and representatives in their adopted country of the Vaad Hatzalah. Recha's maiden name had been Rottenberg and earlier she had emigrated from Poland to Antwerp, Belgium, where she married Yitzhak, a Belgian businessman, originally from a Chassidic family in Bukovina, Romania. After their marriage, they removed to Montreux, Switzerland, where Yitzhak and Eli continued in business.

Their first clandestine work had been in concert with a Swiss police captain, Paul Grueninger, during which they smuggled in eight hundred Jewish refugees from Germany and Austria. The U.S. State Department holier-than-thous and Sir Herbert Emerson notwithstanding, they had used forged Swiss visas.

In fact, Recha and Grueninger, informed on, were actually caught in this endeavor. She was jailed and he lost his police job and pension. But once released, she went right back to smuggling forged passports into Germany and Austria.

Recha used the Polish Government-in-Exile's Swiss branch diplomatic pouch to send messages to her contacts in the U.S. and Turkey. Later she used their codes, which she had to in order to evade McClelland who was dead-set against her negotiating ransoms with the Nazis.

She established good relations with the Papal nuncio in Switzerland, Monsignor Filippo Bernardini. Thus she was also able to take advantage of Vatican couriers to relay information to Jewish underground resistance bodies in German occupied territories. It has been said she was the first to employ South American identity papers.

Apparently, too, she made entry visas available for China.

That is a story in itself. As told by Evelyn Pike Rubin in her book, *Ghetto Shanghai*, the history of the small colony of Jews that made it to safety in the Far East illustrated the Catch-22 horror of trying to escape the Holocaust. When her family finally decided they had to leave their German homeland, their first choice, no surprise, was America. But in applying for a visa, they learned they would have to enter on the Polish quota, because the birthplace of both mother and father had been in Pozna☐, at the time a Polish city. The wait for them would take years and therefore, in their desperation, they turned to Shanghai, no doubt helped by visas that Recha Sternbuch provided.

Shanghai was what in the news world would be called a *side-bar*. It was the end of the earth to most European Jews. "What are you, crazy? Go where?" Evelyn Rubin's family was taunted. There was also a bit of Alice-in-Wonderlandish contradiction about these visas there. They were *not* needed to get into Shanghai; their usefulness was really as *exit visas*. Once beyond the reach of the Nazis, Jewish escapees could go on to other destinations.

At Recha's trial, her lawyer admitted such was her intent. "One should point to the Palestinian transport in the spring of 1939 in which Madame Sternbuch took part," he said. The real goal in that case was illegal entry into Palestine. These Chinese visas were used to fool countries like Italy that demanded to know end-stops. Dr. Feng Shan Ho, the Chinese Consul in Vienna, was only too happy to use these documents to get people out of Austria and even out of concentration camps like Dachau.

It should be noted that the only place in China where these refugees were accepted was in Shanghai, a cosmopolitan city not under Chinese Government control.

In September 1944, Recha approached Jean-Marie Musy, the former president of the Swiss Republic, known as a Nazi sympathizer, and began a chain of extraordinary if ultimately futile events. Musy, the publisher of the arch rightwing newspaper *La Jeune*, had used his friendship with Heinrich Himmler and a sum of ten thousand Swiss francs to free a Jewish couple from a concentration camp. Why could he not do the same for other doomed Jews, the Sternbuchs reasoned.

Musy's turnabout from extoller of Nazis to would-be savior of Jews had an obvious explanation. By September 1944, the Germans were clearly losing the war. An adroit politician who had reached the highest levels of his country's government, Jean-Marie Musy saw his chance for redemption when the Allies won and maybe—although he denied it—the chance to make a little money.

Roswell McClelland considered Musy "a very dangerous person" and labeled the operation he was proposing—a whole swap of Jewish lives for thousands of trucks and equipment—a "counter propaganda on his friend Himmler's behalf."

Musy's own narrative, issued by him in 1945 in a report to the Union of Orthodox Rabbis of the United States and Canada, starts when a Monsieur and Madame Lob came to him and appealed for his help to save her sister and husband—the Bloch family. They had been arrested in France by the Germans. The Lob and Musy families had known each other for a long time, Musy having been Lob's lawyer and their sons having done their Swiss military service together.

Agreeing to aid them, Musy went to Paris and met with General Oberg, chief of the German police in France, who declared to him that "no Jew who has entered a concentration camp has ever come out of it." Whether true or not (my own father-in-law was released from Dachau in 1938), Musy argued that Madame Bloch was a Swiss citizen. His persistence paid off. The couple was freed.

Later that year, Musy was approached again on behalf of the Union of Orthodox Rabbis of the United States and Canada through Isaac and Recha Sternbuch who asked him to use his contacts in Germany to free more Jews from concentration camps.

The most important of these contacts who Musy wrote to was naturally Reichsführer Heinrich Himmler, commander of the SS, the second most powerful man in the Third Reich. They had known each other since the ex-president of Switzerland was helping organize "Anti-Communist Committees" in Europe.

Himmler wrote back, and a meeting was arranged in Berlin. The only way to get there was by automobile, a dangerous trip, since Allied war planes were strafing the roads. But Musy set out on the 560 mile drive accompanied by his son Benoit.

At this point, Musy's "report" turned into a puff piece, extolling himself. Writing in the third person, he gushed: "Nevertheless for Jean-Marie Musy, the danger which he would encounter did not play an important role in his decision to accept the mission. It was with a deep sentiment of humanity and Christian concern that drove Jean-Marie

Musy and his son Benoit to intervene on behalf of the prisoners of the concentration camps," and he pointedly emphasizes: "They have never asked for or received personal compensation."

Then, the writer even put in a quote that he claims Reichsführer Himmler said about him, i.e. "He [Musy] was a man totally unselfish, extremely intelligent and educated who *only had one goal: to save as many lives as possible* amongst the hundreds of thousands of prisoners of the concentration camps."

There is an absolutely surreal quality about this narrative: the very idea of Musy presenting himself to Himmler, the greatest Jew killer of all time, as the agent of the "Union of Orthodox Rabbis of the United States and Canada" blows one's mind.

Perhaps not totally off the wall was the fact that, according to Musy, Himmler agreed to release Jews without authorization from Hitler. But the SS head drove a hard bargain. He didn't want money. He wanted mostly trucks but also taxis, automobiles, machinery, etc. This was a nonstarter for the Allies.

Eventually, Musy was to admit: "General Himmler has definitely desisted from demanding compensation in hardware." A price was negotiated. Himmler said he would settle for five million Swiss francs—about one million dollars.

This whole house of cards was soon to fall apart when Gestapo Chief Ernst Kaltenbrunner got wind of what was happening and told Hitler who, enraged, ordered these talks to cease.

Some Jews *were* liberated, including Recha Sternbuch's Rottenberg brothers, the Berger-Rottenberg family, the families Donnebaum, Cilzer, Dr. Stiassny, Helen Stein, and a few prominent French Jews. In addition, a train bearing 1,200 Jews from the Theresienstadt camp did exit through Konstanz into Switzerland. A second trainload, expected to follow, didn't.

A final loose end was cleared up by Musy in his report—the matter of the five million Swiss francs—the "ransom" scheduled for payment to free six hundred thousand people; that had been raised but never used. Its purpose was to assure the Germans the money was there in the event an agreement could be reached.

It had been banked in the name of Isaac Sternbuch, acting for the Orthodox Rabbis. Since, in the end, it wouldn't be spent, Musy had the entire five million turned back to Sternbuch and the Rabbis.

Meanwhile, alas, as these months had rolled by, thousands and thousands more Jews and others in the clutches of the Nazis had their lives snuffed out.

Musy finished his postwar disquisition by writing: "After the end of the Second World War . . . Jean-Marie Musy thought that the most rational solution [to the "eternal Jewish Problem"] *would be the reconstitution of an Israeli State.*

On McClelland's watch, Jean-Marie Musy was not the only Swiss player.

Saly Mayer was Swiss, too, born in Switzerland, and Jewish. During the war years, he was the director of the Swiss office of the Joint Distribution Committee. Prior to the war, he had been chairman of the Association of Jewish Communities in Switzerland and had also served on the Municipal Council of his hometown Saint Gallen. He earned his living as a textile manufacturer.

Activities in which Saly played a leadership role before the War Refugee Board was created and installed in Switzerland included transmitting funds from the Joint to the rapidly growing (up to 25,000) Jews who reached Shanghai. He participated in the ill-fated "Europa Plan" that attempted to ransom the several million Jews still left alive in Nazi-occupied Europe in 1942. Once Roswell McClelland arrived, Mayer arranged for him to meet SS. Obersturmbannführer Kurt Becher, Himmler's negotiator. The War Refugee Board was the only American governmental entity legally able to conduct negotiations with the enemy.

Just as hair-raising as Musy's adventures were those of Saly Mayer as a Jew in contact with the SS on a regular basis and finding himself in the position of toying with those killers when it was obvious no deal was in the offing. His is a saga that if he were a *gentile* would have earned him the title of a Righteous Gentile who had risked his life.

Toward the end of the war in Europe, Roswell McClelland sent a letter to Colonel William O'Dwyer who had replaced John Pehle as head of the War Refugee Board in order to refute charges made against Saly Mayer. He said he had met Herbert Katski, Ira Hirschmann's successor in the Turkey WRB office, and been told the Board wanted his opinion on claims that Mayer "had sabotaged" Jean-Marie Musy's attempts to bring more groups of Jewish refugees out of Germany into Switzerland. The accusers were Isaac Sternbuch and a Dutch Jewish leader named Gans.

McClelland's highly indignant riposte was that he was not unaware of these innuendoes. Gans, he answered, was "peddling third hand statements" and Sternbuch was basing his attack on "declarations made by Musy," after one of his returns from Germany. The WRB agent went on to add: "To the best of my knowledge such an accusation leveled against Saly Mayer is grossly and flagrantly incorrect. I know Saly Mayer well and can unequivocally state that interfering with Musy's activities would be the farthest thing from his mind. He always applauds other groups' success and has never displayed Musy's tendency to 'monopolize' such rescue activities."

It became an open secret that in the rivalry between Musy and Saly Mayer that McClelland clearly favored Saly. Here was a Falstaffian figure, larger than life, described as a quiet man who became "a compulsive talker and overwhelmed his negotiating partners with long speeches." The SS officer Becher suffered jibes from his colleagues that the *old Jew* (he was 62) "led him around by the nose." Saly's personal life was clouded by the fact that his only son was mentally disturbed. Saly could be very suspicious, grow hostile, throw tantrums. But he and McClelland hit it off well and, as has been stated, "In the warm atmosphere of the McClelland home, together with Roswell's wife Marjorie and three small children, the lonely man relaxed and became 'Onkel Saly.'"

McClelland also declared: "Saly conducted a masterful holding operation for six months. It seems incredible . . . he could have sustained it for so long . . . when he had so little to bargain with." He is described as a tremendous talker and often hard to get him to make his point. "It kept his Nazi interlocutors for one guessing, and it gained time, precious time."

Although, as a possible caveat, McClelland did concede that SS Lieutenant Colonel Kurt Becher in entering negotiations with Saly might have been "disgruntled by Musy's initial success and *attempted* to *discredit* Musy's status as a negotiator."

In reality, on the afternoon of March 24, 1944, the same day that FDR spoke out on war crimes, Musy and his son had returned empty-handed from trying to induce the Nazis to release more convoys of Jews from Bergen-Belsen.

It conceivably may have silently tickled McClelland, who suspected Musy of mercenary motives, to learn that the brand-new Mercedes the Sternbuchs had bought so he and Benoit could drive to Germany in style had been upended and damaged and riddled with bullets.

The American, no mean diplomat himself, subsequently expressed the tactful hope that negotiations through the International Red Cross would "now supersede the previous subordinate negotiations through the Saly Mayer-Becher and Sternbuch-Musy *hook-up*s." The SS negotiator Becher nevertheless made it known he still wanted to "discuss urgent matters with Saly Mayer."

In McClelland's opinion, the Nazi was now interested in "trying to sell certain wealthy Jewish families belonging to the Weiss and Chorin families held hostage in Vienna, and save his own hide."

Saly Mayer's negotiations with the Nazis did not lead him to travel into Germany as Musy had. Even bearing an SS safe passage document, Deutschland was no place for a Jew to be. So the meetings were held on the bridge between Saint Margarethen in the eastern tip of Switzerland and Höchst, Austria, then incorporated in Germany, a dramatic enough setting but perhaps not an ideal place for palavering.

Here it is necessary to raise the question of money in all of this suspenseful drama. Musy had paid ten thousand Swiss francs ($2,500) to, in effect, *ransom* a Jewish couple. Much larger sums soon would come into play, for instance the proposed grandiose Europa Project and later the five million Swiss francs, the ransom intended to pay for one million Jews that was deposited at the Swiss National Bank.

What was the origin of this "blocked" account?

Was it not the War Refugee Board, using the Joint to supply Swiss francs it had paid for with dollars in the U.S.? There was no advertising of the source. But it could be noticed afterward how Roswell McClelland was one of those whose signature could free up the cash. Remember, too, Saly was connected to the Joint.

Whatever, it was pure bait in other words.

Probably more so than the rest of his fellow WRB special attachés, Roswell McClelland found himself caught up in a flurry of competition, conflicting egos, intricate complications, policy disagreements, backbiting, and just about any other impediments imaginable to save victims of essentially deadly kidnappings of innocents on an unimaginable scale.

If dealing with the Nazis weren't tough enough, also sandwiched in was the long-time Jewish rivalry—particularly in the Orthodoxy—between Zionists determined to establish a homeland and fanatically anti-Zionist believers who preached the Messiah would never come if the Jews created a nation of their own. Aside from the personality clashes involved, a major policy was at issue, too. Should the negotiators stall for time, which Saly Mayer was doing, or should the ransom money be paid at once in one fell swoop?

The words of the argument still have a sting after all these years. In Joseph Friedenson and David Kanzler's book about Recha Sternbuch, *Heroine of Rescue*, after depicting that the Vaad Hatzalah could not come up with even one million dollars, the authors wrote: "The results in Switzerland were sadly predictable. Mayer refused to coordinate rescue efforts with the Sternbuchs, refused to grant the Nazis 'good will,' refused in fact to consider the ransom plan at all." Stymied, the Sternbuchs went over Mayer's head to his boss Joseph Schwartz, the European head of the Joint. No dice there, either.

Next, the Sternbuchs with their plan turned to Rudolf Kastner, the Palestine Jewish Agency's man in Switzerland, and he turned them down. According to *Heroine of Rescue*, "They offered him the use of their Polish diplomatic code, so that he could bypass Mayer and the War Refugee Board. However, he still refused. Literally in tears, they pleaded with him for hours to drop Mayer. Again Kastner said no. As a last bargaining chip, a Sternbuch representative said that the entire Musy mass-rescue operation could continue under the aegis of the Joint—as long as it went ahead."

Amidst all this intramural Jewish turmoil, there was no way for Roswell McClelland not to be drawn in. The book about Recha Sternbuch and her husband, Yitzhak, considers him a foe. That is, a supporter of their archrival Saly Mayer. Yet, if the book is correct, the one solid result of the Musy endeavors was the Germans' promise to release roughly 1,200 Jews in a trainload of Jews from Theresienstadt to Switzerland in February 1945. The quid pro quo was: "The Swiss must agree to accept the 1,200 refugees and the United States to support and eventually relocate them and $1 million had to be established as a guarantee for Reichsführer Himmler to show that Musy and 'the rabbi Jews,' as he called the Sternbuchs, were indeed serious."

The final rub, believe it or not, as expressed in the *Heroine of Rescue* book, was: "Most important, though, was that Germany's image in the press had to be mitigated."

A public relations campaign was subsequently launched in conjunction with the arrival of the trainload of 1,200 released concentration camp inmates and carried out in the Swiss press, American newspapers and Jewish publications.

McClelland's position in the eyes of the Sternbuchs can be read between the lines. He is described as "dubious of both Musy and the negotiations" and after stating he was told a large amount of money would be needed for *expenses*, it was frankly admitted: "Sternbuch did not want anyone to know that the money would really be used for necessary bribes . . . Yitzhak Sternbuch also pointed out to Vaad Hatzalah that McClelland simply did not like the Sternbuchs or their tactics." So when McClelland recommended that the War Refugee Board NOT participate in a joint one-million-dollar bank account with Musy, Sternbuch could say he was unsurprised. It was obvious McClelland, according to Sternbuch, "simply favored Mayer's plan to keep the Jews interned under International Red Cross supervision and therefore preferred to wait for the (impending) end of the war in Europe, in a matter of months.

In discussing a proposed second transport of Jews, this time of about 2,000, the statement was made that "a long-standing yet unforeseen obstacle sprung up to prevent its success: Saly Mayer." Sternbuch flatly told the Vaad Hatzalah that "S. Mayer through his agents in Berlin undertook steps to make impossible bringing over of refugees . . . he strives to keep the Jews alive, but he doesn't care to take them out of Germany."

Emphasizing the back and forth—ping-pong-like—essence of the quarrel and its effect on others concerned was a communication from Joseph Schwartz, head of the Joint in Europe, to Moses Leavitt at the Joint's New York headquarters.

Schwartz wrote: "I have followed very scrupulously instructions not to take part in any discussions which Saly Mayer is conducting. However, I want to associate myself with McClelland's recommendation—to keep activities already in progress through Intercross [the International Red Cross]."

The discussions at this time—the end of 1944—involved eighty thousand Jews in Budapest, seventeen thousand in Vienna, "unknown thousands herded on foot toward Austria and those in camps in German-occupied Europe including Belsenberger [sic] . . . I think the highest tribute should be paid to Saly Mayer. The negotiations have gained time."

Six months earlier, Leavitt had received a communication from Europe regarding Joel Brand's mission and that "Saly thinks Brand reliable," further that "Brand and Freudiger [Fulop Freudiger, head of the Orthodox Jewish Community in Budapest] were members of the same committee [the Judenrat or Jewish Council] but unable to combine efforts . . . Schwartz has all the information. War Refugee Board Switzerland knows of reference to Washington of Freudiger-Sternbuch proposition. Sternbuch waiting for an answer."

Somewhere along the line, a joint bank account had been opened under the control of McClelland and Sternbuch for four million Swiss francs, apparently as a part of twenty million Swiss francs held in escrow. Schwartz was eventually reporting to Leavitt that only five hundred thousand francs had been spent—"for the purchase of food, most of which has not been distributed . . . Have asked McClelland to return the balance to New York or turn it over to Saly Mayer."

Apparently Sternbuch agreed because when the account of the first five million (actually $4,662,000) was returned to the Joint's account at the Chase Bank through the Federal Reserve Bank of New York, it was in the names of Roswell McClelland and Saly Mayer.

Following the money, more may be gleaned running through a long message sent by McClelland to John Pehle on November 16, 1944. In it, the WRB special attaché writes that Saly Mayer in his negotiations with the Nazis "could state that he had 20 million Swiss francs placed at his disposal." Conditions on its use were that the money "can only be put up as a deposit held by a neutral third party acceptable to both sides." The funds would be *blocked* until SS negotiator Lieutenant Colonel Becher's assistant, referred to only as K., came up with a list of the "goods desired." In actuality, K. was an SS buying agent named Kettlitz. The Swiss police were hesitant about extending his visa, allowing him to stay longer, and letting the German go beyond Saint Gallen. Saly was doing all he could to allow Kettlitz more time in Switzerland and freedom to travel inside the country so he could shop for what he wanted. Also, Saly asked the Joint office in Lisbon to cable the Joint top command in New York City for the "20 million to be transferred in his name immediately." McClelland was requested to support this request, which he obviously did.

The same message included the news that the daily negotiations by Saly Mayer "have become increasingly strained and difficult" and Kastner (the Hungarian Rudolf Kastner) and Billitz (Dr. Wilhelm Billitz, a Jew converted to Christianity who ran the Manfréd Weiss Steel and Metal Works, a major armaments industry in Hungary) had left for Budapest and B. (Becher) for Berlin on November 6 and would report to Himmler before returning to Budapest. Becher had left behind "his henchman K. in Switzerland to pursue conversations with Saly Mayer."

McClelland then outlined the Allied terms that had been presented to the Germans.

1. The Germans had to cease "mistreatment calculated to bring death, execution and outright extermination with respect to all (repeat all) detainees in German hands regardless of nationality, both Jewish and non-Jewish, aged, invalid and children, remaining in Budapest."
2. All individual Jews specified by the Joint Distribution Committee [members of the Bratislava Jewish Council in Slovakia] to be released.
3. All Jews in Hungary with documents of belligerent countries or neutrals or outside German occupation be allowed to leave [specifically refers to eight thousand Jews at Bergen-Belsen.]

"These stipulations were supposedly submitted to Himmler on or about November 10 by Becher," McClelland informed Pehle and added that Becher was awaiting "word from assistant Kettlitz that Saly Mayer has placed at their disposal 20 million francs."

Behind all of this maneuvering, as McClelland saw the situation, was the German desire to secure "sizeable amounts of Swiss francs," which they would use to buy and export goods from Switzerland "of value to the German war effort." He added: "Trying to get the Nazis to consider goods of nonmilitary value has elicited little or no response."

Reiterating "the original goal of gaining time specifically in relation to the situation of the Jews in Hungary," the WRB's spokesman declared his "considered opinion that Saly Mayer should be instructed to discontinue negotiations as tactfully as possible." His fear, he wrote, is that if the bluff is carried too far, the Nazis might take out their anger on the still surviving Jews in their grasp.

McClelland's superiors in D.C. disagreed and ordered a continuation of the talks.

Two other persons who figured in these complicated discussions were Samuel E. Woods, the U.S. consul in Zurich and Dr. Reuben Hecht, Belgian-born Zionist representing the Revisionist Irgun group in Palestine who connected with the Sternbuchs and through them with Jean-Marie Musy. Thus, with the war in Europe nearing an end, the wild messy drama enfolded the frantic efforts to save what remaining Jews the Nazis still had imprisoned from being slaughtered en masse. Woods, called "one of the most successful intelligence gatherers of World War II," and particularly adept at helping American airmen interned in Switzerland slip away to fight again, and Hecht, who had immigrated to Palestine in 1936 and connected the Irgun to European rescue work, were part of the group whose strategy was to pressure Himmler to countermand Hitler's order to kill all Jews. Hecht had important press contacts in Switzerland and the U.S. He could promise favorable coverage of any ameliorating actions.

However, a wire from Washington to McClelland and U.S. Ambassador Leland Harrison in November 1944 strongly underlined the abhorrence in D.C. of anything that smacked of *ransom*. It doesn't say so exactly but the meaning is clear: "The transaction outlined in your cable cannot (repeat not) be supported by the [War Refugee] Board in any way and further it is the Board's opinion that no (repeat no) funds from any source should be used to carry out such a proposal." It was signed: Stettinius (then Acting Secretary of State).

And followed by another command of no possible ransom: "Schwartz [Joseph Schwartz, European chief of the Joint] will soon arrive in Switzerland. Tell him of the contents of our Number 3932 [cable] of November 18—in which the Board stated its opposition to the transaction outlined in your 756 of November 16." Schwartz was likewise to be told "under no circumstances may he participate in negotiations referred to in 7565 . . . carried on by Saly Mayer as a representative of the Swiss Jewish community."

Rarely is diplomatic language so emphatic.

The cast of real-life characters in Switzerland having been introduced and set in motion as they were in those heady days of 1944 when the war was taking an ever more decided turn in favor of the Allies, we must now take a closer look at other sectors only lightly touched upon heretofore, starting with the Iberian sector and Robert Dexter's responsibilities in Portugal and the problems the WRB had in Spain.

Chapter Eight

In the First World War, Portugal fought on the Allied side along with France, England, the U.S., Italy, Belgium, Romania, etc. During World War II, its strong man, quasi-dictator António de Oliveira Salazar, kept the country neutral. Not quite a fascist (although the former university economics professor had organized a feared Gestapo-like secret police known as the PIDE), he adroitly played both sides, selling wolfram, or tungsten ore, a steel-hardening substance, to the Germans and leasing airfields in the Azores to Great Britain and the United States. Lisbon, his capital, like pre-Free-French Casablanca, became a hotspot of intrigue and espionage that by the time the War Refugee Board had installed one of its special attachés there in 1944, the smart money was betting on the coalition that in this war called itself the United Nations.

In returning to Lisbon with his wife Marjorie, New England raised Unitarian Robert Cloutman Dexter might be considered a surprise choice. He had originally gone to the Portuguese capital for the Unitarian Service Committee, a program that he, himself, had proposed and created as a subset of the Boston based organization. But seemingly Dexter had left in disgrace, fired in a nasty dispute over his leadership. Nevertheless, the War Refugee Board had snapped him up to be their man in Portugal.

Ordinarily Portugal would have been *subordinate*—to use McClelland's word—on the War Refugee Board map. In this instance, however, due to the obstinacy of the U.S. ambassador to Franco's realm, Carleton Hayes, no WRB special attaché could simultaneously be posted to Spain. Hayes loudly declaimed that a separate official to work on refugee problems wasn't needed and would interfere with work he deemed more important. He furthermore even nitpicked that private agencies weren't legally able to do rescue work.

If Hayes sounded at times like a haughty academic, that's because his background was in college teaching. He had been an established, respected professor at Columbia University and chairman of its history department.

Let's listen to a sample of his response to John Pehle. Said Hayes: "It becomes more clearly evident that the War Refugee Board's efforts to stimulate the exodus of unprotected and stateless refugees from German-occupied territories will result in fact in an increase in the number of such refugees entering Spain sufficient to tax the facilities which already exist for their care . . . My strong recommendation is that the Board attempt to take full advantage of the already proven facilities which are in existence . . . from Blickenstaff's organization instead of endeavoring to set up an alternative organization on the assumption that it will be justified by later developments, an assumption with which I am not prepared to agree with as yet."

Carleton Hayes had perfectly filled a ticklish political appointment for the Roosevelt Administration. A person of his stature and a Roman Catholic was needed to represent them in Franco Spain. Hayes was actually a convert, raised as a Baptist but like many converts, ultra-devout in his adopted religion and well equipped to deal with a regime professing the same deeply conservative faith.

The person Hayes referred to as "Blickenstaff" was David Blickenstaff of the Office of Representatives in Spain of American Relief Organizations. One may suspect that he was serving the ambassador in an assistant capacity of sorts, having done prior work for the American Friends Service Committee. Hayes made no secret of the fact he had set up Blickenstaff's agency to unify the rescue groups and feared this work would suffer if Blickenstaff had to do two jobs at once. Besides, unspoken but strongly intimated was that Hayes's annoyance also derived from having his turf infringed upon.

Hayes argued that Blickenstaff, whose wife was Spanish, had "gained the confidence and respect of the Spanish Government and it recognized him as the qualified representative of stateless refugees in Spain." The American envoy also added that the Spaniards had said they would prefer Blickenstaff to someone from the Intergovernmental Committee on Refugees, mixing that group up somehow with the War Refugee Board.

While Carleton Hayes apparently had not been an early fan of Franco (reportedly he had his own name removed from the masthead of *Commonwealth Magazine* when it pledged support for the Caudillo in 1936), in due time he would be of the opinion that Franco was preferable to the Spanish Republicans, and he later incurred the opprobrium of having apparently appeased an obvious if highly religious monarchist dictator.

WRB special attaché Robert Dexter in Lisbon seemingly had smooth relations with the difficult Hayes. Dated November 23, 1944, is a communication in which he tells of speaking with the ambassador about special license H-2153 regarding money used for Spanish guides to bring children and adults over the mountains. These guides were always paid in pesetas, so there was no need for foreign exchange. "Ambassador apparently has no objection on using this money for this purpose to be given Sequerra in Barcelona [Samuel Sequerra, a Spaniard working for the Joint]."

Earlier, back in May, there had been this communication: "Had long conference with Hayes about the War Refugee Board and progress of rescue, with which he is in hearty agreement." The suggestion was made for David Blickenstaff to become the WRB agent in Spain and the understanding had become that he could do both the WRB work and the job he was already doing in Spain on refugee problems.

Defenders of Hayes's recalcitrance pointed to the justification he had obliquely made, himself, for not wanting to rock the boat in Spain with the Spanish authorities He reminded the WRB that its presence in Spain would be dependent on the Franco government. "In the absence of any apparent need for the presence of the numerous personnel mentioned by the Board, a request for admission into Spain might for example prejudice the admission of other personnel whose importance to the war effort is more direct."

Here, in guarded fashion, Hayes was offering clues to his number-one concern: rescuing shot-down Allied airmen and transporting them secretly through Spain back to duty.

Hayes and Secretary Hull had had a series of cable exchanges during the spring of 1944.

On March 24, 1944, Hayes was telling Hull: "Two hundred and ten French refugees in Spain sailed from Gibraltar on March 22 for North Africa." That brought to 472 the total number of "such refugees evacuated since the beginning of the year. It was estimated that 409 French refugees remained at present in Spain."

In addition, Hayes to Hull again: "I should like to be advised further as to the proposed relationship between the work of the WRB and that of the 'representative in Spain of American relief organizations.'" In addition, Hayes was questioned closely: "If Blickenstaff went to work for the WRB, would he have to give up his present work, which was as staff for all the agencies handling refugees?" Hayes's recommendation was for Blickenstaff to serve "concurrently with the WRB agent who might be pushed to give up his refugee work."

Pressing hard, Hayes outlined the refugees in need at that date. Of 1,300 stateless and unprotected fugitives, they included 400 Spanish Sephardics who had been released from German concentration camps in accordance with a Spanish-German agreement and for whom no travel arrangements had been provided in advance. It was expected that some 800 would end up in the former Vichy concentration camp in Fedhala, Morocco.

But it was pointed out that many of those mostly Jewish escapees would prefer to remain in Spain, rather than go to Morocco. The Free French, themselves, were using rough interrogation methods and employing ex-Vichyites.

Hayes told Hull: "If Sephardic Jews were to be assisted by the WRB or other such organizations, Spain would be reluctant to let them go, seeing conditions at Fedhala were so bad."

Carleton Hayes was not high on the French and their bureaucracy in North Africa. He had complained to Cordell Hull that regarding Sephardic Jews who received assistance from the "War Refugee Board or other such organizations," Spain would be reluctant to let them go "if Fedhala, under the French is so unsatisfactory."

He railed at the charge of $25 per person of the screening process at Algiers. The French required six copies of all applications with photographs and thumbprints for prior approval. This procedure, he argued, would be "most cumbersome and especially unfeasible as regards those refugees still detained in Spanish camps and prisons."

On May 20, 1944, Hull was contacting Hayes. The State Department, he said, was deeply concerned over reports that Hungarian Jews were fated to be exterminated. "Approach the Spaniards to get detailed information on this fear as soon as possible through their man in Budapest."

Another part of Hull's communication was that Pedro and Lydia Chaprine and Jules and Anna Grunstein, bearing Costa Rican passports, had been granted permission to enter that country. They would be allowed repatriation aboard the Swedish vessel, the *Gripsholm*.

A list was furnished of those awaiting authorizations in Latin America. Then followed the names of those denied access: in Nicaragua, Otto Wilhelm Strauss and Regina Strauss, née Maier, and in the Dominican Republic, Jenny Muller, née Silverstein. They had been turned down for the *Gripsholm*. These unfortunates could be included in a transfer of refugees to Fedhala, provided support could be arranged by Blickenstaff and paid for by the WRB.

The steps to rescue Spanish Jews in Greece should be "a matter of urgency," the WRB declared. A letter from Hull to Hayes emphasized that fact. The Papal nuncio at Bern was asked to ask the nuncio at Madrid to ask the Spanish Government to inform the Spanish ambassador to Berlin of the "gravity of peril" of Polish Jews with Paraguayan documents and insist that he "urgently give them effective protection." Similar representations were to be made on behalf of Jews and others with Paraguayan or any other Latin American documents, "acting jointly with the Papal nuncio, or on your own . . . and make a progress report as soon as possible."

Word went out to U.S. consular officials in Spain and Portugal to issue one thousand visas to refugee children who had reached the Iberian countries on or after January 1, 1944, and before July 1, 1944. Children must be under sixteen years of age at the time the visas were issued . . . and finally, "children under fourteen years of age need not be registered and fingerprinted.

"You may also inform the Spanish and Portuguese governments that the War Refugee Board will provide financing necessary to provide maintenance for refugees from enemy oppression arriving in Spain and Portugal." Also stressed was concern for Jews holding papers of Paraguay, Peru, Venezuela, Nicaragua, El Salvador, Honduras, Ecuador, Costa Rica, Chile, and Haiti. An attempt in 1943 had threatened to void those holding Paraguayan papers. The Intergovernmental Committee on Political Refugees had then issued assurances that Paraguay had not cancelled its passports. Efforts were made to convince Latin American governments to insist that these official papers not be investigated until after the war.

But back to Portugal. All Americans know that in 1492, Columbus sailed the ocean blue and discovered America. Not too many know that in 1492 also, the Spaniards expelled all Jews—and Muslims—from their kingdom. Practically none, I think, could tell you that in 1497, Portugal did the same thing. In both cases, Jews might avoid forced exile by switching to Catholicism, thereby becoming *New Christians* and eventually spawning, again in both countries, Inquisitions, mostly bent on ferreting out those among the converts who had gone back to their Hebrew roots and were practicing their religion secretly.

Thus it was in 1506 that an ungodly attack was launched upon the *cristão-novo* of Lisbon, accused not only of having lapsed but of being responsible for a devastating earthquake. More than two thousand were massacred. King Manuel I who had actually been friendly to the Jews at the beginning of his reign but had had to expel them in order to marry the daughter of the Spanish monarchs King Ferdinand and Queen Isabella, was not in Lisbon when this spontaneous rampage took place. Upon his return to the city, he had some fifty of the ringleaders executed.

Consequently, the breakout of the Second World War found both Iberian nations pretty much *judenrein*—without Jews, as the Germans would say—until refugees started pouring in from countries elsewhere in Europe.

Since Ambassador Carleton Hayes insisted on running his own solo show in Madrid, Robert Dexter found himself initially the only WRB special attaché on the Iberian Peninsula.

As it happened, Dexter had academic credentials as impressive as Hayes—a doctorate from Clark University in Worcester, Massachusetts. He even taught at Skidmore College. Then, he went to work for the American Unitarian Association in Cambridge, Massachusetts, heading up its Departments of Social Relations and International Relations, and in the latter role made frequent visits to the Unitarian congregations in Europe. Thanks in large part to a Czech Unitarian by the name of Norbert Čapek, Czechoslovakia at that time contained the single largest number of Unitarians in the world. Their ranks were swollen even more when the Nazis took over the Sudetenland in the fall of 1938.

Working out of the First Unitarian church of Belmont, Massachusetts, Robert Dexter started a letter-writing campaign to find people willing to sign affidavits of support for refugee Jews as he had done for the Sudak family. Before Czechoslovakia, itself, was overrun in 1939 by the Hitlerians, he dispatched Waitstill and Martha Sharp to work out of Prague.

In 1941, Robert and Elizabeth Dexter, themselves, went to serve for six months overseas—in neutral Lisbon, where he cooperated with Varian Fry and the Joint Distribution Committee.

A year later, the OSS recruited him, and he was given the code name "Corn." During this period, Dexter helped set up links between the OSS and colleagues cf Fry in Marseille in the French Resistance. Furthermore, on his own, he brought in René Zimmer, the head of the Unitarian Service Committee's medical program in Vichy to work with the Underground in helping refugees reach safety. Before the war ended, Dexter was to resign his Unitarian position and complete his work fulltime for the WRB.

On a somber note, Norbert Čapek had his wife go back to the U.S. early in 1939, while he stayed on in his soon-occupied country. Arrested by the Gestapo, he was taken to Dachau and from there to Hartheim Castle in Upper Austria. This was a little-known euthanasia site where Čapek was gassed and considered a martyr to his religion.

Dexter's experience in Europe and familiarity with Portugal made him a seasoned pro on his new assignment. He gave straight answers. During a prolonged debate in D.C. on issues pertinent to the WRB that started with saving children, one of the staff, Louis Dolivet, an expert on France, pushed for bringing five hundred of these threatened kids to the U.S. and argued: "How can anyone be against it?" Sitting in on the meeting, Dexter firmly demurred: "It won't work. I don't think the State Department is going to give visas unblocked like that." Their boss John Pehle, also involved, said: "Well, that is our problem."

Dolivet responded: "The only new factor is that financially there will be possibilities."

Whereupon Pehle riposted: "That is not the new factor. The new factor is two-fold. One is that you have got a governmental organization whose full-time job this is. The second is that you have a possibility of getting a measure of cooperation out of other governmental agencies, such as the State Department, that you didn't get before."

In further discussion, the term "suction points" was used. Presumably these were the best geographical points for funneling refugees to final safety. The two named were Romania and Portugal.

Another sticky issue arose when Dexter was asked if the Unitarians requested the WRB for visas would they be granted, especially including one for Julio Álvarez del Vayo, the ex-foreign minister of the now defunct Spanish Republic in exile. Dexter answered: "I think we will."

Ansel Luxford, also on the WRB staff, put his finger on the controversial nature of this decision: "The Spanish are not going to like us using our efforts to help the Spanish Loyalists get out of

Portugal. We have to operate under cover on this in order not to get in trouble with the Spanish government."

No one argued the point.

The talk then swung to the use of Portuguese ships in their refugee operations. Dexter thought there was plenty of space on them. Josiah DuBois, representing the Treasury Department, asked if there were "any chance of getting a Portuguese ship into the Black Sea?"

Dexter said he didn't see why not. "One has recently gone into the Mediterranean." But then he warned: "Don't take away your American run, the Lisbon-New York or Lisbon-Philadelphia runs, in order to put them in the Black Sea. That would be tragic for everybody."

Requests to help individuals and their families escape of course were piling daily onto the desks of War Refugee Board special attachés. One of more than ordinary interest to latter-day American readers reached Dexter in June of 1944. It had originally come to McClelland in Switzerland from a Magda Bychowsky in Bern and concerned her parents who were still in Hungary, Vilmos and Jolie Gabor. The plea was seconded by her younger sister Mrs. Conrad Hilton of Beverly Hills, California, better known as Zza Zza Gabor and older sister Eva Gabor, likewise an actress in Hollywood.

This plea was transmitted to Robert Dexter in Lisbon. The elder Gabors had permission to leave Hungary, occupied by the Nazis in March, and to enter Portugal but could not exit with Hungarian papers. They needed some form of Portuguese travel or identity document that only the Portuguese Government could issue. Accordingly, Dexter was asked to arrange through Lisbon to provide them with proper papers. The telegraphed request was sent to him from Bern by U.S. Ambassador Leland Harrison.

Magda credited the Portuguese Ambassador in Budapest, Carlos Sampaio Garrido, with having saved their lives. He is listed as a Righteous Gentile, his office credited with having rescued one thousand Hungarian Jews. At the time she was married to the first of her husbands, a Polish count, Jan Bychowsky, an RAF pilot, who died in action in 1944.

A key project proposed for the Iberian section was the evacuation of primarily Jewish children from France to Spain and Portugal. The proviso from Latin American countries that agreed to accept them was that the War Refugee Board would pick up all the costs. The Dominican Republic said it would take one thousand to two thousand, Costa Rica one thousand, Eire (Irish Republic) five hundred, Guatemala one hundred, preferably French and Belgian, Peru fifty, Honduras fifty, and quixotically Paraguay (under the Stroessner dictatorship) one hundred thousand families.

Isaac Weissman was a delegate from Lisbon to the War Emergency Conference of the World Jewish Congress and the leading proponent of saving five thousand Jewish children by *professional smugglers* across the Pyrenees in a "highly illegal and dangerous project." The Catholic Church in France was going to help and also De Gaulle's Free French and the Zionist Resistance Movement in France along with the American and British Ambassadors in Spain and Portugal and the International Red Cross. In France, those children were in hiding, using false names, pretending to be Catholics. Weissman reported: "We came to terms with the professional smugglers and hired Spanish and French women to take boys and girls through forbidden military zones to the frontiers for a rendezvous with the so-called "brigands.""

Involved in raising financial support in the U.S.A. was a visit to New York by the Free French Captain Pierre Dreyfus, son of the famous falsely accused Alfred Dreyfus, to address three hundred delegates to a gathering in Manhattan for that purpose. Also described by Weissman at such meetings were members of the French underground attempting to get Turkish Jews out of France. Ambassador Steinhardt in Turkey worked on the Vichy Government and "this brought about the postponement of the decision by the Germans to send Turkish Jews to concentration camps."

Weissman reported that "through the intercession of the American Embassy in Lisbon [no doubt by Dexter] 300 orphans were placed in a beach resort six miles from Lisbon." The World Jewish Congress provided funds for building additional homes for children there and Weissman was advised that the World Jewish Congress had authorized him to reimburse Dexter for 22,604 escudos advanced to purchase furniture for the reception center for refugees at Paço de Arcos.

Robert Pilpel, husband of previously mentioned Harriet Pilpel, was receiving cables at the American Legation from the Joint in New York and eventually as early as April 1944 was being queried if he had agreed that "continued evacuation from France of children to Spain and Portugal was unnecessary." Rapid developments in the war were clearing much of France of the Germans. Included, though, was the information that "we might possibly use Portugal's offer later for children from Hungary or elsewhere." The U.S. ambassador, John Gilbert Winant, in London declared: "I find most encouraging the transfer of American visas from children in France to children in Hungary." He had been so informed by the Acting Secretary of State Edward Stettinius in D.C.

At the end of July 1944, Weissman made a "formal request" to the Portuguese Government to receive three thousand "registered Jewish children still in France . . . children probably going to Palestine . . . seeking the War Refugee Board to pay. Ambassador Winant was engaged in this effort." The International Red Cross was needed to approach the French authorities. They "would work independently with the Joint or together with the War Refugee Board."

Earlier apparently, there had been an attempt to have 10,000 children from Western Europe enter Switzerland "temporarily for physical and mental rehabilitation by the Swiss" and that the Swiss Minister to Vichy France would get from Pierre Laval "5,000 exit permits" to Switzerland, but Laval said *Non*.

Working for Weissman in Portugal was a wounded Portuguese World War I veteran named Alves who had a special knack for dealing with children. The evacuation of kids from France was complicated by the fact that some of them were Polish citizens, not French. Alves worked with a top French official Jean Chatain, and they were soon embroiled in what was described as a "very bitter internecine quarrel between Jewish organizations." It had overtones of the Zionist/anti-Zionist split in Jewish society worldwide. The children in contention were described as "enthusiastic Zionists, singing songs and playing games about returning to Jerusalem." Also, Weissman and Alves had been given names of non-Jewish children, offspring of "well-known anti-Nazis." The comment was made about Weissman that "he is somewhat of a visionary" and that "he somewhat talks bigger than he performs but has done something on a shoestring."

Alves and Chatain also claimed that all *Jewish adults* who had recently crossed the Pyrenees came through the World Jewish Congress by "the definite planning of M'sieu Croustillon but once in Spain needed the help of the Joint." The Joint would then claim them as evacuees.

Dexter at the time wrote rather forcefully, "This whole question, indeed the future usefulness of the War Refugee Board's program here in the Peninsula is bound up with the possibility of the Board's sharing a representative with the backing of the Embassy to overcome difficulties . . . issues that could be better clarified in Madrid or Barcelona than from Lisbon." He then pronounced the obvious: "That it was a matter to be decided by the Board after consultation with Ambassador Hayes and lies without the province of this Mission."

In a letter to Rabbi Stephen Wise at the World Jewish Congress, John Pehle was a good deal less diplomatic: "WRB here is still without enough money to meet the extensive rescue work planned. Also no remittance from you and even transfer promised by Kubowitzky [the executive secretary] unarrived."

The yawning donation gap between the two major Jewish organizations was the World Jewish Congress's $300,000 to the Joint's $15 million.

In charge of refugee matters at the Portuguese Ministry of Foreign Affairs was Dr. Malheiro Reimão who agreed in principle "to admit a considerable number of children under 16 coming from France via Spain into Portugal even though these children do not have proper travel documents and are without visas for Portugal." Only three hundred at a time, from May 15 would be admitted and stay temporarily at the Victoria Club in Paço de Arcos. Portugal wanted a *Título de Viagem*, "Voyage Title," to place on their departure visas.

Rabbi Wise in New York was sent names by Weissman: "Max Skowmonsk, 10; Isak and Fanny Bejzbaum, who had an uncle in New York; three Rosenfelds; Annie, Sus, Marcel and Suzanne, children of Abraham and Faja Fajmester, with a grandmother in New York . . . Cable Herman Mandel in Lima, Peru, that his niece Edith Thisberg and Joseph and Civie Margosches are among the rescued children" and arrived in tattered clothing and no shoes and were being outfitted.

Thus did some little fish slip through the nets—thirty to ffity at a time and never more than three hundred.

Dexter was wired from D.C. in May that the Board was relying on him as the WRB rep "to prevent duplication in this important rescue program." He was told the Joint "was licensed to carry on a rescue program from Portugal and has substantial funds available for these operations." He was also told the World Jewish Congress had applied for a similar license but the War Refugee Board had not recommended it—and as long as private funds were available, the State Department "would not recommend use of WRB funds to rescue children or maintain them." The wire was signed by Secretary of State Cordell Hull.

But the WRB did agree to pay a part of the costs of the World Jewish Congress's reception center in Portugal, which held twelve kids, all World Jewish Congress kids.

Joseph Schwartz of the Joint reported that the World Jewish Congress was "taking steps to set up separate children's relief facilities." The existing Jewish facilities were anti-Zionist.

Weissman wired Rabbi Wise complaining that the "Joint says it is rescuing persons from occupied territory." He claimed: "It is not true. The Joint has not brought out a single person. However, to refugees brought over the border by Congress workers, the Joint lays claim. For support, these refugees then go to the Joint. The World Jewish Congress can save hundreds of Jewish children if they get the money."

On May 3, 1944, Ambassador Hayes reported to Secretary of State Hull the "Embassy herewith returns as unused one-third of the block quota numbers allotted for refugee children."

Nowhere in my research have I come across a comment on this scandalous remark. Not even a tut-tut about its callousness. *Leaving one-third of the quota for saving children* UNUSED! Carlton Hayes has had his defenders. A major justification for his snub of the WRB was fear of jeopardizing his program of ferrying surviving shot-down Allied airmen to safety across the Pyrenees by angering Spanish authorities with whom he had reached a *modus vivendi*. This was baldly stated in a letter to Dexter from Pehle dated May 2, 1944.

Pehle's answer: "We assume the channels to be used for evacuating refugees will be different from and not conflict with those using the escape of aviators."

So Dexter was informed and then also told: "We are also sure you will be able to find many non-conflicting opportunities for the rescue of refugees."

Another hang-up on saving these children was the weather conditions in the Pyrenees. They could slow things down temporarily or even protractedly if they got bad snow.

The fate of the Jewish children wasn't the only item that came to Robert Dexter. In March, he was asked to find transportation for 450 refugees from Bukhara (in Uzbekistan today) who had Palestine certificates but were stranded in Teheran (Iran). Sea travel would cost $300 for each refugee. The request was made to approach the Iraqi Government for transit visas through their country, something that they had refused to grant to anyone. The possibility of transiting through

Turkey had been discussed but in that case the difficulty was obtaining exit visas from Bulgaria. Pressure on Bulgaria was recommended but also they would need Turkish transit visas.

The problems seemed endless and mostly consisted of acquiring bureaucratic paper work and paying transportation charges.

The Swiss would take more kids from France but needed guarantees they wouldn't stay long.

The Romanians would give exit visas to Palestine for five thousand kids, but transportation was needed. Negotiations with a Portuguese shipping company estimated a cost of $1 million to $1.5 million.

Six hundred refugees in Tangier (Morocco today) could go to Palestine but required visas and transport.

Hungary, it appeared, was easing up on exit visas.

A Dr. James Bernstein in Lisbon had a plan to get one thousand children to Argentina. Working in Argentina was a Mme. Anita N. de Sandelmann of Buenos Aires, who told the rescue workers to contact the Argentinean consul in Vichy to "hasten the immigration of 1,000 kids."

There were the Sephardics. To the Nazis, it mattered not that they were not stereotypes of the Jews they knew—neither the poor, pathetic inhabitants of the *shtetls* in Eastern Europe they had occupied nor the successful, brainy, sometimes haughty achievers of the Teutonic and Western European lands. These Sephardics (the word came from the Hebrew for Spain) were often elegant, aristocratic types—*grandees* in certain instances. But into the ovens with them! Hitlerians bent on massacre didn't question how twisted, scientifically inaccurate, and morally wrong their racial nonsense was.

Ambassador Hayes in Madrid was charged with convincing the Franco government to grant them the status of Spaniards, notwithstanding they had been long lost since 1492. During April 1944, news was revealed that four hundred Sephardics in Athens had been interned in a concentration camp. Hayes was wired: "It is vital that these Sephardic Jews be given Spanish government protection to forestall their departure to Poland and certain doom." Thanks to Nicholas Franco, brother of Generalissimo Francisco Franco Bahamonde, they were. It has been stated that the Francos through their mother, whose maiden name was Bahamonde, were of Jewish descent, converted in 1492 at the time of the expulsion. Thus, the Caudillo's defiance of Nazi demands to surrender all Jews he had been sheltering at least temporarily until they could be removed to safety.

Initially, the Nazis had moved gingerly against these unfamiliar-to-them Jews. Upon their occupation of Greece and Yugoslavia in April 1941, they arrested the members of the Jewish Council in Salonica, the biggest city, and other leaders in northern Macedonia. Yet after six weeks, these men were released. For slightly more than a year afterward, they unleashed no anti-Semitic measures in this region of the Balkans. By June 1942, however, the SS got started, ordering all Greek and Yugoslav Jews, eighteen to thirty-five, to present themselves for forced labor. Then, diabolically, they blackmailed the overall Jewish community to pay them 1.5 *billion* drachmas to avoid the slave work. On February 7, 1943, the other German shoe dropped. Yellow stars were required, a "big" ghetto created and deportations commenced. Among the 48,000 local Jews in seventeen transports sent off to Poland and never heard from again were even those Sephardic citizens of neutral countries in the area who had contributed to the Nazi shakedown earlier.

On January 7, 1944, the Nazis said the Sephardics considered Spaniards could be *repatriated* to Spain. But Madrid wasn't overly welcoming. They could not all be accepted—*en bloc*—as a single group. Instead, each had to be held for two to three months and investigated individually. It was a system that caused "consternation and despair." Other countries, including Portugal, had accepted repatriation of their citizens *en toto*.

Bergen-Belsen was where the Sephardim were held, but not subjected to forced labor.

Even once in Spain, they were not out of the woods. One group of Sephardics in France were warned they would not be taken unless the Spanish Government was assured they shortly afterward would be shipped to Camp Lyautey in Morocco.

R. Henry Norweb was the U.S. minister [later ambassador] in Portugal. He was alerted in June 1944 that James H. Mann, the assistant executive director of the War Refugee Board would arrive in Lisbon to confer with him about problems in Portugal. So, too, was notice sent to Hayes at the Madrid Embassy that Mann could go to Spain "to confer with you if you so desire." The notification was signed by Acting Secretary of State Edward Stettinius.

Although the parlous situation of noncooperation in Spain was not soon corrected, Hayes allowed two Portuguese Jewish twin brothers

Samuel and Joel Sequerra to do volunteer rescue work from a base in Barcelona. Samuel, a bachelor, unlike his sibling who had a wife and child, earned the nickname of the "Angel of the Pyrenees." He had come to Spain originally as a delegate of the Portuguese Red Cross but really to open an office of the Joint. The escape route opened by the brothers was established through the Lleida Pyrenees via Viella, Sort and La Unatapedera. The Sequerras' office was later attacked and burned by the fascistic Spanish Falangists in July 1944.

It has been lamented that the Sequerra contribution has been *olvidado*—forgotten—or almost so among the heroic tales of rescue—especially of Jewish children.

Robert Dexter in Lisbon seemingly had smooth relations with the difficult Hayes. On November 23, 1944, there was a communication in which he told of speaking with the ambassador about Special License H-2153, regarding money used for Spanish guides to bring children and adults over the mountains. These guides were always paid in pesetas, so there was no need for foreign exchange. "Ambassador Hayes apparently has no objection on using money for this purpose to be given Sequerra in Barcelona." Earlier, there had been this notification from Dexter in Lisbon: "Had long conference with Hayes about War Refugee Board and progress of rescue, with which he is in hearty agreement. Suggests David Blickenstaff for WRB agent in Spain. Understands Blickenstaff could do both WRB job and one he is already doing in Spain."

With $50,000 for disbursement from the Joint, acting for the War Refugee Board under License W-2155, the green light was given to move the threatened Jews and anti-Nazis across to Spain. It would cost 4,000 pesetas ($400) per person. Along with the license issued by the U.S. Treasury Department was the request that its substance be "transmitted urgently to Mr. Samuel Sequerra, the Joint's representative at the Hotel Bristol in Barcelona. In addition, Sequerra was to be informed that the Joint's man in Lisbon, Dr. Joseph Schwartz, would "give him instructions with regard to beginning the operations envisaged by License W-2155." In it permission was given "to communicate with persons in enemy or enemy-occupied territory . . . for the purpose of evacuation . . . This government [that of the U.S.] considers the saving of lives to be of paramount importance."

Earlier since 1943, Portugal's Salazar had been cannily moving toward the Allies, wanting to save Portugal's overseas empire following their now predictable victory in the war. Ambassador Norweb met with the Portuguese dictator in February 1944, making a deal to swap a return of Portuguese Timor in the Pacific liberated from the Japanese for the right of the British and Americans in the Atlantic to use the Azores as a base of operations.

In Barcelona, the Sequerras installed themselves in the Hotel Bristol, collaborating with a man named Sam Levy, not otherwise identified.

An example of their handiwork can be exemplified by the case of little Paul Buchinger. His family in France lived in Limoges. A group of young Jews offered his parents to take Paul across the Pyrenees to assured safety. At the end of May 1944, the boy boarded a train with his brother to Toulouse, closer to the Spanish border. In June, he arrived in Perpignan, even closer, and went to the frontier, itself. There were eight kids who were handed over to Catalan smugglers. It took several days to get across. As Paul Buchinger later explained in Spanish: "*Dormiamos en cobertizos y bebamose agua de los arroyos* [We slept in shelters and drank water from streams]." It was a painful memory for him.

In Spain, he was separated from his brother. His handlers had him lodged at a *granja*—a farm—then taken by train to Barcelona. On the ride, he was told not to say anything so no one could tell he was a foreigner and pretend to be sleeping. It was a long ride and a long time for a kid to keep quiet.

Samuel Sequerra met him in Barcelona. He was deposited in a *pension*. "*Que se desmayo* [I almost fainted]." The kid who opened the door to him was his neighbor from Limoges. Paul next went to a villa that was an orphanage where he stayed three months. He was taught geography, history and Hebrew. Otherwise, he could do what he wanted at the place.

But the scare prompted by a Red Cross official who asked to see the papers of "stateless children" sent him moving again to Estoril in Portugal, to Cadiz back in Spain, to Gibraltar and finally to Haifa in Palestine among a group of 50 kids and 350 adults.

Another documented escape in the same area was that of Gilles Goudchaux, the brother of Serge Weill-Goudchaux who had acted as defense counsel for Herschel Grynszpan, the Jew who had killed a German diplomat in Paris in 1938, the pretext of the infamous *Kristallnacht* pogrom in Germany fomented by Hitler's government. Gilles Goodchaux, himself, had lived in Paris and New York before the war as a buyer for several American department stores.

He spent four years in the French Resistance. At the beginning of this time, there were four hundred thousand Jews in France, half of them French natives, the others refugees. Goudchaux thought only twenty thousand were left by the end of the war.

In December 1943, he was living on the Riviera at Cannes and thought that four thousand Jews had found refuge in nearby Monte Carlo, an independent country whose prince was sympathetic to the persecuted Hebrews.

By the end of 1943, this Jewish *résistant* had to think about fleeing France. The route was south, and his wife followed three or four days later. They reached Lourdes, the world-famed pilgrimage site, and then proceeded to Pau in the Pyrenean foothills and joined a group of Jews in hiding. Goudchaux thought there might be one thousand sheltered in the vicinity. Next, the reunited couple left for Bayonne, practically on the Spanish border, and crossed into a "red zone," where special papers were required. They travelled with a rugby team in a furniture van. At Itxassou up in the mountains, they were met by a Basque guide and accompanied him on foot. For two nights they trekked and hid by day. There were four guides altogether, who were paid eighty thousand pesetas for bringing them into Spain. In the first Spanish town reached, Elizondo, they were arrested by the Spanish police and brought to Pamplona, where they declared themselves British subjects. Removed to a holding facility at Leiza, they stayed there for twenty-five days. But with the help of the British and local Spaniards, they were transferred to Gibraltar and delivered to the Free French authorities in North Africa.

Goudchaux was to say he had heard of different routes from theirs. One was out of the small French city of Foix to Andorra, also an independent country, and another by sea from Nice to Corsica on small fishing boats. U.S. Intelligence was eventually to claim that Goudchaux must have been exaggerating in his narrative. No way could a thousand Jews have been hiding in Pau.

The hike over the Pyrenees, *le Chemin de la Liberté*, was the route most employed. It was estimated that eight hundred Allied airmen plus numerous Jewish refugees risked their lives on a climb of 1,500 feet up and 3,335 feet down. The weather could be dark and drizzly or boiling hot; snow might be underfoot, followed by freezing mists, not to mention enervating heat, depending on the season. The story was told of a Jewish woman carrying her two-year-old daughter in

November through snowdrifts. When the child cried, the guide said she should be suffocated. The Germans might hear the noise. It is not recorded how this crisis ended.

After passing the hat to pay for guides, a young Swiss woman, Mademoiselle Naef, organized a flight across the rugged terrain, while meanwhile down in the foothills, near the Ariège River, a nineteen-year-old girl, Inge Vogelstein, and two other Jewish refugees were waiting to flee. Then, the Germans captured the trio at the Château de la Hille, where they were hiding. Taken to the French prison camp at Le Vernet, originally set up for Spanish Republicans fleeing the end of the Civil War in 1939, which three years later became a transit point for Jews deported to Poland, they somehow managed to escape, got to Spain and settled in Lerida.

The France to Spain to Portugal to safety in North Africa underground railroad, so to speak, functioned under the same rules. Yet Portugal, which had expelled its Jewish population in 1497, appeared more impatient to hurry the fleeing victims of Nazism on. It presently had far less natives of the Hebrew faith than its larger neighbor Spain did, although it had allowed the World Jewish Congress in December 1942 to set up a rescue area at Ericeira, a beach resort twenty-one miles from Lisbon. The status of some 250 stateless evaders was legalized there.

The push-pull in Portugal over this issue went on and on. Edward S. Crocker, counselor of the U.S. Embassy, Lisbon, reported Portuguese pressure to hurry refugees off to Fedhala in Morocco. Doing this, he wrote, will "sweeten Portuguese-American relations." The message should be transmitted to the War Refugee Board, he insisted, and he wanted "an identification of intentions."

The response back received by Crocker may actually have been not what he wanted to hear. The Joint, which was caring for five hundred Jews in Portugal "had no interest" in withdrawing its financial support of their upkeep and felt the Portuguese Government was not pressing for their evacuation. Thus, it seemed "premature at the present time to consider their transfer to Camp Lyautey." The Joint, in fact, rejected the idea of Fedhala.

The War Refugee Board, in turn, declared that very few of the refugees in Portugal were there at its request nor those of private American organizations. Consequently, also, they asserted: "The Board is not prepared at the present time to recommend their transfer to Camp Lyautey."

Reacting, the Portuguese Foreign Office said it was "impossible to admit more refugees without more effective guarantees from the United States that all of the people whether given U.S. visas or not, will be speedily removed from Portugal by the United States if admitted." The motivation behind this bald statement was that the Portuguese Ministry and government feared the impending end of the war and a consequent decline in U.S. interest. The Portuguese specifically objected to the statement that recipients of U.S. visas after July 1, 1941, will only be accepted subject to immigration law and other limitations. They also didn't like the statement that "the United States will evacuate those not given U.S. visas as soon as possible" and wanted a U.S. guarantee of a definite limit "on a stay in Portugal" from Ambassador Norweb.

The British Foreign Office and the Intergovernmental Committee on Refugees in London also added their voices of restraint. Regarding the rush to Fedhala, the Brits cautioned it would be better if the "refugees now in Portugal remain there until it becomes necessary to remove them." The Intergovernmental Committee seconded the motion. Besides, word was received that Fedhala was closed and its replacement at Philippeville, with a capacity for only 350 persons, was *completely full.*

It may have been suspected that the British were simply stalling a movement of refugees who might end up in Palestine. A proposal from London was for a survey to be done of all refugees in Portugal and Spain as part of a combined Anglo-American master list of évadées. The Intergovernmental Committee had promised funding, they revealed, for such a treading water activity.

In the third week of August 1944, Robert Dexter was notified that James H. Mann, the troubleshooter of the WRB's D.C. office, had been appointed special attaché to end the gap in Spain and would work out of the American Embassy in Madrid. Dexter was also told that the Board had designated Mann to be in overall command of War Refugee Board matters for the whole Iberian Peninsula.

Previously, "something of a disturbing nature" had been reported by Mann—that the relations between the World Jewish Congress and the Joint in the Portuguese capital were "not as cordial as I [Mann] would like them to be." This was an understatement. Some pretty harsh language had been used in the charges made during the spat. Money may have been the real root of the problem, rather than competitive personalities. The World Jewish Congress felt it was doing the heavy lifting and wanted financial support from its rival. Isaac Weissman was bold enough to write Pehle the "consequence of the Joint's interference was that children's rescue is suffering." He likewise complained to his employer, Rabbi Stephen Wise, in New York.

On its part, the Joint firmly if politely replied to the request of a "subvention" (i.e. a grant of funds), to the American branch of the World Jewish Congress. The answer was NO. Their expressed reason: "The visit of Joseph Schwartz to Spain has made it clear we shall need all our available funds for our own work of rescue which we believe can best be accomplished through our direct efforts rather than through the intermediary of another organization."

A parting dig was overtly added that the World Jewish Congress had "set up duplicating machinery for the care and maintenance of children." Therefore: "Under the circumstances, the Joint Distribution Committee cannot see its way clear to grant a subvention to the World Jewish Congress."

Pehle expressed the hope that with Mann's help these fiery relations would soon flame out and "mirror that of the full cooperation in the U.S."

The highly capable WRB emissary was soon knocking heads together. Incidentally, James Mann, a former Foreign Service officer, had been a second choice—the first was James G. McDonald of the President's Advisory Committee on Refugees, whose appointment hadn't worked out.

Arriving in Madrid to begin with, Mann quickly learned the political lay of the land from Corey Oliver, an assistant to Ambassador Hayes. He also had a friendly contact with Niles Bond, the junior embassy officer who handled refugee affairs but who, it turned out, was not happy with Samuel Sequerra.

Two other actors in this mishmash were equally as obscure historically as Oliver and Bond. They were a man named Forsythe, "the only American Foreign Service officer in Spain with a real understanding of the [refugee] problem" and an American businessman Daniel Heineman who was friendly with both Henry Morgenthau and FDR. The latter while accompanying Mann to Lisbon briefed the WRB rep on how he should approach the Franco government. Heineman then proceeded to take up the matter with the Marques de Foronda, an aristocrat close to Spanish Foreign Minister Francisco Goméz-Jordana—and Jordana spoke to Franco himself.

In their 1987 book about American refugee policy, authors Richard Breitman and Alan M. Kraut write: "Hayes finally called on Jordana and for the first time mentioned the WRB and its program." Yet as Breitman and Kraut sum up: "Hayes's opposition had cost the War Refugee Board and the refugees a great deal of time."

In Lisbon, Ambassador Norweb was persuaded to sponsor a top-level meeting at the American Embassy of all parties involved. Attending were Elisha Dobkin and David Sealfiel from the Jewish Agency in Palestine, Robert Pilpel for the Joint, Isaac Weissman of the World Jewish Congress, and adding the WRB's Mann and Dexter as *intermediaries and observers.*

The gathering was secret. There was to be no publicity, and its goal was to stimulate "a free and frank exchange of information." It was promised that the "principals" in Portugal would be kept abreast of all operations and no reports of activities made to the U.S., "except through the facilities of the War Refugee Board.

Additional stipulations were that: "All persons entering Spain through the Committee shall be turned over to the Joint; but all children will be sent to Portugal and handed at the Spanish-Portugal border to persons of Portuguese nationality designated by the Youth Aliyah Committee of Portugal." Also to be kept in the loop was Miss Henrietta Szold in the head office of the overall Youth Aliyah immigration program in the Holy Land.

It was agreed that Robert Dexter would keep the original of the "subject memorandum."

When at last at the end of May 1944, it had been decided in Washington to unsnarl the tangle in Portugal, Ambassador Norweb received a cable that James H. Mann of the War Refugee Board was leaving for Lisbon by clipper. "Mann's mission," Norweb was told, "is to attempt to settle the dispute between the World Jewish Congress and the Joint Distribution Committee. He has full authority from me [Secretary of State Cordell Hull]. I am counting on you [Norweb] to advise Weissman and Schwartz to obtain their full cooperation in bringing about a settlement of this matter. Please advise when Mann has arrived." Signed: Hull.

The verbal shots back and forth had occurred in May. With Mann on the job in the middle of June, the situation gradually improved and by the first week in July, a memo from Dexter to Pehle bore the news that "for the first time since the organizations have been functioning in

Portugal, their representatives met in an apparently friendly conference a day or two ago and yesterday they had lunch together."

Before long, there was the glowing report that the WRB and the State Department were "highly pleased the World Jewish Congress and the Joint representatives were finally brought into an agreement."

Another organizational player on this stage was the Comunidade Israelita de Lisboa—the Jewish Community group headquartered in Lisbon. The sometimes heedless Isaac Weissman allegedly made use of its name without ever having contacted these coreligionists of his. He had also set up his own operation with the tongue-twisting title in Portuguese of Commisão de Auxilio aos Transitarios Estrangeiros para a Legalização de sua Estada na Ericeira.

His mouthful referred to refugees he had boarded in the Cliffside Atlantic coast resort of Ericeira who were "clandestines," meaning they had not entered Portugal legally. But somehow Weissman had gotten permission for them to remain there.

This occurred in 1943, before the WRB was organized. And the following year, his *Commisão* was shut down by the Vigilance Police, while allowing him to operate at Caldas da Rainha, another tourist spot and noted for its hot springs. The reprieve may have been due to a meeting Weissman had with the president of the republic arranged for him by a prominent Portuguese Navy admiral.

A letter dated July 12, 1944, from Elisha Dobkin of the Jewish Agency to Ambassador Norweb brought at request for transit visas through Spain to accommodate 1,500 Jews from Hungary, "mostly Rabbis and prominent persons in Jewish communities and organizations." They would be chosen from among many holders of Palestine immigration certificates now still in Hungary. Dobkin was the director of the Immigration Department of the Jewish Agency. His purpose in contacting Norweb was also to ask for Portuguese visas, since these Palestine-bound escapees would have to go to Portugal eventually en route.

In that same July of 1944, Dexter wrote to D.C. about testimony he'd received from two American women who'd been held in a concentration camp: "Both Mrs. Johnson and Miss Flinders seemed to me to be obviously telling the truth, although it is difficult to understand how any individuals could be as they reported the Gestapo and German guards to have been. It seems very much worthwhile that when these individuals arrive in the U.S., they be seen and their stories taken down. Mrs. Johnson's stories are particularly valuable as obviously she is not Jewish."

Another element of the WRB's workload in Portugal was action to secure the release of refugees imprisoned when they had arrived without legal documents. Together with British Embassy officials, they made a "practice of visiting all prisons in which political prisoners are kept." The advice was proffered that "It would make far more of an impression on the Portuguese if the [prison] visitors arrived in a good-looking CD [*Corps Diplomatique*] car than in a broken-down taxi."

Several other proposed initiatives were turned down for fear of antagonizing their Portuguese hosts. Complaints of harsh treatment of refugees born in Russia—possibly considered Communists—were shelved as was pushing for allowing refugees to hold jobs while the question of brutality against jailed inmates was handled as delicately as possible.

This welter of obligations thrust upon the War Refugee Board in Iberia might have lain behind a remark Dexter imparted to Pehle after a month or so of fairly feverish activity. Writing that he'd originally feared the Joint who'd been in Lisbon well ahead of them would have considered the WRB's addition unnecessary, but "nothing like that has happened."

Chapter Nine

Throughout the voluminous material on the War Refugee Board, like veins of marbling in a steak, run mentions of *working with the Underground* in such-and-such a German-occupied country. For the most part, the details of these surreptitious wartime groups in correspondence and communication were necessarily sketchy. Identities revealed could be fatal. Tragedies occurred whenever organizational lists of these brave opponents of the Teutonic conquerors and their satraps fell into enemy hands.

Postwar, their stories could be told and their links of 1944–45 brought safely into print.

A full accounting of all Underground and partisan activity in the European theater has filled many a book. The proliferation and complexity of their composition can be dizzying. Take for instance Hungary, which as a Nazi satellite was left untouched by them until March 1944, when leaks of a possible Magyar unilateral surrender to the Allies led to an invasion by German troops, bringing with them the Gestapo and SS.

Thus we find pushback by the following entities, just among the Jewish population: Ihud Mapaii; Beitar; Bnei Akiva; Hamizrahi; Dror Habonim; HaNoar HaTzioni; Hatzionism Haclali'im; Mizrahi; Hashomer Hatzair; Paratroops of the Haganah; the Shimoni Group, the Communists; the Gordon Circle; the Borochov Circle.

The salient figure of the Hungarian Jewish Underground appeared to be David Gur, whose book *Brothers for Resistance and Rescue* details the events starting even before the Nazis invaded and eventually installed a vicious fascistic government led by the murderous Arrow Cross organization.

Gur had been in Budapest, doing work as a building apprentice in preparation for his emigration (*Aliyah* in Hebrew) to Palestine. Even prior to the German invasion, he had attached himself to the Hashomer

Hatzair faction and was helping refugees from other countries already under Nazi rule.

In response to the new direr situation created by the Axis takeover, the various Hungarian undergrounds created a unified defense committee, and Gur joined a group forging identity cards and other vital papers, one of its prime activities. Equipped himself with "Aryan documents," Gur and his coworkers served Jewish youth movements, Zionist organizations, unaffiliated Jews, and "most of the non-Jewish resistance groups."

The irony of the situation in Hungary brought forth the wry observation that in the birthplace of Theodor Herzl and Max Nordau, the two preeminent promulgators of "Zionism," the concept of a Jewish State "had never struck deep roots" in their native country. These non-Zionist Hungarian Jews referred to themselves as "Magyars of the Israelite faith."

Nevertheless, anti-Semitism had early sprouted in Hungary right after World War I. The *numerus clausus* law of 1918, restricting entry of Jewish students to universities, was the first of its kind in Europe and unfortunately soon spread among neighboring lands.

In 1939, the Hungarian Government of Admiral Miklós Horthy took advantage of the Munich Treaty to help itself to chunks of Poland, Romania, Slovakia and even Yugoslavia that it claimed belonged to them from the days of the Austro-Hungarian Empire. The areas of South Slovakia, Carpatho-Ruthenia, Northern Transylvania and the Banat, boosted the number of Jews already within their borders. So in early 1943, pre Nazi invasion, the framework for the unified underground Magyar Relief and Rescue operation was erected.

Admiral Horthy, considered a "moderate anti-Semite," presided over a population of Jews that expanded from four hundred thousand to nine hundred thousand under his mildly dictatorial regime. There were confiscations of Jewish wealth, estimated at thirty million pengős; by comparison, the entire 1942 debt of Hungary was five billion pengős. Brushed aside in 1944 after the Germans arrived, Horthy was helpless once the deportations of Hungarian Jews to the death camps were carried out between May 15 and June 28, 1944. A newspaper report in the *Swedish Stockholm Tidings* of April 25, 1944, stated that three weeks earlier, the preparations were underway. Large numbers of Jews were arrested. "The sight of young SS men taking Jews out of trains became a familiar occurrence in the streets of Budapest." In the first ten days,

25,000 Jews were expelled to Warsaw. The wealthy Jew Franz Harin hid in a Benedictine monastery but had to leave to tend a sick daughter and was caught. Mass conversions of Jews to Christianity took place, so much so that there were complaints. Bishop Béla Kapi of the Trans-Danubian Evangelical Districts openly questioned the Jews' sincerity. *The Magyar Courier* exhorted priests to make sure the Jews weren't just after a baptism certificate.

Unlike other areas of Europe where partisan groups had thick forests and rugged mountains in which to operate, Hungary was primarily a flat plain, not conducive to armed resistance against a stronger foe. Thus the concentration on forging documents in a main workshop, characterized as "unique in all of occupied Europe."

These surreptitious anti-Nazis also ran the Tiyul, the name given to the smuggling of Jews across the Hungarian border into Romania, who travelled via the Black Sea and eventually to Palestine. Some efforts were made to get the Magyar Jews to join the partisans in Yugoslavia. About fifteen thousand Hungarian Israelites did reach Palestine before the end of August 1944, when the Tiyul was discontinued due to a change in Romania. Some of the Hungarians were to join in the heroic but ill-fated Slovak Uprising of August 1944, and most were killed in battle.

Bunkers were established where Jews could be hidden. Children's homes—fifty-two of them—accommodated eight thousand youngsters and their teachers. An especially noted one of these was the "Glass House" at 29 Vadasz Street in Budapest, which was under the auspices of the Swiss consulate, as were most of these hiding places. Some three thousand Jews found refuge in them and were fed there, and a branch of the Glass House was also opened at 17 Wekerle Street.

Despite his excellently forged Aryan Identity card, David Gur was apprehended by police detectives of the fascistic Arrow Cross regime.

Its head was Ferenc Szálasi, a retired army officer who replaced Admiral Horthy whom the Germans were to keep under house arrest. Szálasi's gang, also a political party, formed "mob patrols" mainly of trigger-happy teenagers whose "wild behavior" terrified the city of Budapest. As soon as the war tapered toward its end, they murdered at will. In the final week of December 1944, the underground forgery laboratory on Erzsebel Boulevard was discovered and its three members taken to Arrow Cross headquarters. One died under torture and the other two were lodged in the downtown military prison where David Gur was being held. The underground Dror Habonim and Hashomer Hatzair decided to free them. Their whereabouts was learned from an Arrow Cross man nicknamed Tony. This was on December 21, 1944. The would-be rescuers also found an officer in the Hungarian Army who for thirty Napoleon gold coins would release the incarcerated men. On December 23, the fascist gendarmes left in the city tried to break out of the Russian encirclement. They failed in their attempt and consequently returned to Budapest. On Christmas Day, David Gur and his fellow prisoners were lined up in the military prison courtyard. An officer with a list of names read them off for the prisoners called to step forward. Initially, none of them budged.

That is, until the name of Rapos Farkas Tibor was reached. David Gur among the prisoners recognized his pseudonym, which he'd used while living in hiding with a friend and fellow underground member, Moshe Pil-Alpan. Surmising that Pil-Alpan had provided the list, David Gur stepped forward and the rest of the prisoners followed him. En masse, they were moved in a column up to the Chain Bridge over the Danube but not stopped on its banks for execution as expected. Instead the march was continued on and into a house at 17 Wekerle Street, which happened to be a branch office of the Swiss legation, and there they were united with their comrades.

The next day, this daring deception was repeated and ninety-seven more prisoners were taken to a protected house at 32 Pozsonyi Street.

These frantic days in Budapest were full of such incidents. Possibly the most dramatic occurred when Jews who had gathered in the Yellow Star House in a section of the city known as Népszínház were startled by the arrival of a pair of Arrow men in uniform bearing Hungarian fascist emblems.

They said they were looking for the Jew Alpan, David Gur's friend. His mother was present and terrified. She was told to go down into the cellar and stay put.

Out on the street, however, the Arrow Cross disguise of the two was penetrated by a genuine Arrow Cross street fighter, who had been a neighbor of one of the men and cried out: "You're a Jew!" A crowd gathered. But the two fake fascists kept their cool and chased away the forming mob. Actually they were members of the Dror Habonim movement.

It wasn't always this easy to escape tragedy. One crushing blow happened when a body of Polish refugees in one of the safe houses, not understanding Hungarian, shot at an Arrow Cross storm trooper. Holed up in a house, the insurgent Jews had to face units of the German and Hungarian armies who arrived with tanks and fired upon them. Mortars were brought into play, too. In the bloody shootout, all of the Poles were killed.

As for the War Refugee Board's role here, it has never been delineated precisely. One may see its hand in the famous speech delivered March 22, 1944, by FDR on War Crimes punishment awaiting the Nazis. Specific reference was made to the surprise German occupation of Hungary three days earlier. After his stating that the "wholesale murder of the Jews of Europe goes on unabated," there is added in the president's words: "As a result of the events of the last few days, hundreds of thousands of Jews who while living under persecution have at least found a haven from death in Hungary and the Balkans and are now threatened with annihilation."

Special intense psychological pressure was put on Hungary. A group of seventy-three prominent American Christian leaders headed by Al Smith, the prominent Roman Catholic ex-presidential candidate, expressed their indignation over the atrocities the Nazis were committing in Hungary, particularly against the Jews. The Archbishop of New York Francis (later Cardinal) Spellman added his eloquent words in a moving appeal to Hungary's large Catholic population: "Abraham is called our patriarch, our ancestor. Anti-Semitism is not compatible with the sublime reality of this text . . . Spiritually we are Semites." And after adding that Saint Stephen, the patron saint of Hungary had stated that no minority should be oppressed, he finished by frankly stating: "It would be all the more tragic, therefore, if a people so devoted to Mary, the Jewish maiden who was the mother of the Messiah, should freely countenance cruel laws calculated to despoil and annihilate the race from which Jesus and Mary sprang."

Most likely, too, the WRB was involved in financing funds for a *first priority* of the Magyar Underground: the mission of "supplying, transporting and delivering food to the children's houses and the Glass House."

Six months after the war in Europe ended, Rudolf Kastner, a key figure in the Hungarian Underground, in a letter to Saly Mayer, elucidated his point of view of the situation that had existed in his native land during the hostilities. Then living in exile in Geneva, Switzerland,

Kastner had been head of the Hungarian Zionist Organization from 1942 to 1945. He was, in effect, contradicting an account of Mayer's role that Mayer's employer, the Joint, had just issued. Kastner wrote that "for truth's sake," and as chairman of the Budapest Committee, he had to respond.

His preamble stated: "It was not exactly you who persuaded Hitler's agents to cancel the deportation of Jews from Hungary."

The *actual facts*, Kastner claimed were:

a) After the total evacuation from provincial towns . . . following the intervention of the Pope and King of Sweden . . . but first of all . . . the energetic and dignified step of President Roosevelt . . . it was Regent Horthy with an order to the Hungarian administration . . . prevented the deportation of the Budapest Jews.

b) Those of us in Budapest played some role in the calling into existence of the Hungarian resistance and Samuel Stern, Aulic [sic] Councilor, could tell some tales of it. The Germans, however, insisted on the evacuation of Budapest . . . Becher informed you *it was a definite decision*. He made this information clear on August 21, 1944, at our first meeting on the bridge between Saint Margarethen and Hoechst. Your answer thereupon was: *"The deportations would not be a great catastrophe if you would only stop that damned gassing."*

c) After the removal of the Horthy Government [October 15, 1944] and coming to power of Szálasi, Aitchmann [sic Eichmann] arrived by plane to Budapest to organize the deportation . . . It had to be done in *a great hurry* due to the approach of the Russians. The Arrow Cross were soon forcing Jews to walk toward the Reich.

Kastner's indictment of Saly Mayer continued with disappointment voiced that despite their hopes that the Swiss negotiator would convince the Nazi Becher, "We returned to Hungary without your having expressed a single wish. Then Kastner rued the fact, in his words, that he "was left to fight out by himself . . . He had had to go back to Budapest at the mercy of the Nazis and to the terror of the

Arrow Cross Party. You, the independent citizen of Switzerland, left the task to me . . . It is not exact that you browbeated [sic] the agents into releasing another 1,700 Jews from Bergen-Belsen."

On Kastner went, like a prosecutor summing up testimony and accusations: "We were those who organized this transport consisting of province Jews rescued and brought to Budapest from the ghettoes by us—of Budapest Jews, Polish, Slovak, Yugoslav etc. refugees living in the Hungarian capital . . . The sine qua non of the transport: We made available the necessary funds [from the WRB?] . . . before your first meeting with Becher, the realization of which was due to my exertions in Budapest . . . 318 of them were allowed to leave for Switzerland . . . This was the first compact group of Jews that the Nazis let out of their grip since the outbreak of the war."

Then, *whammo!!* "It is not true that you ever at the risk of your life entered Nazi Germany to carry on discussions."

Following upon this politely phrased tirade was a listing of Jewish heroes in the region: Gisi Fleischmann of Bratislava [Slovakia] "who suffered martyrdom"; Chaim Dov Weissmandl, the Rabbi of Nitra [in Slovakia], "this resistant of unequaled audacity who jumped out of the train deporting him"; Ottó Komoly, chairman of the Hungarian Zionist organization, "shot by the Arrow Cross when smuggling food in the ghetto . . . Samuel Stern, Dr. Karl Wilhelm . . . and my friends in Budapest, Samuel Offenbach, Hansi Brand, Audor Bics, Dr. Juraj Revesz of Bratislava who organized food suppliers of Jewish 'bunkers' . . . and of Dr. Emil Tuchmann of Vienna and of thousands of young liberating children from the ghettoes and from Jewish houses."

A touch of Jewish sarcasm was added toward the close of his screed: "This letter is not being written in order to interfere with the rivalry of the different Jewish organizations, which even in the darkest hours of greatest peril and destruction did not cooperate."

Finally, kudos to the WRB, which did indeed involve itself in Hungary: "It was fortunate that we could profit by the background of the War Refugee Board for a diplomatic ploy in which, you in any case, were standing on the safe side—in neutral Switzerland."

Left unspecified in this particular missive was the preventing of the murder of another 84,000 Jews trapped in the Budapest Ghetto, the 6,500 children locked up in Jewish "houses" whom *chalutzim* "kidnapped" to safety, sixty-nine Jews arriving from Bratislava bunkers and Austrian camps to Switzerland in April 1944, and the surrender by the Nazis without a fight of Bergen-Belsen, Mauthausen, and Theresienstadt concentration camps.

Copies were sent to a long list of Jewish dignitaries including Chaim Weizmann, Moshe Shertck, Gerhart Riegner, and once more Samuel Stern who served as chairman of the *Judenrat* of Budapest.

Added to the Hungarian film stars, the Gabor sisters, was another of their compatriots in Hollywood, the character actor Bela Lugosi, who had occasion also to contact the War Refugee Board. He had been born—where else?—in Transylvania, then part of the Kingdom of Hungary, and his stage last name, forever associated with *Dracula*, was derived from his hometown of Lugos. Having emigrated to the U.S. well before World War II, he was writing John Pehle for information on an official statement sent to the Red Cross that the British and U.S. Governments were prepared to give asylum to Hungarian Jews. "There are a lot of false rumors being spread about this question and many people are being taken in by them."

His letter was on behalf of the Hungarian-American Council for Democracy, located at 23 West 26th Street in downtown Manhattan.

Slovakia directly borders Hungary along its northwest boundary. Although the two citizenries speak altogether different languages (Hungarian has somewhat of an affinity with Finnish and Estonian, while Slovak is purely Slavic), we have seen they have interrelations.

An individual who has already surfaced in underground connections was Rabbi Weissmandl. The city he served, Nitra, was located on the Nitra River, a tributary of the Danube, not far from Bratislava. Jews from Nitra and Trnava were sent to Auschwitz in Poland to build the infamous concentration camps and crematoria the Nazis erected there. In 1942, Rabbi Weissmandl became active in the Hashomer Hatzalah organization in Bratslava. The martyred Gisi Fleischmann was on it too. When the Nazis started deportations to Lublin in Poland, the Slovak underground bribed the SS commander in charge, Dieter Wisliceny, giving him the equivalent of $50,000. For two years, the expulsions to the death camps were halted.

Helping Jews still free in Poland, they sent items for these impoverished victims to sell and even used German officers and soldiers to transport the goods. However, one of these German messengers was caught in 1943 and had a list of designees on him. Rabbi Weissmandl was arrested.

But the major story of the underground in Slovakia did not occur until the Slovak National Uprising at the end of the summer of 1944.

On the next-to-last day of August—the 29th—the brewing revolt burst into the open in the small city of Banská Bystrica. Under the leadership of General Ján Golian, the rebels marched that evening and by the next morning had captured the place. The Germans, counting on a puppet Eastern Slovak army, saw it dissolve. Golian's troops, 47,000 strong by September 5, moved out to occupy large portions of central and eastern Slovakia. They took two airfields in the region, which were then used by their Soviet allies to bring equipment. The Americans also joined in by early October, landing Flying Fortresses bearing more supplies and more OSS agents. In addition, they evacuated fifteen Allied airmen, whose planes had been shot down, and disembarked Czech units from the Soviet Army.

Still, despite these early victories, the Slovak Uprising was to prove a mixed blessing.

Support for the outbreak was not universal among Slovakians. The ultra-nationalists who wanted Slovakia detached from the Czechs deemed it an attempt to restore Czechoslovakia as it existed before the German invasion. Thus the statement that "the large rebel units did not have *unambiguous popular support.*"

On the other side, the pro-German government of Father Jozef Tiso, a fascistic-minded Roman Catholic Monsignor, remained in power at Bratislava and dispatched forty thousand troops to disperse the insurgents. Apologists for Father Tiso have tried to soften his image, arguing that he was only a diehard Slovakian for independence from the Czechs, not an anti-Semite. But Hitler was heard to have said: "It is interesting how this little Catholic priest is sending us the Jews." The oncoming Soviets, most likely because they couldn't control these non-Communist Slovaks, grew less cooperative and finally actively hostile. They actually blocked Western aid from getting through and ordered their own partisan Slavic contingents out of the fight. Postwar, a first order of business for them was having Tiso convicted of treason and executed.

In any case, the Red Army, reaching Dukla Pass on the Slovak-Polish border, made a botch of the battle there and had their advance halted.

Worse still, the Czechoslovak Government-in-Exile was unable to convince the Allies to ignore the Soviet obstructionism and continue sending supplies to the rebels in what was still a part of their country.

The German counteroffensive was powerful. Eight divisions—48,000 troops—were sent into combat and included four elite Waffen SS formations buttressed by a pro-Nazi Slovak outfit.

Initially, the rebels had seen themselves holding out for two weeks. In point of fact, they did better than that. The whole month of September went by and half of October until the Axis launched its full-scale attack, beginning on October 17–18, when 35,000 German forces entered from Hungary.

The Russians, stopping their offensive, sat by and watched. On October 27, Banská Bystrica was abandoned, and the OSS and British SOE (Special Operations Executive) units retreated into the mountains.

Almost all resistance had ceased on October 27, yet at the higher altitudes the fighting continued. Several villages were burnt to the ground. One of them, Kremnicka, entered the atrocity lists of municipality sites along with more-publicized towns like Lidice and Oradour-sur-Glane. Its body count was 747 slain, and this was even surpassed by neighboring Nemecka, where the Nazis massacred 900 souls, taking seven blood-soaked days to do so.

On the third of November, General Golian and his subordinate Rudolf Viest were taken prisoner and summarily executed. Christmas Day, the OSS and SOE men fell into a German trap. They, too, were shot on the spot.

At the start of this episode of revolt, it should be noted that Rabbi Weissmandl, who had been released from his first imprisonment, was rearrested along with his five children—four girls and a boy. The Rabbi had been assisting refugees since 1938, once the Nazis had overrun Austria. His most famous coup in starting had been to find refuge for sixty rabbis from Burgenland, whom the Nazis had stuck on a ship that—in a forerunner of the infamous *SS Saint Louis* incident a year later—was turned away from port after port. Weissmandl flew to England, enlisted the help of the Archbishop of Canterbury and the Foreign Office and acquired entry visas to Britain for all the rabbis. Unfortunately, he wasn't so lucky later that year, after Munich and the Nazi occupation of Vienna, in helping Jews expelled into the no-man's-land between Slovakia and Hungary. Weissmandl, living in Nitra, contacted the Archbishop of Canterbury again and Samuel Hoare, the foreign minister, but this time the answer was NO.

In a sense, Rabbi Chaim Dov Weissmandl was a victim of the Slovak Partisans' Uprising. The event triggered the German decision "to put an end to Slovakia's Jews." After that day of September 7, 1944, when he was hauled off to incarceration, Rabbi Weissmandl simply vanished forever.

Six months later, the Red Army entered Banská Bystrica and a little more than a week later conquered Bratislava, capping their triumph in Slovakia a month or so prior to the ultimate German surrender.

What has been said about the Slovakian Uprising, tragic in the end though it was, is that it did help the Allied war effort by tying up German military units they might better have used on the Russian front.

This revolt also saw the formation of fighting Jewish bodies within the overall Slovak forces. The best known was the Novaky Brigade composed of former inmates of the Novaky concentration camp. The Order of the Slovak Uprising was awarded to 166 Jewish partisans.

Among the very rare escapees from the Auschwitz complex were two young Jewish Slovakians, Rudolf Vrba and Alfred Wetzlar, who slipped out in April 1944 but whose report was not released by the War Refugee Board until November. Their depiction of what went on within the notorious killing site, although disbelieved in some quarters initially, was soon being told throughout the Free World.

Here are some excerpts from a spine-chilling account whose details are so real and full of verisimilitude that they have to be believed.

They had been in Auschwitz and at neighboring Birkenau for two years and had also transited from Lublin, one of them sent through the "assembly camp" of Sebed to Auschwitz and then Birkenau in April 1942, the other from the Novaky camp to Lublin in June and then on to Auschwitz and later Birkenau. Both these notorious death centers were located in Poland.

The report details the start of the horror show on April 13, 1944, when a thousand men were herded into railroad cars at Sebed (in Slovakia). The narrative begins: "The doors were shut so that nothing would relieve the direction of the journey . . . When opened, we realized we had crossed the Slovak border and were in Zwardoń." The train had been guarded by Hlinka men (followers of a virulent Slovak Nationalist and also a Catholic priest, Andrej Hlinka, who had died in 1938) and were replaced by the SS. "A few cars were uncoupled there. Then we proceeded to Auschwitz. We stopped on a side track. Placed in rows of five, the count came to 643 of us. We walked 20 minutes with our heavy packs. We had reached Auschwitz."

The prisoners were led into a huge barracks. They had to leave their luggage on one side of it. Forced to undress, they went naked to an adjoining barracks. Their bodies were shaved and disinfected. In a third barracks, they were tattooed. "The extreme brutality of the process made some men faint." Led in groups of one hundred into a cellar, they were taken to yet another barracks and given striped uniforms and wooden shoes. This whole process lasted until ten a.m. "In the afternoon, they took away our prisoners' clothes that were replaced by the ragged and dirty remains of Russian uniforms. Then, we were marched off to Birkenau."

The well-known color coding of the prisoners was explained, done by cloth triangles sewn onto the prisoners' clothing: red for political prisoners; green for professional criminals; black for "antisocial labor slackers," pink for homosexuals, violet for members of the *Bibelforscher* (Bible seekers), and the Jews, of course, marked with a Star of David, its six points yellow within a red triangle.

The whole huge Auschwitz complex is delineated: several factories within Auschwitz itself, a war production plant, Krupp works, a Siemens operation. Outside the gates was a "tremendous plant covering several kilometers—the infamous Buna.

"If you touch the fence, you are machine-gunned.

"If the escapee is caught alive, he is hanged in the presence of the entire camp but if he is found dead, his body wherever it may have been located is brought back to camp, seated at the entrance gate, a small notice in his hands reading: 'Here I am.'"

The nearby forest, we learn, was called Brezinsky, and that the local Polish natives referred to Birkenau as *Rajska*.

There was one humungous kitchen for fifteen thousand people.

The buildings had been built by twelve thousand Russian prisoners, most of whom had died of exposure in the severe winter weather.

The French Jews were described as being "in terrible shape." Out of 1,320, only 700 were alive. Within a week of their arrival, 600 had died.

The *Prominencia*, those prisoners who ran the camp for the Nazis, were mostly professional criminals and older Polish political types.

As the report explained, the mortality rate was so high "that every day our group of 200 had 30–35 dead." Some were beaten to death by the *kapos*, fellow prisoners assigned to guard them.

A group of 300 Jewish Slovak girls was described "dressed in old Russian uniforms and wooden clogs, their heads shaved."

There were examples of prisoners killing each other. "Once I was an eye-witness," one of the reporters wrote, "when a young Jew named Jossel demonstrated *scientific murder* on a Jew in the presence of an SS guard. He used no weapon, merely his bare hands, to kill his coreligionist."

During February 1943, a new modern crematorium and gassing plant was inaugurated at Birkenau.

"On principle, only Jews were gassed. Aryans very seldom, as they are given 'special treatment' by shooting.

"Prominent jurists from Berlin were present at the installation of the first crematorium in March 1943 . . . On the *program* was the gassing and burning of 8,000 Kraków Jews . . . The guests spied through peep holes. They were lavish in their praise of the newly erected facility."

There were Greek Jews sent from Salonica—ten thousand of them—who mostly died of malaria and typhus . . . Some Jews were killed by "intracardial phenol injections administered by a lance corporal of the medical corps."

German professional criminals were named: Alexander Neumann, Albert Haemmerle, Rudi Osteringen . . . and political prisoners Alfred Kien and Alois Stahler . . . "They had to make written declarations that they had killed so and so many prisoners."

The main killers, according to the report, were Tyn, a Reich German from Sachsenhausen and Polish political prisoner number 856, Mieczys□ aw Katarzy□ ski. An SS Hauptsturmführer, the unnamed son or nephew of the police president of Berlin, "outdid all the others in brutality."

One group was kept at the camp for six months and not mistreated except by "a certain professional criminal by the name of Arno Bohm, prisoner number 8." The authorities even allowed a Czech prisoner Fredy Hirsch from Prague to set up a school. Fredy talked of leading a revolt but never did and instead he committed suicide by poisoning himself with luminal.

SS Untersturmführer Schwarzhuber, commandant of Birkenau, revealed he'd been told "that many Polish Jews were crossing to Slovakia and from there reaching Hungary and that the Slovak Jews were helping them." This Nazi was from the Tyrol in Austria, described as "an alcoholic and a sadist. His superior was Rudolf Höss, later hanged as a war criminal.

Until February 1944, fifty percent of the "block eldests" who ruled the roost in the barracks were Jews. The Nazis made them all resign and kept only three deemed indispensable. Franz Danisch, prisoner number 11; 182, a political prisoner from Königshütte, Upper Silesia, was the "undisputed master of the whole camp and has the power to nominate or dismiss block eldest and block recorders and hand out jobs."

Among the guards were Lithuanians, all armed with automatic pistols.

There was a camp song that the Germans made the prisoners sing over and over again. Its lyrics contained much of the smarmy motto of the camp that has received so much attention for its rank hypocrisy: "*Arbeit Macht Frei*" (Work Sets You Free). The theme is set right from the first stanza:

> From the whole of Europe came we Jews to Lublin
> Much work has to be done and this is the beginning
> To manage this duty, forget all about the past
> For in fulfillment of duty, there is community
> Modern times must teach us. Teach us all along
> That it is to work . . . And only to work we belong.

The kapos were Reich Germans and Czechs. The Germans were brutal but the Czechs helped wherever they could.

One of the adjutants was a Jew from Sered' named Mittler, and very brutal.

The brutal death of a Rabbi Eckstein from Sered' was pictured. He was one minute late for assembly. His captors thereupon stuck his head into a latrine, poured cold water over him and shot the poor man. He had been transferred to Auschwitz from Lublin and enrolled as a political prisoner.

Workers in the Buna factory were "terribly mistreated." The prisoners were forced to paint skis. Each was given a quota of 120 a day. "If you missed, you were flogged." A "brutal and vile individual" was the commander of this squad. He often struck women. His name for the record was SS Scharführer Wykleff.

On May 10, 1944, the first transports of Hungarian Jews arrived at Birkenau. Names of some of these new victims have been recorded. Among the women: Ruth Lorant, Mici Lorant, Ruth Quasztla, Irene Roth, Barna Fuchs, and from other parts of Hungary, Robert and Erwin

Waizer, Chaim Katz, a person surnamed Stark, another Ehrenberg. We need always to be reminded that not all the victims were faceless, nameless bodies.

The lesser villains, too, the real murderers, need recognition as well. At Auschwitz and Birkenau, Schwarzhuber, Weiss, Hartenstein, Kramer and Höss led the list.

In the individual executions, the condemned were put against a wall. "The executioners shot their victims in the back of the head with a short-barreled rifle which made a muffled report." The bodies were taken to a nearby stable, "thrown into a heap of straw . . . bloodstains removed and the emplacement prepared for the execution of two further victims."

The murder of the famous Polish actor Witold Zacharewicz was cited. He received a deadly injection while ill in bed.

A mother was shot with an infant in her arms.

Both Slovakia and the Czech regions, primarily Bohemia, Moravia and part of Silesia, had belonged to the Austro-Hungarian Empire, whose existence was extinguished following World War I. Under this jurisdiction for half a century, the Slovaks had been treated as somewhat of a second-class minority and the better-educated Czechs somewhat more respectably, Slavs as well, but with a certain Germanic orientation. In one sense, World War II offered the Slovaks their desired independence from the Czechs, except it was under the auspices of the Nazis. So enemies changed, as it were. Focused on the Germans, who held them newly in thrall.

On the Czech side, their story of resistance during World War II has been deemed "a scarcely documented subject." The Czechs did form partisan units. But because of the land's less rugged terrain and heavily urban settings, the opportunities for full-scale operations were minimal.

Tipping off the Nazi intent was their first decree, after the swift German takeover in March 1939, banning all Kosher food preparation and cooking.

The Czech underground's most sensational exploit, needless to say, was the ultimately successful attempt on the life of Reichsprotekter Reinhard Heydrich, made on May 27, 1942. Heydrich, one of the ultra-top Nazis, commander of the Gestapo, had been sent to the Protectorate of Bohemia, Moravia and Silesia, to crack the whip as only he knew how and keep the all-important production of

Czechoslovakia's military industry flowing to Germany. It hadn't taken Heydrich long to earn the nicknames, *The Butcher of Prague* and *The Hangman*. Only pure blind luck, perhaps, kept the four-person, London-based Czechoslovak army-in-exile parachutist assassination team from bungling the affair.

After a pistol fired in ambush jammed, Heydrich's green Mercedes touring car abruptly stopped. Seated in the open back, Heydrich was then only wounded by a specially altered antitank grenade tossed at him. He staggered out, his own weapon drawn, a Luger, and shot at his assailants—and missed.

Then, he collapsed on the hood, obviously in serious pain. A delivery van drew up, and he was loaded aboard (the tires on his own vehicle had been blown off, and his chauffeur had been wounded by the attackers), and he was driven into Prague to the Na Bulovce Hospital. There, he overcame a high fever and appeared to be safely on the mend when, sitting up one day in his hospital bed, he keeled over and soon expired. The prevailing, slightly bizarre explanation was that horsehairs from the upholstery on the Mercedes back seating had penetrated his body and caused an eventually fatal inflammation.

Consider the code name the assassins and their British handlers at SOE had given beforehand to the attack: *Operation Anthropoid*, most unusual in those stiff-upper-lip quarters.

There was nothing risible, though, about the aftermath. Nazi massacres of innocent civilians commenced immediately. Two entire communities—the world-famed Lidice and the almost totally unknown Ležáky, were burned to the ground, false intelligence having linked them to the assassination. Their populations were killed en masse or some, the women and children of Lidice, sent to concentration camps. Of thirteen young boys so treated, only two survived the war. Mass retaliations elsewhere saw 550 more Czechs murdered between May 15 and July 13, 1944.

The First Czechoslovakian Partisan Brigade was named after a fifteenth-century hero Jan Žižka of the religious Hussite Rebellion, in which Jan Hus, its leader, became an eventual Protestant martyr. Two other local groups likewise used Jan Žižka in their titles: Jan Žižka Moravskoslezský in the north and the Czech Brigade of Jan Žižka in the south.

One aspect of the Underground/partisan warfare in Czechoslovakia was its direction by their government-in-exile, headquartered in

London. The home-front warriors were in direct contact with its leader Edvard Beneš, a former president of the country and hero of its independence. Working with Beneš there was the chief military intelligence officer, František Moravec. A unified command linked the men in England with separate bodies of freedom fighters under the German occupation, originally just non-Communist groups, bearing the rubric of UVOD—"Central Leadership of the Home Resistance." As it was, they did cooperate with the Communists eventually. In differences that existed in this coalition, the major one was an argument over what should be done with the sizeable prewar minority of ethnic Germans. The UVOD wanted them entirely expelled, while Beneš preferred only a partial purge.

In the Hostyn-Usetim Mountains, fighting broke out and urban areas soon experienced sabotage activity such as that of the White Lioness operation. Silesia was another scene of defiance. The Communists did their training outside the country, in Ukraine near Kiev. Most of the initial trainees were Slovaks. Some were deserters from the pro-Axis Hungarian Army. It took considerable time before these budding forces could go into action. Their military weakness could be seen in a skirmish against German border guards near the mountain town of Velke Karolva. Their unit was forced to retreat. They only had 130–140 operatives and their commander was a twenty-three-year-old youth.

But gradually their ranks grew to more than 1,500; with 927 of them Czechs and Slovaks, 257 Soviets, plus Ukrainians, Azerbaijanis, Georgians, Kazaks, Tajiks, etc., and even anti-Nazi Germans, Belgians and Russians.

Foreigners in the fight were also in the enemy ranks. The Germans tried to set up fake partisan outfits, one in conjunction with Vlasov's turncoat Russians and another with ethnic Germans fluent in the Czech language.

František Moravec, who had taken part in the planning of Heydrich's assassination, had a namesake or relative to face throughout the conflict, Edmond Moravec, the puppet protectorate's minister of national enlightenment. At the war's end, this quisling-type traitor committed suicide.

The men who had killed Heydrich were hunted down and eradicated. Four of them participated in the ambush and three more had parachuted into Czechoslovakia with them. All were members of the Czech Army, mostly sergeants. Best remembered by history are Warrant Officer Jozef Gabčík, whose British-made Sten gun jammed, and Staff Sergeant Jan Kubiš, who threw the ultimately fatal grenade. The end came in a fierce shootout in a Prague church. The besieging Germans suffered casualties in this firefight: fourteen dead and numerous wounded.

They are revered to this day, especially in the present-day Czech Republic, now separated from Slovakia, which was created as a separate nation after World War II.

While direct evidence of WRB support to the undergrounds of the three countries just discussed is scanty, there are snippets in the records. They detail financial support, in effect bookkeeping, of the primary and perhaps only help the War Refugee Board could tender.

We find, for example, that twelve thousand Swiss francs were paid to bring "special courier service" to a number of occupied territories including Hungary and Slovakia. On June 12, 1944, there is an entry of two thousand Swiss francs sent to Nathan Schwalbe for the Hechaluz Jewish youth groups in Hungary, Slovakia and Romania. Schwalbe also received—a rather startling fact—five thousand in Swiss money to Jews in hiding in, of all places, Berlin, the capital of the Third Reich. The ubiquitous Mr. Schwalbe also turns up in connection with the Hechaluz Labor group for Hungary, Slovakia, Romania, and Poland.

Stefan Eisenberg, leader of the Hungarian student organization in Zurich was another recipient for his work in obtaining Palestine certificates for refugees. He needed to send wires to Palestine and the WRB paid for them. Also operating from Switzerland was Dr. J. Weill, providing medicines through the Pharmacie Nouvelle in Geneva and needed by Hungarian refugees in Yugoslavia. Dr. Jean Kopecky of the Czech Resistance Movement was listed, too, given money to aid Jewish refugees in Slovakia.

The Germans did place one major concentration camp in Czechoslovakia. They located it in the small town of Terezín near the western border with Germany. World War II buffs know it as Theresienstadt. Although thousands died there, it was not originally targeted to be a death camp. Rather more, a Potemkin Village, the "Show Ghetto," a false façade, appearing as a holding tank for distinguished enemies of the Third Reich. Neutral observers were brought in to see how well those interned were treated. It was civilized, it was cultural . . . an orchestra had been formed to play classical music, concerts were arranged, art allowed. This veneer fooled many people. It was bruited about that Theresienstadt wasn't a horror show, quite the contrary. Here was refined Nazi hypocrisy at its finest.

It has to be added that a personal peep of my own into wartime Czechoslovakia and the Hitlerian mentality was provided years later through the marriage of my first cousin, Dr. Edward Rolde, to a fellow psychoanalyst everyone called Sasha (given name Alexandra), who had lived with her mother through the occupation in Prague. They were Jewish, but the Germans could never prove it. They knew that Sasha's Mom had been born in the United States in some small town in Kansas. Repeated letters to the authorities there asking for her birth certificate, which they erroneously believed denoted religion as in Europe, needless to say went unanswered, and so Sasha and her mother were left unmolested and postwar moved to Canada and then the U.S.

Poland is next. This Slavic country may well be labeled the epicenter of the concentration camp world. Auschwitz, the granddaddy of them all (Oświęcim in Polish), was there and next to it was Birkenau. So was Treblinka, the second most deadly of the killing sites. In fact, all the six death camps were in Poland. Chełmno was the first to operate exclusively for extermination, using gas exhaust from trucks on victims in sealed vans and managing to asphyxiate 150,000 of them through this crude method. Improvements were made with the more up-to-date equipment of the gas chamber, and Bełżec was able to reach a total of 600,000.

Treblinka took 900,000 lives before an uprising in August 1943 put a temporary halt to its murders, although the facility was to resume them for another three months.

Majdanek, located in a suburb of Lublin and reachable by trolley car accounted for 360,000 more victims, of whom only a third were Jewish. Many Soviet prisoners were dispatched and other Slavs, particularly, from Belorussia, Ukraine, and Poland.

Auschwitz-Birkenau accounted for one to two million lives snuffed out. The earliest experiments with gassing were carried out on its premises, involving 250 Polish and 600 Soviet POWs, and the huge complex only ended its ghastly business in November 1944.

At Sobibór, an attempted uprising was also ferociously squashed, and at Auschwitz, itself, yet another mass effort to escape failed.

The above were only the best-known camps. In October 1944,

the War Refugee Board received a communication about one less-publicized operation in Poland, left nameless, ostensibly a forced labor camp. but horrific all the same. Extracts of a letter from Dr. S.G. of the Underground Jewish National Council in Warsaw vividly pictured the atmosphere of this terrible time and place.

Here's the opening paragraph: "Dr. L.S. is supposed to be working in a factory for enamel dishes [along with 2,000 others] . . . H.J. and T. are in a punitive camp, covering the areas of the new Jewish cemeteries . . . The guards consist of the most blackguardly Ukrainians who behave with bestial cruelty. They are headed by Baron Gett (from Vienna), a cruel sadist who murders people with his own hands for the slightest breach of camp law."

Very few Jews comparatively were left alive in Poland, according to the Underground document—200,000 in all—150,000 in punitive camps and Łódź and 50,000 in hiding, a precipitous drop from the close to three million of the prewar days.

And comments were added about a certain Dr. Weichart in Kraków accused of being a Jewish cuisling. His "enterprise is useful only to the oppressors and deliberately gives the impression in the world that the Germans do not oppose Jewish self-help measures."

Then it went on: "At the Plaszow camp, the Germans "steal" everything sent, although Dr. Weichart sometimes sends medicines such as aspirin and so on. No disinfectants, insulin, etc." Dr. Weichart is "regularly the guest of the camp commander, Dr. Baron Gett . . . as well as the German police führer who is stationed at Oleandrym . . . people in the camps believe he [Weichart] is guilty of co-operating, plain and simple, with these devils." The Underground's worry is that the Americans will contribute large donations to Weichart.

This was not an idle fear. A report from Kraków stated that only the Judische Unterstutzungstelle, a relief group directed by Dr. Michael Weichart and Hilfstein (probably Dr. Chaim Hilfstein), was allowed and confined to labor camps since "German authorities have barred all assistance to Jews outside of the camps. Help from Weichart sent to the camps is mostly limited to medical supplies, which it receives from Jewish relief organizations abroad." Weichart called his outfit the Central Jewish Relief organization for those in labor camps scattered throughout Poland."

Names of the three worst tormentors at Auschwitz were revealed: Franz Wileiczik who beat Jews senseless; Sub-Lieutenant Wilhelm

Retschke who sent people to crematoria to be burned alive; and Michael Jurstacko, a Ukrainian officer who killed a Jew for smoking a cigarette.

In Birkenau, which operated under the shadow of Auschwitz, the gas chambers were started in February 1943. A month later, after a trial period, the efficacy of the gas process was demonstrated to the Nazis' top echelon. Important guests came from Berlin to the *opening*. For the occasion, eight thousand Kraków Jews were subjected to the new technique. "The guests were exceedingly satisfied when they saw the destructive machinery in operation and spent a long time peering into the gas chambers [through peepholes]."

The forced laborers at Birkenau labored as slaves for German companies renowned worldwide, Krupp and Siemens especially. Additionally, the prisoners were engaged in building a factory to produce synthetic rubber. The mortality rate among them was thirty to forty a day, due simply to exhaustion. Many were killed out of hand by the kapos.

After one two-week period, a mere 150 out of an original 650 were still alive. Others were assigned to the hospital, where the death toll was 150 a day. In the hospital's Block Seven, 2,000 died in seven days. "We worked night and day in two shifts," a survivor later stated. "We had to be kept from the other prisoners on account of the stench emanating from us."

Under such conditions, a pushback was inevitable. Partisan groups formed, Jewish and non-Jewish. It wasn't only Jews who were slaughtered at Auschwitz; three hundred thousand Polish Catholics also perished there. Nevertheless, it was rare for a Jew to be accepted into the Polish Army-in-Exile (I did once, however, meet at a friend's wedding the bride's Jewish father who had been a colonel in the elite Polish cavalry). Friction between these religiously based entities was therefore not surprising, harmful though it might be to the anti-Nazi cause.

History was to see this dichotomy played out in two separate revolts against the Hitlerians that have engraved themselves on the world's consciousness—the Warsaw Ghetto Uprising, which was followed by the Home Army Warsaw Uprising beyond the ghetto, both crushed after heroic fighting.

But the battles in Poland were not just in the capital city. The Hechalutz (Pioneer) youth groups became partisans. In Western Galicia, they called themselves The Fighting Hechalutz. They dynamited bridges, attacked prisons, liberated inmates. One of them named Frumke and four others (they often fought in groups of five) had a shootout with the Germans and all were killed. Yet they took Germans down—eight hundred in the Warsaw outburst alone—and served notice that from then on all Jews would not submit quietly to the universal death sentence imposed upon the Jewish people. In battered Warsaw, several thousand Jews remained alive, disguised as Aryans. It was even claimed that several hundred German soldiers had deserted to the Jewish side in the first of the outbreaks. The Nazi high command had to send in tanks and aircraft to squelch this minimal upheaval. Later, a Gestapo report was said to have bumped the number to 1,800 of the German officers and soldiers who fought for the Jewish Resistance, led by a Wehrmacht colonel who managed to escape capture.

The Nazis had roared into Poland in September 1939 and unspoken was their hush-hush *Aktion Reinhard,* code name for the goal of eradicating Jewish Poles entirely and reducing the Slavic Roman Catholic population to the indignity of slaves. This was the newest version of the *Drang nach Osten* movement to the East, which long before the Nazis had been a pronounced Teutonic ambition. While Poles were considered *subhuman* in the Nazi lexicon, Jews were seen as *inhuman.*

Admittedly many Poles were anti-Semitic. It is an overstatement to say, as some have, that they were worse than the Germans, for there was never a Polish blueprint for exterminating this generally unloved minority in their country.

But the Nazis in Poland were to set a record for *the largest single massacre of World War II.* They gleefully called it Operation Harvest Festival. In November 1943, they wiped out the entire prewar Jewish population (prewar 42,000) of the Lublin Ghetto and its surrounding area of the Lublin Reservation.

The object of this Nazi annihilation was to clear the path for a centuries-old pet project. They were creating a German "settlement area" within the General Government, the rump state they had erected in their occupied Polish areas. The local Poles—one hundred thousand, mostly farmers—would be forced out (or killed) and twenty thousand ethnic Germans moved in to take over their property.

To be sure, they were resisted.

The *Armia Krajowa,* the Home Army, in touch with the Polish

Government-in-Exile in London, was formed and attracted other groups of fighters that had independently formed. These included the National Armed Forces, the Peasant Battalion, the Confederation of the Nation (far-right politically), the Peoples Guard of the Socialist Party, and the Camp of National Unity. In the end, the only group to spurn this coalition called itself the National Armed Forces.

A major haven for them was in the Parczew Forests, near Lublin, within the Germans' General Government zone. The capture of the city of Parczew in April 1944 was a combined effort of the Peoples Guard and the Jewish Partisans.

The impact of these acts of defiance reached beyond Poland's borders. The *New York Post* in that same April ran the following headline on the 19th.

RIVINGTON STREET MOURNS WARSAW KIN
15,000 JEWS MARK THE BATTLE OF THE GHETTO

Leading the march from this strongly Jewish and Italian neighborhood on the Lower East Side of Manhattan were Shya Wattenberg, his wife Lena and two daughters Mary and Anna. Mayor Fiorello La Guardia addressed crowds at City Hall and Carnegie Hall. Ironically enough at the same time, his sister Gemma was languishing in a Nazi internment camp, the one for women at Ravensbrück, with her daughter and infant grandson. On the personal orders of Himmler and Eichmann, she and her husband and entire family had been imprisoned. She survived along with her daughter and grandson. Meanwhile her brother was head of UNRRA.

Another American subjected to Nazi brutality was Miss Fanny Flinders, originally held in Poland. Her New York address was 1561 Longfellow Avenue in the Bronx, but she had gone to Poland in 1938 to visit her Jewish mother. In May 1939, still in Poland, she took sick and was unable to leave before the war broke out in September. When apprehended by the Nazis, she was badly mistreated. They placed her in a holding tank with ninety-four other women. In the twenty minutes they were allowed to exercise, they "had to run like horses" and were hit with whips if they didn't move fast enough. More than once, she was beaten. The prison was full of filth and lice. Many died or committed suicide. Transferred to Berlin, she was again packed into an overcrowded cell. The guards made them dance on broken glass. She was told she would be hanged. Young girls she knew were raped and tortured by the Gestapo. At length, she was transferred to Liebenau, a *women's internment camp for enemy nationals*, near the Swiss border, where conditions were better and the elderly guards not so brutal. Some three hundred British citizens living in Poland had been brought there.

Poland, in a sense, was the end of the line, the final stop, where much of the "dirty work" of the Holocaust was carried out. The trains rolled in from all over Europe to this Hellish destination. For example, on June 26, 1944, a cablegram sent by Dr. Ignacy Schwarzbart of the Polish National Council, specifically reported that seven thousand Jews had been transported out of relatively benign Theresienstadt to Auschwitz and gassed to death upon arrival.

This news had been addressed to Rabbi Stephen Wise of the World Jewish Congress and immediately conveyed to the War Refugee Board. A month later, a follow-up report declared that since mid May at least thirteen trains a day had been rolling in. Two gas chambers were asphyxiating one thousand victims a day, while four crematoria burned the bodies to ashes. A smaller group of two thousand had been rerouted to Gleiwitz (Gliwice in Polish), who were first forced to write optimistic letters to their relatives and friends still alive back home in Hungary. On the platform at Auschwitz was a heap of the valises 300 meters (1,000 yards) long, 5 meters (15 feet) high and 200 meters (600 yards) wide.

There is an often maddening complexity to the resistance in Poland that this steady drumbeat of German atrocities provokes. The proliferation of fight-back groups, however, can be lumped into three main categories: the Jewish response of which we have seen a sampling; the Home Army of the Polish Government-in-Exile, non-Jewish but having a Jewish member, Dr. Emmanuel Scherer on its Polish National Council; and gathering momentum, especially after the Nazi invasion of the Soviet Union in June 1941, the Communists, who used the banal title of the Polish Committee of National Liberation.

They were not insignificant groupings. The Armia Krajowa, the Home Army, was said to have had half a million soldiers at its peak, to have caused 150,000 German casualties, destroying one-eighth of German transports heading to the Eastern Front and engaging in *full-scale battles* with the Teutonic occupants in 1943 and 1944. The Communists, once the Soviet-Nazi Pact became a dead letter, emerged as an ever more powerful component of the Red Army. And the

Jews—sometimes they had to fight against the others, especially Polish nationalists, a component of the Home Army that included vicious anti-Semites. Stalin's minions also took aim at the Home Army: the atrocious "Katyn Massacres," in which thousands of Polish Army officers, intellectuals, and prewar politicians were mercilessly slain and buried deep in the forest to which they'd been herded. Passed off for years as the work of the Germans, it was decades later finally acknowledged by Moscow to have been perpetrated by the Russian NKVD secret police.

By January 1945, these other forces—the Jews and the Home Army—had pretty much disbanded, and the Polish Communists were left to rule the roost under Soviet dominance.

Polish refugees were scattered throughout the world from Bombay to Mexico. They were in touch with the War Refugee Board. Their main Polish-American organization, the Rada Polonia based in Chicago, was said to have been asked by John Pehle to raise $500,000 for the WRB effort in Poland and promised $100,000. One claim afterward, which seems most dubious, was that Pehle turned down the offer on the grounds it was from a *sectarian* (Roman Catholic) source. Hardly a credible excuse, it seems, since the prime donors to the WRB were *sectarian* Jewish organizations, the Joint especially.

It is known that Pehle did meet with Francis Sweetluk, a Polish War official and Franklin Roosevelt met with Władysław Sikorski, the first prime minister of the Polish Government-in Exile and commander-in-chief of the Home Army, and an estimated three million dollars was raised among Polish-Americans. The Polish leader died on the Fourth of July, 1943, and his successor was Stanisław Mikołajczyk, not as towering a figure as his predecessor.

Almost a year later, June 1, 1944, the Joint Distribution Committee launched a campaign for the raising of three to four million dollars for the relief of all Jews in Poland, not just Polish Jews, with sixty percent of the money earmarked for the Polish Government-in-Exile. They were acting in concert with Dr. Emmanuel Scherer, who was one of the rare Jewish members of that body's governing council.

My own acquaintance with the Polish diaspora, especially those who could not go back to a Stalinist country, occurred in Paris when I was a college student. I will never forget those huge, strapping, red-faced, blondish guys we encountered in a café, who spoke English well because they had fought with the British in North Africa. They were giving up on Europe, they admitted to us, leaving to start new lives in Canada, since it was now obvious they could never return to Poland nor root out the Communists. We talked well into the night.

Another contact of mine was with Felix Ziffer, who had the room next to mine my senior year at Yale. Despite his Germanic sounding last name, he was totally Polish, physically big, too. His father had been a prestigious diplomat before the war and served on the governing body of the Polish National Council during the hostilities. Felix was a lot older than the rest of the undergraduates. He, too, had fought the Nazis.

The name Jan Karski is frequently encountered in works about the Holocaust. It was this elite Polish cavalry officer who told his eyewitness story about Auschwitz to Supreme Court Justice Felix Frankfurter and wasn't believed. Karski had also served in the prewar Polish Diplomatic Corps. In 1942, he was asked by Jews in Poland to carry the message of the German annihilation of Poles and Jews to the outside world. His real given name was Jan Kozielewski and he had been raised as a Catholic and remained so. In his country's army, he was trained as an artillery specialist. Captured by the Soviets during their 1939 invasion of Poland in tandem with the Germans, Karski was traded to the Nazis while they still had their alliance with Stalin. En route to a POW camp in November 1939 in the German dominated General Government enclave, he escaped or was liberated by his fellows (both versions exist). At any rate, he joined the ZWZ (Związek Walki Zbrojnej), Union for Armed Combat, the forerunner to the Armia Krajowa, while becoming Jan Karski.

Under his *nom de guerre*, Karski organized courier missions inside and outside of Poland and served in the dangerous role of a courier. In Poland and France, he was taking his life in his hands. Visits to Great Britain were not hairy in and of themselves, but any travel in an age of air raids was always chancy. He met with noted figures like the Hungarian-born novelist and essay writer Arthur Koestler. In addition, he had an audience with Franklin Delano Roosevelt in the Oval Office.

His talk with the president he felt was a failure, he later confided to John Pehle. But Pehle disagreed and told him he *had* made a difference. It was due to his visit, Pehle reminded him, that FDR had agreed to establish the War Refugee Board, and he declared the Karski mission "changed U.S. Government policy from . . . indifference at best to affirmative action."

Treblinka may be the best place to round up this brief survey of Underground and Resistance activities in Poland, before moving on to the experiences in other countries not yet covered.

It was the Nazis' boast that at the newly modernized Treblinka camp the whole killing operation there ran from "door to door" in "45 minutes," from "opening the cattle cars to slamming shut the gas chambers."

Efficiency in such regard was not really Treblinka's distinction. Its imprint on history, faint as it might seem now, is based on the fact of a revolt *within* a major concentration camp that succeeded—at least to an extent.

It might be useful in focusing on this war crime to follow the drama on the inside through several real-life individuals who played leading roles.

Two names to remember are Max Bialis, the chief SS bully and Meir Berliner, an Argentinean Jew caught up in the war, whose nationality was ignored. As if in a movie thriller, they ended their lives together on the camp's parade ground in a death-throes struggle on September 11, 1942. When the Nazi passed by him, Berliner struck out with a knife he'd concealed and stabbed Bialis under his left shoulder blade. Immediately, Nazi guards pounced upon the vengeance seeker and pummeled him to death with their rifle butts. After his death it was revealed that Bialis, a homosexual, had kept a harem of young Jewish boys in a private house, all of whom were immediately put to death. It has also been said that the dying SS Untersturmführer was heard to mutter while being carried off: "Kill all Jews."

An unnecessary admonishment, certainly, given that this was precisely what Treblinka had been put in business to do.

Actually, there were two Treblinka concentration camps—I and II—as they have been labeled. Treblinka I was for forced labor; Treblinka II where you ended up if you no longer had the strength to work—the last stop. It held the gas chambers, which started with three and within a short space of time reached ten.

It has been stated that Rudolf Höss, the commandant at Auschwitz, criticized his fellow SS at Treblinka because the prisoners there knew they going to die.

Consequently, the three Jews who had first conceived the idea of not going to their deaths quietly met together on the parade ground and plotted. In his illuminating postwar volume, titled simply

Treblinka, the Frenchman Jean-Paul Steiner creates an imagined dialogue between them.

> "My name is Galewski," said one [his first name was Marceli and he had been an electrical engineer in Warsaw].
> "My name is Berliner. I was a businessman in Buenos Aires [first name Meir]."
> "My name is Choken. I was a Jew [first name Itzhak]."
> By a kind of reflex, each put out his right hand. Their hands joined in a confused knot.
> The Committee of Resistance of Treblinka was born.

The "First Victory" of this Committee of Resistance reported by Galewski was the smuggling of Itzhak Choken into a railroad car that was transporting out the clothes of dead inmates, piles of them the height of a two or three story building in which Choken easily hid.

Escapes multiplied. Steiner wrote: "This will to escape that drove the prisoners was stronger than their fear."

Some individuals were cited: Abraham Bomba, a barber, escaped in 1943. Yechiel Berkowicz and Yechiel Cooperman escaped with him. Isadore Helfeg, just a kid, hid in a pile of bodies, stayed with partisans until the war's end. Chil Meyer Rajchman fled from Łódź to Pruszków, worked in a labor camp, was beaten, deported to the Warsaw Ghetto, escaped and hid until rescued in January 1945.

But such escapes were like the pump priming for a much more spectacular result in August 1943 at Treblinka. Again Steiner writes: "The Jews had transferred all the energy and all their hopes to an undertaking that was insane, grandiose, and almost unique in the history of the camps; an armed revolt."

Marcelli Galewski was the chief kapo at the camp. He had volunteered for the position after the new German camp commander Kurt Franz had threatened the Judenrat that they had to provide a name to him or else. Galewski was described as "a man in his 40's, tall, slim, with dark hair who looked and behaved like a Polish aristocrat." Another leader with him was a former Czech Army officer, Zelomir Bloch, a Slovak. At Treblinka I he had been the foreman of the labor detail that sorted clothing. Because of a missing bundle unaccounted for, he had been transferred to Treblinka II. Also listed as original plotters were Zvi Kurland, the white-haired "elderly amongst us,"

Moshe Lubling, a Dr. Chorazyzki, and Rudek Lubremitski, a driver mechanic in charge of the gas pumps of the garage.

The date chosen was August 2, 1942.

The signal that would be given was "Revolution in Berlin."

But before we reach this climax, we must backtrack a bit to the astounding history of Itzhak Choken following his escape from Treblinka, for it had a bearing on the ultimate act of rebellion, itself.

After a few adventures, Choken had reached Warsaw. There he came in contact with the Jewish Resistance Organization. He had once before then, in a bad moment, actually entertained the idea of going back to Treblinka and seeing Galewski. Then he had gone into battle in the Warsaw Ghetto Uprising. The bunker from which he was fighting held out for three hours before his commander ordered a retreat. In the course of doing so, Choken broke his leg, took a bullet in the chest and was recaptured. Ergo—with sadistic irony—was his crazy fantasy fulfilled. He was back inside Treblinka and seeing Galewski. Before he soon died of his wounds, he did get to Galewski and inspired the latter's vow to fight to victory and thus plan the *Revolt*.

At a chosen gathering of the prisoners that same evening of Choken's death, Galewski introduced those present to a man named Djielo. He became the military leader of the plot.

The exact spark that lit the pending attitude of Enough! No More!—into a blazing conflagration burst on August 2, when a particularly brutal SS man by the name of Kurt Küttner, better known simply as Kiwe, discovered some contraband gold the prisoners had hidden. He had to be killed at once. Galewski called for a volunteer. Every hand rose. Galewski chose Wolomanchik, an ex-thief from Warsaw. Out of their small store of arms, Wolomanchik picked up a rifle, and from a corner of the barracks that Kiwe was approaching, fired. Kiwe fell. Another shot went off and the Nazi lay still. The actual signal for the action was the explosion of a grenade tossed by the Jewish fighters and cries of "Revolution in Berlin!"

Rudek and his combat team rushed to a parked armored car. The German guarding it was cut down. Rudek, himself, climbed up the turret to open the hatch, dove in, moved its machinegun and peppered the onrushing Nazis. A Jew named Yatzhek and his unit captured the garage. He stayed alone there and let out a river of gasoline, which he detonated with a grenade, and the resulting flames engulfed the camp.

The motor that had pumped the deadly Xyklon B gas into the

death chambers was destroyed by an inmate named Wiener. He was killed by the explosion that demolished it.

Adolf, another inmate, a scrawny man, was strangled to death in a tussle with Ivan, a giant Ukrainian guard, but not before he, in turn, stabbed the brute to death.

One of the SS men, despite his cries of "I'm your friend Karol Petzinger!" was stomped to death by a mob of inmates all rushing for the nearby woods now that the gates had been opened.

It has been estimated that 600 of them reached the thick forest.

But Jean-François Steiner ended his book by writing sadly: "Of these 600 escapees there remained on the arrival of the Red Army a year later, only 40 survivors. The others had been killed in the course of that year by Polish peasants, resitants of the Armia Krajowa, Ukrainian fascist bands, deserters from the Wehrmacht, the Gestapo and special units of the German army. Those 40 survivors are alive today."

The famous French novelist and philosopher Simone de Beauvoir has written in her preface: "But so far as I know, except for Treblinka, there exists no story presented from the *inside*—the business as usual and the demise of a major death camp (xiii)."

Finally, among the correspondence of the War Refugee Board, there are some from the American Embassy that touch upon the horrors of Poland.

On February 6, 1945, the WRB received a description of the thousands of tortured inmates of Auschwitz "rescued by the Red Army."

"They are described as being people whose age is impossible to tell . . . as being exhausted to the point where they swayed like shadows in the wind."

The WRB did make an inquiry then about the situation in Łódź and learned through an American correspondent returning from there that only 829 Jews remained alive in that large city. There had been 250,000 Jews in Łódź before the war.

A month earlier, Secretary of State Edward Stettinius had wired George Kennan at the U.S. Embassy in Moscow: "Urgent. Try to get the Russians to prevent massacres at Auschwitz and Birkenau." The response from Kennan included: "The interest of the War Refugee Board in the welfare of these people [concentration camp inmates] and in such measures as can be taken for their protection has been expressed by me."

Chapter Ten

Poland and Lithuania's connections with each other are primarily historical. The two countries currently abut each other along a shrunken common border only a little less than fifty miles in length. Yet in the past they were fused together into a single political entity originally known as the Grand Duchy of Lithuania and Kingdom of Poland. Formed in the thirteenth century, this union lasted almost to the end of the eighteenth century. Two hundred years before, its nomenclature had been changed to the Polish-Lithuanian Commonwealth, and its demise in this status occurred in 1795 when it was forcibly incorporated into the Czarist Russian Empire.

After many vicissitudes, Lithuania achieved its independence after World War I. It took a three-cornered battle against the Red Army, Polish troops and the Bermondt Army composed of Czarists led by German officers. The leader of that freedom-fighting effort, Antanas Smetona, took office as the first president of the republic in 1919, lost reelection, but led a coup in 1926 that kept him in office as an authoritarian strongman until the Soviet invasion of June 15, 1940, when he fled to the United States.

With the Nazi invasion of the Soviet Union in June 1941, the picture was scrambled again. Out of Lithuania went the Red Army and in swarmed the Germans, greeted to an extent as liberators from the hated Russians. But with all that, the Nazis had trouble raising an SS Division from these folks. Nazi arrogance and ill treatment soon led to the rebirth of an underground, or rather, more than one. Aside from the independence-seeking Nationalists, who in certain cases aided the Teuton invaders, there were Lithuanian Communists, led by Antanas Smietus, creating a force of five- to ten-thousand, and the Jews whose commander was Abba Kovner, who had moved to Vilnius when it was still a part of Poland and often referred to as Vilna. Once the Nazis on July 21, 1940, attacked the city destined to be Lithuania's capital, young Kovner escaped the ghetto with friends and hid in a Dominican convent sheltered by Sister Anna Borkowska, a Pole.

Kovner, a tall, gangly, striking-looking youth with angular features and a wild crop of curly hair, looked like the poet he was in actuality (postwar called "one of the great poets of Israel"). His ringing cry of defiance and motto was: "Let us not go like lambs to the slaughter."

A book about Abba Kovner, entitled *The Avengers* (which is what they called their partisan group), describes how the movement started. After Abba moved out of the safety of the convent into Vilna, he set up a meeting at the Judenrat office. It was here that he told the assembled crowd of Jewish adults and teenagers not to go quietly to their deaths. "Destroy your illusions," he told them. "Ponar is not a transit camp. Everyone there is murdered. Hitler intends to destroy the Jews of Europe, and he has begun with the Jews of Lithuania (50)."

One day soon afterward, a note was delivered to Abba in his ghetto apartment. "We must meet," it said, and was signed: "Wittenberg." The name was well known, Itzhak Wittenberg, as a diehard Jewish Communist and anti-Zionist. He invited Abba to meet with him and the leader of Betar, a rightwing Zionist group, Joseph Glassman, for the purpose of forming a common front, an army of Jews to sabotage the Germans.

These three young men then proceeded to set up the United Partisans Organization (UPO) with Wittenberg as its leaders and the other two his lieutenants.

They set about collecting arms. Mother Superior Borkowska, disguised as a poor Jewess, brought Abba three hand grenades. Unexpected help came from a German officer, an Austrian named Anton Schmidt who, turned off by the slaughter he'd seen of Jews, dreamed of engineering a wholesale escape of Jews across the Baltic to Sweden. Meeting Abba, he convinced the Jewish leader of his sincerity and the two agreed to work together. He was found out eventually by the Nazis and shot during the winter of 1942. Abba's group soon included two young women who figured prominently in the underground activities of the UPO: Vitka Kempner and Ruzka Korczak. The former, among other things, was to marry Abba Kovner after the war, and Ruzka committed allegedly the *first act of sabotage in occupied Europe.* She blew up a German troop train and killed more than two hundred Wehrmacht soldiers.

Within the next year, Abba and his followers moved into the

Rudnicki Forest, twelve miles south of Vilnius. It was a swampy, mosquito-ridden area of true wilderness, although still close to Lithuania's largest city. They had to go for miles to find an encampment of partisans who'd preceded them. This destination was actually an island in the swamp. Some Jews from Narocz, who had survived a fight with the Germans, were there already. In addition, two camps of Russians, two of Lithuanians, and one of the Polish Home Army members existed.

It was a combustible mixture. Not only did they take potshots at each other or even engage in full-fledged internecine firefights—the Soviet partisans have been described as "dangerous enemies of the Polish Underground"—but the Jews were at a particular disadvantage. Falling into the hands of either of the rightist Lithuanian or Polish anti-Nazis might be as lethal as if they'd been captured by the SS. Even the Markov Brigade, the major Soviet unit, primarily non-Jewish, is described as "anti-Semitic."

Prior to their retreat from Vilna, there had been a searing drama centered on Abba's leader, Itzhak Wittenberg. The Nazis, seeing him as the kingpin of the local resistance, put an extraordinary price on his head. Either Wittenberg was turned over to them or the entire Vilna ghetto would be destroyed by tanks and bombs. The inhabitants still alive within the Jewish Quarter were frantic. Led by Jacob Gens, the head of the Jewish Council and its police force ordered Abba to turn over his commander. A mob of ghetto residents screamed for Wittenberg's head. Abba's arguments that the Nazis wouldn't be satisfied just with Wittenberg—he would simply be the start—fell on deaf ears. Abba and his comrades were labeled "fanatics" for shielding him. But they hid Wittenberg, anyway, and let the mob rave.

In an ending as florid and gripping as any tragic opera, Wittenberg announced he would give himself up and handed over his gun to Abba.

Once he'd surrendered to Gens who would deliver him to the Gestapo, the latter slipped him a capsule of prussic acid, in case the torture the Nazis inflicted to make him talk became too unbearable, and told him to hide it in his ear.

As Wittenberg walked through the ghetto streets to meet his captors, he has been described as "a sacrificial lamb on whom the people had loaded their guilt and sin."

The next morning in his Gestapo cell, Wittenberg was found dead. He had swallowed the poison.

It was on July 27, 1943, that Abba's group, calling themselves *Leon*, which had been Wittenberg's code name, took to the woods. They had originally been slated for the Narocz forest region to the north, except the Germans since had occupied that district. They were directed instead by a Russian partisan chief named Yurgis to the Rudnicki Forest. Disguised as woodsmen, they made their way south, not without a few hair-raising close calls.

Jacob Gens meanwhile was shot by the Germans. His crime in their eyes was that a partisan group had formed in the ghetto on his watch.

There were about two hundred Jews who formed the Jewish Brigade, subdivided into four divisions that bore histrionic names: Death to Fascism, Struggle, To Victory, and The Avenger, in which Abba, Vitka and Ruzka were included. The overall "commander" was Abba.

On the island in the swamp, they built their camp. New recruits began showing up every day, including other women fighters from a Vilna fur factory that was still in operation. Before long, the Jewish Brigade had three hundred members.

One day, a burly, thick-mustached Soviet officer arrived and asked to see Uri, using Abba's code name. He was Yurgis, a forty-year-old Communist and former school teacher from Vilna. He told Abba the Jewish Brigade had to be disbanded and folded into the Lithuanian Brigade.

After the argument Abba gave him that "we must fight as Jews," Yurgis warned they would have trouble with the other partisans, the Russians, Lithuanians and Poles.

"You are a Lithuanian," Yurgis insisted. "You must fight as a Lithuanian."

Abba's rebuttal was that the Lithuanians wouldn't have them. "They see us as Jews."

The stubborn young man won in the end, and eventually he came to realize that Yurgis, himself, was secretly Jewish.

While their home base was the Rudnicki Forest, Abba's troops often roamed afield, specialists at blowing up trains. It was reported that in 1944, they accounted for fifty-one wrecked trains, hundreds of trucks demolished, and dozens of bridges blown up.

It was also estimated that guerrillas like Abba's brigade all across Europe destroyed 1,000 bridges a month and millions of dollars of Nazi equipment. They diverted 250,000 Axis troops, mostly Ukrainian,

Polish, Lithuanian, Estonian, and Latvian auxiliaries, but also 20,000 (three divisions) of the German Wehrmacht.

As Abba's force solidified and proved its mettle, the Soviets responded, air-dropping supplies to them. These included vodka, chocolate, condensed milk from the U.S., and of course guns, bullets, and grenades.

But the Soviets also arrested Abba, threatened him, yet he stood up to them and (possibly thanks to Yurgis) they finally released him unharmed. His command, however, was taken away and given to a non-Jew who quietly still allowed him to run the show.

During the summer of 1943, the tide started turning on the Eastern Front. The Germans lost the largest tank battle in history at Kursk. By October, the Nazis had been run out of those areas of the Soviet Union they had occupied in 1941 and 1942.

That winter, the partisans in Rudnicki could see evidence of the Nazi failure. Nearby roads were filled with retreating Wehrmacht trucks and German soldiers, as Rich Cohen described them, "ice-burned with red faces and red ears," whom the partisans jeeringly dubbed "Frozen Apples (138)." On July 8, 1944, *The New York Times* reporting from London printed that "advanced Soviet troops, nearing the border of Lithuania, drove within 20 miles of Vilna." Red Army units previously had arrived in Rudnicki.

Abba and his outfit would now fight as part of the Red Army. They were praised for what they had done with such limited resources and given rifles, machineguns, pistols, rocket launchers, vodka, cigarettes, and meat. On July 7, 1944, to be exact, the partisans marched in ranks to Vilna and joined the Russians already battling there.

Again, *The New York Times*: "Today, well-organized Partisan brigades are helping mop up the Germans. Mountain Partisans passed by, sitting on Netherlands, German or Hungarian saddles and carrying arms from all the nations of the world."

A bittersweet, touching moment occurred on the outskirts of the city. In the presence of Ruzka and Abba, a young woman was holding a crying child. When the weeping ceased, the youngster said something, and spoke in Yiddish.

Ruzka, the most hard-bitten of all of Abba's brigade, burst into tears, sobbing uncontrollably.

"What is it? What is it?" Abba beseeched her.

Finally, tear-streaked, she answered: "I thought I would never again hear a Jewish child cry."

On July 14, *The New York Times* announced: "Russian troops yesterday captured Vilna, capital of Soviet Lithuania."

Wandering through the desolate ruins of the ghetto, Abba, Vitka and Ruzka ran into Ilya Ehrenburg, a world-famous Soviet journalist, writer and poet, also Jewish. They told him their story and posed for his camera.

A day later, the Jewish partisans gathered the bodies of Jews killed in the street fighting, loaded them in carts, wheeled them out to the ancient Jewish cemetery and buried their coreligionists in appropriate Jewish fashion.

The war was not over for Abba and the others, not even after it ended on VE Day. Calling themselves "Avengers," they sought revenge, but that narrative leads us into the *Bricha*, the Jewish postwar exodus from Europe and the fight for Israel in the Holy Land.

Abba's poetry was published in a book with the quizzically strange title of *Sloan Kettering*, named for the hospital in New York City where he was operated on for the throat cancer that was eventually to kill him.

Two books of Abba's poetry in Hebrew: *Ad Lo Or* (Until No Light) and *Ha-Mafteach Tzalal* (The Key Drowned) were based on his wartime experiences and received major Israeli literary prizes.

DEATH IS NOT TO BE PREFERRED is one his most quoted poems, beginning:

> When leading a band of harried fighters
> Or standing face to face with the enemy
> Holding out in a siege
> And standing alone
> On the ramparts
> He never said death is to be preferred

In the archives of the War Refugee Board, not much can be found concerning Lithuania, and neither, for that matter, regarding the neighboring Baltic states of Latvia and Estonia during these harrowing World War II years.

Perhaps the earliest mention in their archives was a suggestion by Dr. A Leon Kubowitski of the Rescue Department of the World Jewish Congress on April 18, 1944, in a letter to L. S. Lesser about having

Lithuanian Jews escape to Sweden, an idea that Lesser presented to John Pehle.

The WRB's man with prime responsibility for these three countries was Ivor Olsen, the special attaché stationed at the Stockholm Embassy in the autumn of 1944. Olsen was to bring 1,200 persons "under this program, which had many tragedies . . . across the Baltic Sea." Five of the vessels he used were captured by the Nazis. Storms in the frigid waters endangered others. The Lithuanian program was said to have had the greatest losses. A key operator was lost on the first trip to establish underground connections and develop routes to Sweden. After 135 Lithuanians successfully reached safety in Sweden, the operation ceased in October 1944, because the Russians military had effectively occupied Lithuania.

It was not just in Vilna where the Nazis conducted their *Einsatzgruppen* massacres. Kovno (Kaunas) was Lithuania's second largest city and the independent nation's capital after 1920, when Vilna was occupied by the Poles. Here the Hitlerians were just as ruthless as they were in Vilna, although the numbers were smaller: 10,000 slain as opposed to 25,000. The Ninth Fort was to Kovno what Ponar had been to Vilna—a convenient, tucked away killing field where the victims were shot. Gas was not yet the execution weapon of choice then, not until the Germans realized they could conserve ammunition, which as the war continued appeared ever more necessary for them to do.

On a different tack, the WRB records contain a cable they sent to Lithuania, asking for information about specific individuals. This was on October 15, 1944, and the Naval Bureau of Censorship refused to let it through. The telegram would have gone to a Samuel Tchobrusky in Moscow regarding the whereabouts of Fania Berkowitz and her children Adela, Menucho, and Benjamindavid, all born in Brest-Litovsk, Poland, and whose last address was care of Rabina Krinicka Trompojio in Lentvaris, near Wilno, as the Poles called Vilna (today Vilnius).

Those names have come to us of individual human beings, poking up, you might say, through clouds of statistics and generalizations. We know not whether those named as being in Lithuania survived or not. Mr. Samuel Tchobrusky in the safety of Moscow presumably did.

Names of Lithuanian nationals who led the early killings have been handed down in history. Algirdas Klimaitis, called "infamous" and "a rogue," appears frequently. He headed up a separate detachment of

Lithuanians, 600 strong, who shared his hatred of Jews and Russians. They wore white armbands with black lettering and may have killed 26,000 Jews between July and December 1941. Klimaitis, himself, was born in Kaunas and had been a Lithuanian Army officer prior to World War II, when his country enjoyed a period of independence. Once the Nazis drove out the Soviets in June 1941, he teamed up with SS Brigadeführer Walter Stahlecker, whose sole task was the massacring of Jews.

Technically, Klimaitis was a *partisan*, but his resistance group became exclusively pitted against the Soviet Union. Had Abba Kovner fallen into their hands, he would have been slaughtered at once. Of like pro-Nazi status was Adolfas Ramanauskas, who had grown up in a Baltic seaside resort now called Klaipėda but because of its large prewar German population was then known as Memel, a free city, which the Nazis incorporated into Germany. During World War II, Ramanauskas did not fight the German occupiers but simply worked as a schoolteacher. Yet as soon as the Soviets returned, he took up arms against them in guerilla warfare that did not end until the later 1950s. Captured by the Security Forces of the Lithuanian Soviet Socialist Republic, Ramanauskas was executed in 1958.

Others who briefly fought the Germans, but mostly against the Soviets, included Benediktas Versila, who survived an execution and fought with the Lithuanian Freedom Army against the Russians until the resistance ended. The Nazis had counted him as dead since 1942; in actuality, he lived until 1983. Juozas Lukša was another Lithuanian non-Jew who started out the same way. He joined the anti-Nazi underground in 1941 yet like many of his comrades ended up in battles against the Red Army. The non-Communist underground leader Povilas Plechavicius has been cited, too.

Latvia had about the same *percentage* of Jews killed as in Lithuania, except the number of Jews in prewar Latvia was much smaller. In Riga, the nation's capital, about ten thousand perished, shot down execution-style in the nearby Rumbuli Forest.

In 1933, the same year Hitler came to power, an ultra-nationalistic group, though one not yet affiliated with the Nazis, was founded in Latvia by Gustavs Celmiņš. It was called Pērkonkrusts (Thunder Cross), outlawed in 1934 with its founder banished into exile. This political party, which used a swastika as its emblem (the sign is called a "Thunder Cross" in Latvian) survived underground until Celmiņš returned to Latvia to work for the Germans as a *sonderführer* (special officer). Eventually, the rightist leader turned against the Nazis, was arrested by the Gestapo and taken to the Flossenbürg concentration camp. Liberated by the U.S. Fifth Army in May 1945, he was to live out his postwar life mostly in the U.S., where he taught at several universities.

For the record, the most egregious murderer of Jews in Latvia was Viktors Arājs, leader of the Nazi-affiliated Latvian organization named for him, the Arājs Commando, more officially the Latvian Auxiliary Security Police. He joined with SS Brigadeführer Walter Stahletter on July 1, 1941, and by November 30 to December 8, 1944, their masterpiece of slaughter in Rumbuli was accomplished.

It was later specified that the Arājs Commando, alone, exterminated half of Latvia's Jewish population. Arājs was actually a Baltic German on his wealthy mother's side and his father a Latvian blacksmith. During the period of Latvia's first independence after World War I, he was a provincial police officer.

A portrayal of him at apparently the Rumbuli massacre is the following: "Viktors Arājs, who was drunk, worked very close to the pits supervising the Latvian men of the commando, who were guarding and funneling the victims into the pits."

Horrific descriptions of those pits dot the annals of the Holocaust, the jumbled, undressed bodies heaped on top of each other in layers of dead and still writhing humans, and the killers shooting single shots into those living their last moments standing on the brink awaiting a bullet in the back of the neck.

Viktors Arājs only belatedly paid for his crimes. Caught up with finally in West Germany, he received a life sentence and died in his solitary confinement cell in 1988.

Of like stature was Herberts Cukurs, an adjutant to Arājs. Prior to World War II, he was literally internationally acclaimed for his exploits as a long-distance pilot in the early days of aviation, the "Latvian Lindbergh." Another less palatable nickname conferred on Cukurs during the war was the "Butcher of Riga," a title he shared with SS Unterscharführer Eduard Roschmann, the commandant of the Riga Ghetto. Those who in these later years proclaim Cukurs' innocence in the deaths of Latvian Jews admit he was part of Arājs's unit but protest he was merely the supervisor of a garage. Incontestably true was that Herberts Cukurs slipped off to Brazil once the war ended and the Israeli Mossad lured him to Montevideo where he was assassinated.

References in the War Refugee Board papers are even scantier for Latvia than for Lithuania. It was noted that two separate groups formed to fight the Nazis in the period 1941 to 1945. One was dedicated to reactivating the independence the country had enjoyed after World War I. The other was pro-Soviet, directed from Moscow, and dedicated to making Latvia, as was to happen, into a Soviet Socialist Republic.

Consequently, the Latvian Central Council was established, a military unit known as the Kurelians (after its general, Jānis Kurelis), formed originally to fight the Soviet partisans, although it did take on the Germans at times. One of its major activities was conducting "boat actions" to Sweden. In the end General Kurelis was deported to Germany along with 545 men, and they were imprisoned in the Stutthof concentration camp.

The dangers of these "boat actions" was brought home tragically when one-third of a twenty-four-person crew in Latvian rescue was reported dead or missing in action.

A major Nazi operation in Latvia bore the surname of its commander SS Obersturmführer Hamann and operated out of Daugavpils, Latvia, and contained a number of Lithuanians as well. The Jews it hunted could not but be struck by the hideous irony of the name. Although spelled slightly differently—one *n*, not two—Haman was the arch-tormentor in the Bible of the Jewish exiles of Persia, until Queen Esther intervened to stop his planned holocaust, and he was hanged by the King.

Iver Olsen in Stockholm agreed to fund a $2 million effort to rescue two thousand Latvian Jews in the summer of 1944. The offer had come from an SS commander named Kleist. Until then, only one Jew in the country had been saved by Latvian partisans and delivered to Sweden. Another survival in Latvia, it turned out, was of a Jewish couple, Israel and Frida Michelson, who hid in forest dugouts. Frida's book: *I Survived Rumbeli* was published in New York in 1982. Others lived by hiding in piles of clothing of those shot in the Rumbuli Forest. There were more—134 of them in Latvia— hidden by Righteous Gentiles, who were later recognized by the State of Israel.

Estonia and Finland are two other major Baltic countries linked together by their Finno-Ugric heritage, Uralic languages and geographical propinquity. Their more distant cousins in speech and background are the Hungarians. It was also the WRB's Iver Olsen's responsibility to rescue threatened populations—especially Jews— from Estonia, which had been occupied by the Nazis in July 1941, shortly after their invasion of the USSR the previous month. Specific WRB work within Estonia, if it happened, is not recorded in the archives. The major WRB operation in this region appears to have been engineering the successful escape of fifteen thousand Norwegians from the Nazi occupation of their country to safe haven of neutral Sweden. The War Refugee Board planned and organized the effort and contributed $50,000, in cooperation with the American Relief for Norway Inc. and the AF of L's Labor League for Human Rights and the CIO's War Relief Committee. Carried out from Sweden, this rescue was done, in the WRB's words, "by a group of highly competent Norwegian labor leaders working with Olsen." The WRB declared: "This project was one of the most successful undertaken."

The northern Baltic States, Estonia and Finland, were the last to be reached by the German war machine. Between July 7 and 9, 1941, the Wehrmacht crossed the Estonian border. Local men who had been drafted into the Red Army deserted and fought the Russians. In one instance, the Germans held back and let the Estonians rout their former occupiers from the key city of Tartu. At the end of that July, the Germans and the Estonian Forest Brothers advanced, and by the end of August 1941, took two other major cities of theirs: Narva and Tallinn, the capital. Down came the hammer and sickle, replaced by the Estonian banner of blue, black and white. The latter didn't remain waving for long, with the Nazis switching to their black swastika on a white circle framed by scarlet red.

Estonia then was promptly incorporated into the German Reich and given the name of Ostland.

German recruiting of Estonians was not particularly successful. An SS division of them was eventually organized, yet in 1942 more than three thousand Estonians men fled to Finland and became an infantry regiment of the Finnish Army.

It was in Stockholm at the beginning of 1943 that the Estonian escapees created a government-in-exile to continue the Republic they'd had since the end of World War I. By June 1944, secret meetings were being arranged in Tallinn. Specific WRB work there, if it happened, is not recorded in the archives.

Concurrently a number of stateless Jews in Finland were taken to

Sweden, plus 150 Finnish Jews were spirited there, too, once Finland had cast its lot with the Nazis and declared war on the Soviet Union. The Swedish Mosaic community was also involved in this successful endeavor. It also may be remembered that in 1943, before the WRB's creation, all nine thousand Danish Jews were daringly spirited away to Sweden, following the Nazi's undeclared overnight takeover of their homeland.

Shifting from the Baltic to the Balkans, we find frequent contacts between the WRB and the partisan groups in Yugoslavia, especially the Communist effort led by Marshall Tito (real name Josip Broz), which emerged as this ethnically divided country's dominant anti-Nazi, anti-Fascist force.

Yugoslavia's very name derived from its location—they were the South Slavs—put together in 1918 as the Kingdom of Serbs, Croats and Slovenes, a title it kept until 1929. The latter of its two principal ethnic entities had been part of the Austro-Hungarian Empire, dismembered at the end of World War I and attached to Serbia, a fully independent state, since the Congress of Berlin had declared it such in 1878.

This South Slav mix of peoples, although similar to each other in language and cultural traits, was not harmonious. They especially had religious differences: Roman Catholics in Croatia and Slovenia, Eastern Orthodox in Serbia, and Muslims in Bosnia, with a small smattering of native Jews. When conquered by the Nazis and Italian and Croatian Fascists in 1941, they remained restive. The first rebellion was mostly Serbian and royalist, the *Chetniks* of Draža Mihailović, but was soon surpassed by Tito's more inclusive anti-Nazi partisans. His became the largest, most successful European underground movement in World War II and stayed in power afterward, even eventually asserting its independence from Soviet Russia's imperialistic grasp.

Working with Tito's forces and the Allied military, the WRB was able to move seven thousand Jews from Hungary through Yugoslavia to Italy.

Money was sent to partisan groups along the northern border up against the Hungarian border. The funds were split for medical and "restorative" needs and between their own (Yugoslav) people and incoming Hungarian Jewish refugees.

The comment was made that "Although it seems difficult to believe, the lines of communication between Switzerland and northern Yugoslavia were better than between Italy and this region [Switzerland]."

It was added that "considerable amounts of medical goods were sent from Switzerland via Chiasso and Trieste [to Yugoslavia] with the collaboration of Italian Resistance groups."

The island of Rab has been briefly mentioned before in connection with the work of WRB representative Leonard Ackerman. It is a jewel of a place at the northern end of the Dalmatian coast and changed hands several times during the war. I spent a delightful week there, age twenty-two, in the summer of 1953. The boatmen who took me around on a variety of trips were no doubt the same who brought four thousand refugees to liberated areas of Italy in the last few weeks of 1943 and the first month of 1944. I remember those jolly guys with whom I conversed in a halting pidgin-German, when they started talking to each other in a sing-song, crazy-sounding language and laughing their heads off. It was somehow finally conveyed to me that they were speaking Czech or rather making fun of the Czechs who were now starting to come back to this tourist spot they'd frequented before the war.

But back to 1944. By February of that year, when the Nazis recaptured most of the Dalmatian coast, some fifteen thousand Yugoslavs, as we have learned, had crossed the Adriatic on these small schooner-type boats to Italy. The only place left open here to Tito's partisans was another island—the island of Vis, off the southern Dalmatian coast. The number of refugees being handled had dwindled from two thousand a week to one thousand a week.

Once the WRB appeared on the scene, they funneled $50,000 (five million Italian lire) to be spent on refugees from various areas of Yugoslavia, including northern Dalmatia, western Bosnia, eastern Bosnia and a fascinating area called the Lika, a barren, rugged, sparsely settled, chalky karst (limestone) area just inland from the Adriatic Sea.

Of the Yugoslavs who eventually were successful in reaching Italy with WRB help, slightly more than 28,000 were sent to camps in Egypt, while another 7,000 stayed in Italy.

When it was proposed that this influx from Yugoslavia be halted, Leonard Ackerman, who also had the WRB's responsibility for Yugoslavia, batted away the idea eloquently if not succinctly: "The issuance of an order restricting the rescue and movement of Yugoslav refugees, coming as it does immediately after the time when the partisans have consented to aid the Hungarians, appears to be extremely unfortunate and very inopportune."

Apparently, as the war began winding down and postwar tensions were on the horizon, the refugee situation in Yugoslavia deteriorated. The British started having trouble with Tito, who allegedly, at Stalin's backstage urging, restricted their rescue activities. Of the group they wanted to get out through Slovenia, Serbia, Montenegro, etc., only twenty-nine made it.

Italy, of course, had its partisan activity, much of it led by the Italian Communist Party, which had existed underground since Benito Mussolini's rise to power in 1922. They were responsible for Il Duce's execution along with his mistress Clara Petacci in April 1945, shortly before the end of World War II in Europe.

In addition to being outspoken, Leonard Ackerman was also pushy. He let the home office in D.C. know they should have a special attaché like himself sent to Italy, now that much of it had been cleared of the Axis and was a haven for refugees.

Nothing came of the idea, however.

The WRB and the OSS worked very closely together and in tandem with the Italian partisans, as well. The British Intelligence headquarters in Bletchley Park, London, was likewise involved and postwar issued a statement saying: "But little credit was given to the vast amount of detailed intelligence collected and transmitted by individual Partisan spies in Italy."

The OSS, itself, ran individual partisan agents landed by submarine behind German lines. One young agent, twenty-year-old Mino Farnuti, set up a secret radio at the foothills of the Apennine Mountains, just south of Ravenna on the Adriatic coast. The liberation of Ravenna has been declared: "No better example of coordination between regular troops and Partisans."

From a dead German major who was carrying plans for the eastern half of the defensive Gothic Line erected by the Nazis in northern Italy, the Allies received the information they needed for a breakthrough, which occurred on September 17, 1944. The 36th Garibaldi Brigade of 1,200 men led by an artillery lieutenant code-named "Bob" captured the key point of Mount Battaglia and let the Allies push into the Santerro Valley.

A three-man team, dropped high into the Alps close to the French border was led by Marcello di Liva, son of an Italian admiral and the great-grandnephew of the English poet, Percy Bysshe Shelley.

An Italian partisan uprising also led to the capture of the major

Mediterranean city of Genoa. Likewise, the important industrial center of Turin.

Among the directions to Ackermann, given him on November 4, 1944, were to work with the Resistance in northern Italy to help Jews and others escape. In this connection, he was sent to Italy to select refugees for the Oswego project and bring them to embark at Naples. Since northern Italy remained under German occupation, the Jews who lived there were in great peril. The idea of enlisting the Pope's help was suggested. Sir Clifford Heathcote-Smith and Myron C. Taylor did speak to the Pontiff, and he agreed. However when His Holiness had the papal nuncio in Berlin plead for an end to deportations of Italian Jews, the attempt "brought nothing but an evasive response."

Seven months earlier in April of the same year, his North African territory had been amended to cover the entire Mediterranean, and Ackerman's first assignment was to "act under and in cooperation with the American Representative to the Free French Comité français de Libération nationale." In addition, Robert Dexter, who in 1942 was recruited by the OSS, had set up contacts with Varian Fry's colleagues in Marseilles, now connected to the budding French Resistance. His work at the Unitarian Service Committee made a perfect cover. And toward the end of 1944, he went full-time for the WRB, helping the underground in France assist refugees.

The French Liberation has received far more publicity than the Yugoslav, although perhaps not as significant militarily in the long run. There were, as in other countries, splits in the anti-Nazi groups but none as one-sided as in Yugoslavia where Draža Mihailović's Serbian *Chetniks* could not compete with Tito's all-encompassing ethnics. In France, to be sure, there were the Communists but also the De Gaullists, eventually more powerful. It was common knowledge that FDR had no love for De Gaulle. But his backing of General Henri Giraud, a staunchly conservative escapee from Nazi captivity, fell flat, and De Gaulle essentially took charge of the French opposition to Vichy and the Nazis.

There were many heroes of the French Resistance. The most celebrated arguably was Jean Moulin, martyred in July 1943 by Nazi torturers. In regard to liaisons with the War Refugee Board, a name we have already encountered was Frenay.

Henri Frenay at the time was in Algiers as a top official of the Comité of the Conseil Nationale de la Résistance. He was especially known for having co-organized Combat, both an underground organization and publication that was one of the main components of the overarching council that Jean Moulin had put together. It has been called "the most important of all the early French Resistance groups."

At the time of France's capitulation in 1940, he was a Captain and company commander in the French Army's 43rd. Corps on the Maginot Line and bewilderingly obeying the orders to retreat given by his superiors.

Within a few weeks, Frenay wrote a personal manifesto that declared: "Our struggle is by no means over. It is first and foremost the struggle of the human spirit against barbarism and paganism while we prepare for the day of our liberation (38)."

"This was my first clandestine act," the future De Gaullist leader would declare.

Ironically, he initially saw Maréchal Philippe Pétain as France's savior. He even briefly worked in the Pétain regime. Frenay would live to see him tried and imprisoned for treason.

His manifesto, when he discreetly exposed it to select others he could trust, became a recruiting tool. Thus did Henri Frenay painstakingly set the stage for the Mouvement de libération nationale, the earliest of the Resistance groups.

On the other side of the coin, his disillusionment with his idol Pétain grew apace. One blow was his learning that the Maréchal had allowed the Germans to place *Gauleiters* as governing officials in Alsace and Lorraine without a word of protest. Frenay was then an officer in the Armistice Army the Germans had allowed France, and Pétain was his commanding officer. But the truly violent jolt was when the headlines in his morning newspaper revealed that Pétain had met with Hitler in the small French town of Montoire. The next day's edition painfully underscored that shocking revelation by publishing a photo of the French World War I hero shaking hands with Der Führer.

Born in Lyon, Frenay came from a staunchly Catholic family of military officers and was a graduate of Saint-Cyr, France's equivalent of West Point (so was De Gaulle), and he also attended l'École supérieure de guerre, the French War College. Naturally, when captured by the Germans while retreating, he tried to escape, and in his case succeeded on the first attempt. Reaching the unoccupied zone, he went back into the rump Army the Nazis had left France and was garrisoned at Marseille. There in conjunction with a French Protestant feminist named Berty (Berthe) Albrecht, he started his underground connection in August 1940. In July 1941, he met Moulin who'd been parachuted back into France after escaping to England. The assignment De Gaulle in London had given Moulin was the "delegate for the non-occupied zone of Metropolitan France" in charge of Gaullist communications with the South Zone and eventually the Nazi-controlled North Zone.

Henri Frenay had joined the Gaullists in 1941. Still, he did not shrink from criticizing his superior. He was quoted as saying: "General De Gaulle decided alone, without taking the advice of any of us, without listening to our observations or criticism, to give a single man entire responsibility for liaison with the Resistance and in fact for its direction." A full-front photo of Frenay's countenance immediately displays a pugnacious sense of fearless innate determination, not in awe of anyone.

It was in November 1943, after Moulin and General Charles Delestraint, head of the Secret Army, were captured by the Gestapo that Frenay decamped for Algiers. De Gaulle made him minister of prisoners, deportees and refugees in the Provisional Government. He was also awarded the Liberation Cross from the great man, himself. Since Frenay was a "ferocious adversary" of the French Communist Party, he was wildly attacked in the pages of their newspaper *L'Humanité*. The abuse was so bad that he sued them for defamation. That is, until he had to flee to Algeria.

Following his service, Frenay dropped out of public life, became a businessman, wrote a trio of books, and died in Ponte Vecchio, Corsica, in August 1998.

Other personalities that arose out of the "night and fog" of the Nazi years in France include the couple Lucie Aubrac, a schoolteacher, and her Jewish husband Raymond Aubrac, whose prewar last name was Samuel, noted for their sabotage planning; Emmanuel d'Astier de La Vigerie, a former *Action française* member, who later also ended up in De Gaulle's wartime cabinet; Serge Ravanal, an ex-French Army colonel, chief of Groupe, a commando of tough Resistance fighters called Groupe Francs; and Jean-Pierre Levy, head of the Francs-tireurs, not to be confused with Francs-tireurs et partisans français, an arm of the Communist Party of France.

A unique feature in dealing with the French Resistance was the ancillary factor of Allied control in North Africa once they had taken over various parts of the French Empire. In the archives of the War Refugee Board, documents can be found relating to conditions at the time there. In a February 1944 communication to Selden Chapin, counselor of Embassy in Algiers, from H. Earle Russell, American consul in Casablanca, we learn about refugees allowed to enter Morocco. These *"evades de France"* (escapees) were being admitted from Spain through the French Red Cross and the French Committee of National Liberation. In fifteen months, 25,000 had entered Morocco and other parts of French North Africa. Almost all (ninety-five percent) were French and 20,000 had entered the French Army. Others, stateless persons, preponderantly Jewish, were not treated so well, especially by the Sûreté. The able-bodied among them were forced into the French Foreign Legion or kept in prison. Somehow between 500 and 800 were coming every month. "Many Jews and other anti-fascist refugees have a real dread of French administration and officialdom, which is based on past suffering in France, especially during the Vichy period . . . In Morocco, where persecution of Jews is still not unknown, especially in outlying districts . . . there is already anti-Semitic feeling that exists both on the part of certain of the native population and of certain officials in the Protectorate."

An opposite if limited view was expressed in another letter to Chapin, this time from William W. Schott, the American consul in Oran, Algeria. "I have to say that there are no manifestations of persecution of Jews or other minorities in the Department of Oran."

The War Refugee Board nevertheless did make a large monetary contribution to the French Resistance and its unified groups. It was paid to Charles Guillen, who was a representative of the relief section of the Conseil National de la Résistance, and Madame Andre Philip, a delegate of COSOR, Comité des Œuvres Sociales des Organisations de la Résistance. A donation of two hundred thousand Swiss francs became twelve million French francs. Among the groups receiving aid were the social services and relief activities of the MUR, Mouvements unis de la Résistance, the Front National and France D'Abord (France First).

The city of Lyon was considered an epicenter of the French Resistance, and a good deal of the WRB money went to it. The État Major (General Staff) des Postes, Télégraphs et Téléphones was a prime recipient, whose employees provided "excellent information and sabotage work" and many of whom were killed. The Lyon Resistance group of SNCF (the French railroad workers) was similarly aided and so was the Œuvres des Prisons de Lyon and likewise the Amitiés Chrétiennes (Christian Friendships) of Lyon, an inter-confessional group formed in Lyon to help French Jews. Of the five million French francs spent in Lyon, half a million went to Father Godard, the representative of Cardinal Gerlier, to pay bribes for the release of wounded prisoners awaiting execution. Funds were also funneled to "Mr. Royall Tyler," an American born in Massachusetts, educated in England (Harrow and Oxford), U.S. Intelligence officer in World War I, living in Geneva and working for the U.S. in World War II. The money was for "aid to the French in the Lyon region for those sought by the Milice (French fascist police) and the Nazis."

John Pehle was later to say: "I should perhaps not have made so substantial a contribution to the Conseil National de la Résistance in France if I had known at the time that the major part of our WRB discretionary funds had been generously contributed by the JOINT [since it was a Jewish organization]. On the other hand, knowing the JOINT and the spirit in which they have always done their work, I feel they would approve."

Money was sent also even to small operations like that of Jean-Jacques Jaeger, head of the Francs-tireurs and partisans in Haute-Savoie, a man who was "extremely helpful in hiding refugees in France and getting them across the nearby border into Switzerland." Parenthetically, this is the area of France I know best, *mon pays*, as the French say, my second homeland. Well do I remember *un vieux*, an old gentleman I met in the bar at L'Auberge Ensoleillée in Peilloneix, a village of three hundred, where I spent a whole year on and off plus numerous visits. We passed several hours discussing the war years in the region. One of the episodes he related over drinks I have retained to this day—that of a local boatman on the Haute-Savoie side of Lake Geneva, who would take money to transport Jews across to the Swiss side but land them in what he said was Switzerland but was really still France and right into German hands. The local *résistants* killed him, my conversational partner declared with an unmistakable sense of satisfaction. He also told me about his collection of news clippings and memorabilia from that era, which ruefully someone had stolen.

An unattributed postscript of sorts on the French situation was:

"The situation of people who escaped from France was not very good *until lately*. Active résistants meet 'a double deception when they arrive here. Had expected a warm welcome. Got at the very best only kind words.' Two groups were taking care of escapees. The Union for the Escaped and The French Aid." Then was added: "It is only in Corsica (a part of France liberated from Italo-German control in September 1943) that we can do anything. They would ask the Germans to exchange 'deported Corsicans' on Isola d'Elba or in northern Italy for Germans interned in Corsica."

One matter raised in several of the WRB documents was that of Jewish children. There was a secret memo, dated March 1, 1944, referring to them as "refugee children." The problem in France seems to have been exacerbated by the surrender of Italy to the Allies in September 1943. Hitherto, the Italians had been in control of parts of southern France, and their relatively benign treatment of the Jews was replaced by the stone-hard anti-Semitism of the Nazis.

Alluded to in the WRB materials is the fact that well before its inception, FDR in 1942 considered allowing with no publicity five thousand children from France outside of the U.S. quotas, but the plan was rendered impossible when the Nazis occupied Vichy in November of that year.

Roswell McClelland, in his Swiss post, was helping to finance an effort of L'Œuvre de Secours aux Enfants (the Work of Assistance to Children) and the Joint as well as giving money to the Fédération des organisations juives. He did say that more could be done in France, if the different groups would work together. He was asking for the equivalent of $250,000.

An American was working with the French OSE in dealing with the plight of Jewish children in France. His name was Noel Field, and he was to achieve a definite notoriety after the war when it was discovered he had been a Soviet spy. In 1941, he became the director of the Unitarian Service Committee's relief mission in Marseilles. His efforts included setting up kindergartens at Camp Rivesaltes and working to liberate Jewish kids from this and other French internment camps. Establishing medical programs for Jews in hiding was another of his projects. Robert Dexter recruited Field to pass on information to the OSS, and he travelled with the Maquis, the resistance fighters in the rural areas. Perhaps it was a cover for his secret work for the Soviets, but the Communists in France considered him an American spy. Noel

Field, a Harvard graduate, was born in England of American parents. His father was from Brooklyn.

Raising hackles in the State Department on this issue was an April 9, 1944, broadcast by the sharp-tongued radio personality Drew Pearson, who reminded his audience that on February 26, 1944, the War Refugee Board had sent a cable abroad to aid Jewish refugees in French Concentration Camps. They had Latin American passports but were kept incarcerated. On that February 26, the War Refugee Board specifically asked the State Department to have its staffs abroad help those unfortunates. Six weeks went by, Pearson said, and only pressure from above convinced State to release the cable. Pearson's acrid comment was: "Unfortunately, the 238 refugees who awaited the cable may now be dead."

On February 21, 1944, five days before the date the thwarted cable bottled up by the State Department was supposed to have been sent, the WRB received a request for funds to be sent to France for a supply of matzos (unleavened bread) needed for the Passover celebration. The price tag was 1.5 million French francs ($25,000 then).

It was in August and September that most of the German troops were routed from France, although a few diehard detachments in isolated places fought on until almost the end of the war the following May.

We find in the WRB annals a letter from John Pehle to James Saxon, then a U.S. Treasury representative at the American Embassy in Paris, thanking the latter for two reports he'd forwarded on the situation of the Jews in France. While still at the Treasury Department, before joining the War Refugee Board as a special attaché, Saxon dispatched an additional digest of information from the French capital. This cabled document had apparently been formulated with the help of the Joint's director for France, J. Jeromykin, and an associate, Maurice Brenner. Incidentally, Brenner, who had been in France throughout the occupation, had never heard of the War Refugee Board.

Revealed in the communication was that at the start of the war, there were 320,000 Jews in France, split fifty-fifty between native-born Israelites and foreign Jewish refugees. An earlier letter from these Joint activists overseas stated: "Jewish participation in the various Resistance units has been considerable, both in the FFI and FTP [French Forces of the Interior and Francs-tireurs et partisans] as well as the Secret Army . . . Not much Jewish participation in the political resistance." Jewish youth formed in 1941 the Armée Juive, later called "Organisation Juive de Combat." Jews were active in the liberations of Paris, Albi, Toulouse and Castres. "Casualties were proportionately higher than in other fighting units, not only on account of the Germans but also on account of the Vichy militia."

It was reported that of the 100,000 French Jews who were deported to Nazi concentration camps only 2,500 were alive at the end of the war in Europe.

Chapter Eleven

Belgium is next. This bilingual (French and Flemish) country, small as it is, did have a lively underground. Prominent among its leaders was the outspoken Burgomaster of Brussels, Joseph Vandemeulebroek, who openly refused to obey German orders. Naturally the Nazis jailed and deported him and leveled a fine on the capital city of five million Belgian francs. But first he issued a proclamation that declared: "Contrary to what has been said, I have neither abandoned my position nor submitted my resignation. I am, I remain, and I will remain the legitimate burgomaster of Brussels." On a happier note, Vandemeulebroek was alive and back in office on September 4, 1944, to welcome the Allied forces that liberated his beloved city.

The Belgian Resistance had two major escape routes, one known as the *Comete*, founded by Countess Andrée de Jongh (Dedee) that ran from Brussels to Bilbao in Spain and the other leading to southern France called amazingly *Pat O'Leary*, the nom de guerre of another Belgian patriot, Albert Guérisse. In actuality, his Irish alias was the name in real life of a Canadian friend of his. Both of these patriots were eventually captured by the Nazis. Dedee de Jongh died at Ravensbrück. Pat O'Leary survived—just barely—after captivity at the Natzweiler-Struthof camp in Alsace and at Dachau.

Within Belgium itself, there was a concentration camp set up at the century-old stone fort of Breendonk. Although barely known to the outside world, it is considered to have been on a par with Dachau and Buchenwald and contained a gas chamber. Especially singled out for his cruelty was SS Sturmbannführer Philip Schmitt, who terrorized the prisoners with his ferocious dog called Lump. The German SS ran Breendonk, and additionally there were Flemish SS guards. After the war, Schmitt was executed by firing squad.

A notation in the records of the War Refugee Board documents that money was given by them to the Belgian Resistance.

One prominent resistance group in Belgium was called the "White Brigade" because of the white overalls its members wore. They used false papers not only in Belgium and France but also once they entered Switzerland. Families they referred to were entirely fictional. One of their leaders, Mendel Wilner, never broke off contact with his cohorts in the Belgian Underground, even from Switzerland. He and a comrade, Siegbert Daniel, had been previously arrested by German military police in 1943, but Wilner, anyway, had managed to flee to safety.

On November 26, 1944, the WRB released of a report on Jews in Nazi concentration camps, informally referred to as "a 60 page horror story," which mentions Belgian Jews who had died.

Included, too, was an incident wherein four Dutch Jews were invited to Auschwitz as an "Investigating Commission" in the summer of 1943. There they were treacherously shot to death. The Germans blithely lied they had been killed in an automobile accident.

The Dutch Resistance has been called "One of the fiercest of all the underground movements in Nazi-occupied Europe"—this despite the fact of its smallness, proximity to Germany and lack of rugged terrain where guerilla forces could operate more easily. Still, the Dutch patriots were bold enough to strike in broad daylight, as they did in one famous incident. Here, the Dutch partisans ambushed a German military truck, not knowing that inside the cab was Lieutenant General Hanns Rauter, the head of the SS in the Netherlands, who answered directly to SS boss Heinrich Himmler. In the mêlée, Rauter was shot but not killed. German retaliation was vicious—263 Hollanders were summarily executed.

A key figure of the Dutch Resistance in contact with the War Refugee Board was a Dr. S. Pollak-Daniels, co-director of the Committee of Dutch Jews. He secretly slipped into Switzerland in the latter part of 1943 to set up arrangements for Dutch Jewish deportees rescued from Bergen-Belsen. His group, which included his co-director W. H. Gans, was described in the WRB material as "a small but well-organized relief committee for Dutch Jewish refugees and other Jews from Holland." The needs of this Dutch organization, it was reported, were "fairly well covered by grants from Mr. Saly Mayer of the Joint Distribution Committee, who gave small monthly contributions to pay for *passeurs* along the French-Swiss border—two hundred Swiss francs a month went to a Swiss customs officer who served in the *refoulement*—"sorting camp" of Cropette in Geneva, where illegal arrivals were kept and often sent back to occupied France. It was said that with a "few hundred francs a month in the right place about 30 people a month who might otherwise have been *refoulés* were admitted to Switzerland."

The Nazis had taken over the Low Countries of the Netherlands, Belgium and Luxembourg in the spring of 1940. When in 1941 Dutch workers went on strike nationwide to protest the roundup of four hundred Jews, Rauter ordered his SS men and German troops to fire on them, killing eleven Netherlanders. Needless to say, these fellow Jewish citizens of theirs were gassed at Buchenwald.

Shooting hostages wasn't just the province of the Germans. Among their collaborators was the former chief of the Dutch General Staff, General Hendrick Seyffardt who, not to be outdone by the SS, had 250 of his anti-Nazi compatriots shot.

Out of 140,000 Dutch Jews, 75 percent or 105,000 were killed.

Holland also suffered from the fact that the military government imposed on them was run by the SS, not by the usually less fanatic Wehrmacht, the German Army.

Caught up in the Nazi web in Holland was an American couple named Johnson. When they were released by the Germans in July 1944, these non-Jewish U.S. citizens spoke of the horrors they had experienced and witnessed and "assumed it would be of interest to the War Refugee Board."

The food given to Dutch Jews and non-Jewish Dutch captives was "so inadequate that most of the prisoners appeared starved, the skins having turned yellow."

Mr. and Mrs. Johnson were first confined in Amersfoort, Holland, and then moved to locations in Germany. They had been living in the Netherlands, and near their house was a synagogue and they had seen Jews being beaten outside it by Dutch Nazis. Mrs. Johnson's story, said the WRB, was "particularly important because she is not Jewish."

Interestingly enough, the Communist Party members in the Low Countries seemingly jumped the gun on resistance ahead of the Soviets, who had a pact with the Nazis until June 1941 when Hitler, without warning, invaded Russia. In Holland, after the first Nazi raid on the Amsterdam Jewish quarter, these Communists led the way in fomenting the general strike of February 1941. The following year, Luxembourg also had a general strike, starting with the city of Wiltz, which was suppressed brutally—twenty-one strikers were sentenced to death.

Another workers stoppage affecting the Low Countries was actually started in the Pas de Calais section of northern France the Germans had lumped in with Belgium for administrative reasons. The French newspaper *Le Monde* many years later in an historical review referred to the event as "one of the most spectacular acts of the Resistance." It lasted for eight days before it was broken.

The Dutch Resistance was described as "small scale decentralized cells engaged in independent activities. People who hid people were called *onderduikers*.

The movie star Audrey Hepburn, as a teenager in Holland, took part in the Dutch Resistance.

We all know about Anne Frank.

We all may not know much about the Resistance in Romania, Bulgaria and Greece, which are like outliers in this story of opposition to the Nazis from within the countries they occupied.

Ironically, Romania could well be cited as a factor in the eventual, if belated, forming of the War Refugee Board. The cause célèbre in the showdown within the Roosevelt Administration leading to its creation was the scandal that relief funds for Jews in Romania (and France) and for the evacuation of Jews from Romanian occupied Transnistria had been held up by a long series of discussions and cables at the State Department that amounted to total inaction. The trio of Treasury Department officials who forced the issue believed the State Department stall was deliberate and outrageous and that the political consequences of its revelation would be harmful to FDR's 1944 reelection bid. Their scathing memo on the issue made the president see the light and resulted, as we know, in the announcement through an executive order of a new and highly experimental agency of the U.S. Government.

A major accomplishment of the War Refugee Board listed in an account of its history was "the ensuring of 48,000 Jews" trapped in Transnistria to be able to transfer to a still-hostile but less-deadly-to-them Romania.

This feat was allegedly accomplished through the influence of Alexander Cretzianu, the Romanian Minister to Turkey, who as we have seen earlier on was promised sanctuary in the U.S. by WRB special attaché in Ankara Ira Hirschmann.

Also there is a discussion of the numbers of Jews involved, how many were *actually* left alive in the Transnistrian "killing field for Jews," until allowed into Romania. Figures have ranged from the 48,000 already quoted to 51,000 or as high as 65,000.

The WRB's special concentration on saving Romanian Jewish children has likewise already been cited.

Romania, of course, was one of those countries that started the war on the Axis side and finished on the Allied side. Meanwhile, the country had much to answer for.

The prime culprit in Romania's deadly persecution of the Jews was an unsavory organization called the "Iron Guard." As early as 1927, this proto-fascist group had committed several pogroms in Transylvania— five synagogues destroyed in Oradea Mare and eight more in Cluj, and numerous Jews murdered. Its founder was a handsome, dark-haired, charismatic young man named Corneliu Codreanu. The King of Romania, Carol II, saw Codreanu as a threat and had him arrested. According to an official notice, he was "shot while attempting to escape." This happened on November 30, 1938.

Replacing the *martyred* fascist was a career soldier, Ion Antonescu, who was chief of the Romanian Army's general staff and minister of defense during the 1930s. On September 4, 1940, after Romania had lost one-third of its territory, Antonescu was made prime minister with absolute powers. An outspoken anti-Semite, he brought the Iron Guard into his government but later suppressed the unruly radical organization and reigned as a military dictator. Naturally, he gravitated toward the Axis. Thus he declared war on the Soviet Union and sent Romanian troops to fight in Russia and Ukraine. His reward was the return of Bessarabia and Bukovina, and he donned for himself the exalted title of "marshal of Romania."

The Odessa Massacres were the most notorious of the Romanian actions on the eastern front. One estimate by the U.S. Holocaust Museum is that one hundred thousand Jews were killed by Romanians and Germans in that Ukrainian city and its surroundings. It seems hardly accidental that the acronym given by Nazis fleeing justice in postwar Europe was O-D-E-S-S-A— Organisation der Ehemaligen SS-Angehörigen—(Organization of Former SS Members).

The records of the Joint Distribution Committee show that by January 1944, just as the WRB was being formed, the "gateway of escape from the Balkans" came into existence—by boat from Romania across the Black Sea to Turkey and by rail through Bulgaria. Also there was "the expansion and financing of underground operations in the

Balkans," including indirect pressure to obtain exit visas from Romania and Bulgaria.

Well before the War Refugee Board came into existence, efforts had started in 1943 to bring threatened Jews out of Romania to Palestine. Eri Jabotinsky, son of the famed Zionist firebrand Vladimir Zev Jabotinsky, entered the scene in 1944 and traveled to Ankara in an American bomber that Congressman Will Rogers Jr. arranged to have take him. En route, in Jerusalem, young Jabotinsky gave the impression that he was an agent of the WRB. This unwarranted use of the WRB name was brought to John Pehle's attention and confirmed by U.S. ambassador to Turkey, Laurence Steinhardt in Ankara. It no doubt put a question mark on another claim by Jabotinsky—i.e., that he had helped 2,400 Jews from Romania get into Palestine.

The whole rescue effort was always fraught with suspense and surprises. None were more acute than an incident in this corner of the world involving a number of Jews from Romania who had made it safely to Turkey, but the British, "without warning and without consultation with Ambassador Steinhardt refused to issue permits to go to Palestine," and these persons were returned to Romania. Peter Bergson was outraged that the War Refugee Board wouldn't intervene. But Pehle told him that by the terms of the executive order creating the agency, they couldn't. This late in 1944, Romania, having gone over to the Allies, was deemed a *liberated* country, and Jews were no longer in danger of their lives, at least theoretically.

Capturing the world's attention, however briefly, was a complex true story involving the *Struma*. It was one of a series of essentially obsolete, unseaworthy "rust buckets," also dubbed "coffin ships," that carried refugees, Jews primarily, from the Romanian seaport of Constanța across the Black Sea to Istanbul. The *Struma* was described as a seventy-four-year-old hulk that had been refitted and carried 764 passengers crammed into space meant to accommodate a very small percentage of that number. Thus, dangerously overcrowded, she left Constanța on December 12, 1940, headed to Turkey, did reach Istanbul and then perforce stayed anchored for more than two months with the passengers kept aboard by the Turks in squalid conditions that can only be imagined.

The sea route leading from Romania to Turkey and then hopefully to Palestine was not a slam-dunk. Even if the often-turbulent waters could be mastered, there was the matter of British reluctance to allow

Jews into Palestine. The notorious White Paper that His Majesty's Government released in 1939 set a limitation on Jews allowed to settle in the Holy Land at a mean-spirited mere five thousand. One reason given by a U.S. State Department supporter of this paltry quota was a paucity of shipping. So another unsung villain to add to the likes of Borden Reams, Jimmy Dunn, Avra Warren, and Howard Travers was the bureaucrat Cavendish W. Cannon, who worked in the notably hostile if not outright anti-Semitic European Division.

Discussion had been underway on a Turkish proposal to the U.S. that espoused the idea of transporting three hundred thousand Jews to safety. But instead of a flood, the obstructionists in the State Department reduced the successfully saved into a pitiful trickle.

The *Struma*, after being held up for so long, finally received permission to leave port. This happened on February 24, 1942. The creation of the War Refugee Board was a tad less than two years away.

If you feel an impending tragedy as the rickety old boat heads out to sea, you will be clairvoyant. BOOM! The *Struma* blew up and sank precipitously. There was only one survivor, a twenty-one-year-old Romanian Jew, David Stoliar. The currently estimated death toll is 791. All sorts of speculations have led to a general conclusion that a Soviet submarine torpedo sent her to the bottom. The nationality of the suspected perpetrators wavered between German, Russian, Romanian or Bulgarian underwater war craft.

One name that has drawn praise in this entire gloomy episode was that of Abraham Galante, a Turkish Jew with important connections. For one thing, he was an elected member of the Turkish Parliament, besides being a journalist, scholar and linguist, and he was able to bring the support of the whole Turkish Jewish community to make the torturous captivity of their coreligionists aboard the *Struma* as bearable as possible.

The memory of this two-year-old travesty had not been forgotten by the time Ira Hirschmann took up his WRB duties in Istanbul in January 1944. The specter of an exploded vessel hung over the efforts of Hirschmann to direct further shiploads onto the sea route from the Balkans. All but one of the ships he paid for were successful—the exception being the *Mefkûre*, which in August 1944, was sunk. Once again, the culprit was declared to have been an unidentified submarine whose crew machine-gunned passengers struggling in the roiled waters. Only five escaped alive. Eight ships were able to succeed unscathed and a total of just shy of three thousand Jews made it to Turkey and eventually Palestine.

From Switzerland, money was being sent to Romania and—of all places—Austria, Hitler's birthplace. These were "substantial financial grants from the Board in Switzerland," plus the International Red Cross and Catholic and Protestant groups helped in its distribution. Funds were expended on buying food supplies in Romania. Medicines and condensed milk were purchased in Switzerland, and the fares for steamer passage to Palestine for Romanian Jews were picked up by the WRB.

Ira Hirschmann, actually in Ankara, working out of the U.S. Embassy, was carrying on projects based in Romania and Bulgaria as well. Iver Olsen from his post in Sweden also pitched in on efforts within these two former Nazi satellites. By the fall of 1944, both Romania and Bulgaria had abrogated their anti-Jewish laws. They were simultaneously putting pressure on "individual concentration camp commanders and their underlings" who showed signs of ignoring orders from Berlin.

The Nazi grip was loosening. From Theresienstadt 700 Romanians and Hungarians escaped to Switzerland in the fall of 1944. A single boatload of Romanians that reached Turkey had 340 asylum seekers aboard. Cretzianu, the influential Romanian bureaucrat, was instrumental in allowing refugees from Hungary to pass through Romania, which was signaled as a "big help." The story of the boat *SS Belacite* was told, wherein ten Romanian families leased her, paying to carry 130 children released from Transnistria. It was a matter of pride for the Romanians that "no refugees from Romania, as distinguished from Romanian nationals, had to pay for transportation."

The same Catch-22 that had thwarted the WRB's assistance in Romania after its "liberation" also applied to Bulgaria. Milton Handler, a well-known New York lawyer, had written to Treasury Secretary Morgenthau on October 3, 1944, about the sad condition of the Jews in both Romania and Bulgaria. The letter was bucked to John Pehle to answer and his reply had to be: "The persons who have survived German occupation and who are now in the liberated portions of the Balkans are, of course, no longer any direct concern of the War Refugee Board and we are confining our operations to the protection of persons still in occupied territory."

It was through the Bulgarian underground that exit visas were procured for Romanians—especially Romanian Jewish children—who, most of them, succeeded in getting to Palestine.

However, the issue of Bulgarian behavior during the Holocaust appears to be quite complicated and controversial. This is illustrated by the reaction in Israel after its creation in 1948. King Boris III, who reigned in Bulgaria during the war period yet, in spite of his country's membership in the Axis coalition, would not send Bulgarian troops to fight the Soviets, was memorialized at Yad Vashem for his support of the Jews in his country. Yet after it was proven that he had authorized the deportation of more than eleven thousand Jews from the territories Bulgaria had annexed, the monument was removed in the year 2000.

The train travel through Bulgaria to Turkey produced results, too. An exact count was 1,392 refugees brought to safety and whose exit permits had been obtained through the Bulgarian underground. Their transit visas across Turkey to Palestine, on the other hand, had been granted by the Turkish Government, anxious to rout them out of their country.

Turkey and Germany, which had fought together in World War I, played footsie in the earlier years of World War II but became estranged as the conflict inexorably turned in favor of the Allies. Yet after the long-hoped-for break occurred, a new problem immediately undermined the thrill of victory. The Turks now regarded the individual anti-Nazi Germans, Austrians and Czechoslovaks in their midst to be "technically seen as "Germans" and *enemy aliens*. Threatened with expulsion from Turkey to God-knows-where, the benighted refugees appealed to the War Refugee Board to intervene. This time they did. One reprieved woman, facing deportation, had lived in Turkey for twelve years and had a one-year-old child.

In Bulgaria the exact number of Jews saved has varied from 48,000 to 50,000. Given credit for this effort were, besides the king, the then Deputy Speaker of the Bulgarian Assembly and former Minister of Justice Dimitar Peshev and leaders of the Bulgarian Orthodox Church, especially Metropolitan Stefan of Sofia and Bishop Kyrill of Plovdiv. The latter hid Jews and threatened to throw himself across the tracks to keep death trains from leaving, and the former sheltered two major local rabbis in his home. The ambiguity of the Bulgarian Holocaust experience was aptly summed up by Michael Berenbaum, professor at the American Jewish University in Los Angeles: "The Bulgarians were heroic rescuers, cruel prosecutors and brutal killers, all at once."

The real villain of the piece was Alexander Belev, a dyed-in-the-wool anti-Semite who controlled the Commissariat of Jewish Affairs. Before the war, in 1936, he had put together a fascistic organization known as "Ratnik." In the Bulgarian language, the word means "warrior." King Boris dissolved this hate group in April 1939. Then, less than a month after the Nazis invaded Poland on September 1, 1939, the suppressed Ratniks and their Hitler-Youth-type group called "Brannick" staged an imitation of the *Kristallnacht* mega-pogrom from the previous November 1938. They, too, smashed Jewish shop windows, roughed up Jews and killed some.

Yet although Bulgaria, like Romania, joined the Axis coalition, they unlike the Romanians had fought on the German and Austrian side in World War I. And in World War II, unlike Romania as well, they refused to send troops to fight the Soviets. (The Bulgarians were fiercely Russophiles.) King Boris was inflexible on that point, although he did not live out the war, dying in 1943. Ruling for the six-year-old heir to the throne, Prince Simeon II, was a regency that only lasted until August of 1944, when Bulgaria changed sides and fought the Germans. The anti-Semitic "Law for the Protection of the Nation" was immediately revoked.

The final comeuppance for the Nazi stooge Alexander Belev followed soon after. He had been fired in October 1943 as commissioner of the Jews and knew he was a marked man. Intending to flee to Germany, he reached Kyustendil, a small city in the westernmost part of the country, but was captured by partisans and sent back to Sofia. Under the armed guard of a Jewish partisan, he was shot to death as soon as they left for the capital. His body was dumped in a ditch and not reported for several years—*sic semper tyrannus*.

A snippet of related information found in the War Refugee Board files refers to Nicholas Balabanoff, the Bulgarian minister to Turkey, whose country had gone to war against the Allies, and as fortunes changed, turned friendly and more and more portrayed his country in the best possible light, presaging their change of sides.

Let us now turn to Greece, another component of the Balkans. One of the first communications to the War Refugee Board about it came from Cairo and stated *the EAM should be connected with and gold made available to them.*

Immediately we are introduced to the alphabet soup of initials for the various underground operations in Greece, made all the more confusing since most of them begin with E, standing for *Ethnikos*, meaning *National.*

On the one side, during the German occupation 1941 to 1945, we find EAM, the National Liberation Front, essentially a large-scale Communism-professing political party, and ELAS, its military wing, the Peoples Liberation Army. Opposed to it was EDES, a military group in Epirus, a northwestern area, and EKKA, whose territory was central Greece. These latter groups were either Royalists or supporters of a republic that would replace the king and queen, who had fled to Egypt.

Even while the Nazis and Italian fascists still occupied their land, the EAM-ELAS and the EDES-EKKA *fought each other* and after the Axis defeat engaged in a ferocious civil war.

Prior to September 1939, Greece in the city of Salonica and surrounding area contained the largest community of Sephardic Jews in the world. It was in the neighborhood of sixty thousand people. Moreover, there was also a sampling in various locations of a very little-known (at least I had never heard of them) minority of a population of distinct Jews called Romaniotes.

These were descendants of Jews who were deported to Rome after the destruction of the Second Temple in Jerusalem in the year 70 CE, spread throughout the empire and kept their separate identity and a Judeo-Greek language, called Yevanic. In Greece, they were clustered mainly around the northwest city of Ioannina, with a sprinkling in Athens and on the close-by island of Aegina.

Ioannina was founded by the Byzantine emperor Justinian in the sixth century CE and is the capital of the Epirus region. A Romaniote synagogue still exists there and is opened by request. Every summer, Romaniotes from around the world return and use it for services, and in the year 2000, a bar mitzvah ceremony was performed inside. The Romaniote Ioannaiotiki Synagogue in Athens sees use on the High Holidays (Yom Kippur, Passover, etc.) and can be visited upon request. In addition to the Romaniote place of worship on Aegina, there is a Romaniote congregation, Kehila Kedosha Janina in Manhattan on the Lower East Side (some 3,000 Romaniotes are said to live in the tri-state area of New York, New Jersey and Connecticut) plus two Romaniote synagogues in Israel, the Yanina Synagogue in Jerusalem and the Zakynthos Synagogue in Tel Aviv.

A particular Greek hero of Romaniote ancestry was Colonel

Mordechai Frizis, killed on December 15, 1940, fighting the invading Italians of Mussolini.

This fierce Greek resistance led Il Duce to call upon the Germans to bail him out, and the Nazis were able to overwhelm the heroic defenders, despite assistance from the British. Britain had always had a special interest in Greece. Therefore, it was no surprise to discover a letter dated August 21, 1944, from the British Embassy in D.C. to George Warren at the U.S. Department, blasting EAM and ELAS, the Communist Underground, for efforts to save Greek Jews via the *Euboea route* past Greece's second largest island.

Snippily the writer, identified as J. W. Russell, telegraphed his hostility both toward Greek leftists and Jews, using haughty, unfriendly language.

EAM and ELAS, Russell pontificated, "are receiving undeserved credit for the evacuation of Jews from Greece and are receiving excessive compensation for their efforts to rescue Jews." Following which, Mr. Russell really goes into high gear: "These are mostly rich Jews who have paid large sums of money for their escape and that in each case ELAS takes a cut of 20%. ELAS has consistently hampered the escape of recruits for the Greek forces in the Middle East but is apparently prepared to assist Jewish refugees in view of the profits to be made and of the improbability of these Jews joining the Greek forces in the Middle East." Joseph Goebbels couldn't have worded it any better.

Three days later, after John Pehle had read this communication, he sent a memo to Edward Stettinius, then the number-two man at the State Department and his immediate boss. He wrote he didn't think the British idea of having accredited representatives work out new plans to rescue Jews in Greece would be feasible. "We are inclined to believe that this suggestion would not be calculated to facilitate the rescue of Jews from Greece," was how he nicely put it in bureaucratic speak. And then, judging the British initiative to be a reprimand of partisan Underground routes in Greece, Pehle offered a stinging yet mildly phrased rebuke of what may well have been London's underlying motive, to wit hoping: "The rescue of refugees might actually be prejudiced."

The murder rate of Jews in Greece percentagewise was . . . well, *murderous* . . . in certain locations and less so in others.

Salonica, with its 56,000 Jews, was the hardest hit. Only 1,200 survived the deportations to the death camps, less than three percent. Athens, on the other hand, which had many less Jews—only 3,500— did much better. The *survival* rate there was sixty-six percent, thanks to the city's police chief, Angelos Evert, and Orthodox Archbishop Damaskinos who faked IDs and baptismal certificates. Conditions varied. On the island of Kos, all Jews were wiped out. On May 21, 1944, fleeing Crete, 260 Jews drowned when their boat sank. Yet on the Ionian island of Zakynthos, thanks to Orthodox Bishop Chrysostomos and Mayor Louka Carrer, all 275 Jews were saved. On Volos, there were 882 Jews whom the Germans sought to deport. Orthodox Archbishop Joakin and Rabbi Moshe Pesach, a Romaniote, teamed up to thwart them. One hundred and thirty of these Jews were shipped to Auschwitz.

The major German concentration camp in Greece went into operation only late in September 1943, although the Nazis had already shipped off the major population of Greek Jews located in Salonica. Until September 8, 1943, the date Italy surrendered to the Allies, a large part of Greece had been occupied by Mussolini's Fascists. Two days later, September 10, the Germans took control of the transit camp already in existence at Haidari, and it was run briefly by Wehrmacht army officers until the SS moved in. The commandant installed by them was an "Old Fighter," Nazi street fighter from Hitler's Munich days—one Paul Radomski. He promptly started off his career at Haidari by personally killing a Jewish Greek Army officer named Levi in front of all the prisoners, and he proved such a loose-cannon brute that the Germans relieved him of his post. Among other things, while drunk, he had even threatened to shoot his own adjutant.

The volatile situation in Greece apparently did not receive much attention from the War Refugee Board. There is a notation in its files perhaps to remind Americans of an uncomfortable fact. Under the Johnson-Reed Immigration Act of 1924 that set quotas for entry into the U.S., the Greeks had been allotted a mere 307 places per year.

We will now move north to Scandinavia—that is, to the two countries conquered there by the Nazis—Denmark and Norway.

The most salient feature about Denmark's wartime experience was the almost overnight evacuation of the country's seven thousand Jewish citizens and seven hundred of their non-Jewish relatives. It has been estimated that ninety-nine percent of Jewish Danes escaped the Nazis and less than five hundred fell into their hands. Alerted by a sympathetic German diplomat, George Ferdinand Duckwitz, that a giant pogrom was in the offing, the Danish Underground acted first. Duckwitz, who was an advisor to Werner Best, the Nazi Gauleiter in Denmark, learned of the impending *Aktion* on September 11, 1943, while on a trip to Berlin. The kickoff was scheduled for October 1, 1943, less than three weeks away. During his return to Denmark, where he had lived before the war and been stationed because he spoke fluent Danish, Duckwitz detoured to Sweden, met with the Swedish president and was assured the Swedes would take in any Danish Jews who could be rescued.

The Nazis had subjugated Denmark in April 1940. It had been Hitler's hope that the Nordic Danes, *Aryans* to the core, if treated leniently, would embrace his Nazi superman dogma. By the fall of 1943, having lost patience with the stubborn Danes, he decided to move at least against the Jewish population.

It is interesting to note that even after the mass escape, the less than five hundred Danish Jews and relatives were sent to the Theresienstadt concentration camp, where conditions were not as purposefully deadly as at, say, Auschwitz or Birkenau. The figure given of those from Denmark who died was fifty-one.

Afterward, Duckwitz tried to give credit to his superior Werner Best, an SS Obergruppenführer, by the way, for suggesting the escape route to Sweden. In any event, Best showed a sense of humor unusual for an SS officer. He declared that he had carried out the Führer's Final Solution. There were no more Jews in Denmark.

By September 1943, the Danish Freedom Council, the brain trust of the Underground, could count on more than twenty thousand supporters. When the Normandy landings occurred in June 1944, they were able to tie down German troops, who could better have been used in France as reinforcements to repel the invasion.

A story came out of Denmark about the heroism of the Danish king, Christian X, who did not leave the country. When the Germans tried to impose their usual anti-Semitic indignities upon the Danish Jews, he was said to have donned a yellow armband with the Star of David on it, as did most other Danes.

That narrative has been debunked to an extent by claims that Danish Jews never had to wear the hated star, nor did the King and populace ever do so. But every morning, King Christian would ride on horseback through the center of Copenhagen, alone, without bodyguards or any hint of security, and show himself in this silent support for the resistance of his countrymen.

It was said that when the great escape took place, some German soldiers looked the other way. This does bring to mind an incident reported to me by a close Danish friend, Finn Falck Madsen, when during the war, as a small boy, he and his mother were walking on the beach near their summer home at Rødvig and encountered a German soldier. Said Finn, who was violently anti-German, this man in green-grey uniform who spoke Danish seemed sympathetic in that he bewailed, almost in tears, the atrocities his fellow Germans were inflicting on people.

The impact of the Underground in Denmark was vividly brought home to me, when on a ferry taking my wife and me from Norway to Denmark, we met a young couple around our age then and became friendly enough so that he invited us to his parents' home to show us some souvenirs from the war. They included the pistol his father had carried (he had been a courier), and perhaps most memorable was an elegant white-painted house he pointed out nearby. There still lived, he said, a rich man who had collaborated with the Nazis. He had not been harmed after VJ Day but simply left in his quasi-mansion, shunned by all his neighbors.

In Norway's case, there was a goodly difference from Denmark. The latter is a small nation of two main islands and a swath of territory next to a piece of northern Germany. Norway, of course, is gigantic, stretching up into the Arctic Circle. It was much, much more conducive to conducting resistance warfare.

Nevertheless, there was never the counterpart in Norway to the Danish rescue of its Jews. The number of Jews was less than a third of Denmark's Israelite population. At least 775 of this very small minority was arrested by the Gestapo, of whom 742 were murdered in the camps and 23 more perished at the Nazis' hands. But the Norwegian Resistance was able to smuggle out 900 Jews, mostly to nearby Sweden but some by water to Great Britain.

Again, unlike in Denmark, the King Haakon VII and queen and royal family left the country, passengers on a British Navy cruiser. They remained in London, where a Norwegian Government-in-Exile was formed. Almost at once in the kingdom, a resistance group developed known as Milorg that was in touch with the exiles.

Entering the scene accompanying the Nazis on April 9, 1940, was a onetime Norwegian politician named Vidkun Quisling. With the Nazis' help, he mounted a coup and seized power in Oslo.

Quisling was not only an outstanding collaborator but his surname would become a worldwide synonym for "traitor" and is remembered so to this day. Nor was his rule on the Norwegian domestic scene an easy task. The underground fought back, and the German exacted brutal reprisals. One of them, the entire wiping out of the town of Telavåg, has been ranked with the much better-known slaughter at Lidice in Czechoslovakia and Oradour-sur-Glane in France.

The most daring of the Norse exploits was the destruction of the heavy water facility at the Vemork Hydro plant in the town of Rjukan.

A good sample of the atmosphere in Norway under the Nazis comes from a document in the WRB collection, emanating from a publication by the Quisling Norwegian Nazis, called *Fritt Folk*. It was a response to a broadcast by the Norwegian Government-in-Exile's minister, Terje Wold, and dated February 28, 1944.

The Norwegian quisling, not identified, fulminated as follows: "Terje Wold's speech on war criminals clearly inspired by the Jews was intended as part of the war of nerves. The whispering campaign is supposed to bring the speech to the Norwegian people, especially to National Socialists. Wold and his fellow refugees say that every member of the National Socialists is a 'war criminal' and will be punished. The most Semitic of our opponents look forward to heads rolling on the ground or 'on every Norwegian tree hanging one member of the National Socialists.' Others rejoice at the thought of deporting National Socialist members to Bear Island when the war is over . . . Nobody laughs more heartily at these gloomy predictions and nobody is more above them than the National Socialist member . . . Wold's Jewish statements on punishment and retaliation therefore have the same effect upon us as water on a duck's back . . . The 'war criminals' however refuse to be frightened either by the Minister of Justice Wold or by other mouthpieces of Jewry."

A final word about Vidkun Quisling, before he was executed in October 1945, after an extensive trial. "Believe me," he said, "in 10 years' time, I will have become another Saint Olav."

Who was Saint Olav?

It turns out he was a driving force behind the conversion of the pagan Norse to Christianity. In doing so, it was acknowledged that he used coercion and force.

Beatified (made a saint) in the year 1031, he was a quisling before Quisling, so thought Quisling.

Finally, we have two unlikely places in Europe where their resistance movements received money from the War Refugee Board—Germany and Hitler's birthplace, Austria.

In a list of its wartime expenditures, the War Refugee Board included an entry that might have seemed startling: $5,000 to Berlin, Hitler's capital. It was directed to an organization called *Freie Deutschland* (Free Germany). The recipient was N. Schwalbe, a Zionist connected to the Hahelutz group in Palestine.

What did *Freie Deutschland* do? When one thinks of resistance to the Nazi leader within Germany, the immediate connotation is the failed July 20, 1944, bomb attempt on the Führer's life at his bunker in East Prussia. But not much has been heard about anti-Nazi Germans' parachute jumps into the same East Prussia and committing acts of sabotage until they were caught and executed.

The White Rose was another small resistance operation in Germany. A brother and sister, Hans and Sophie Scholl, were its founders, and its main activity was creating and distributing anti-Nazi leaflets. The Scholls were eventually caught and executed, beheaded by guillotine. So were other members of the group. But some remained free and active until the end of the war. The last pamphlet they smuggled out was printed in the millions by the Allies and dropped by bombers over Germany.

As for Austria, there was the anti-Nazi Austrian Committee headquartered in Algiers. The War Refugee Board collections include a communication from its president, C. G. Mattersdorf, saying that the group was deeply moved by FDR's March 24, 1944, speech threatening punishment for German war crimes.

Herr Mattersdorf wrote that more than five hundred Austrians had been executed for aiding "deserters and refugees," but people still resisted. He also expressed the committee's hope that the American president would give Austrians forced to serve in the German Army who were now prisoners of war "a chance to take up arms in an Austrian army at the side of the Allies."

The Nazis' biggest Austrian opponent was Otto von Hapsburg, a descendant of the ruling family of the Austro-Hungarian Empire. Sentenced to death in absentia by the Nazis, Otto helped fifty thousand Austrians, including many Jews, escape the country as he had.

Eventually there were thirty thousand Austrians in exile in London. Also, some came to the U.S. like my friends Don and Tom Wallace (formerly Wallach von Puttkamen). Their family had been court Jews in Vienna, and their father was a famous war hero of World War I. Singlehandedly, he had captured many Russians, a feat for which he was made a Baron.

Finally, the Austrian Committee did get a chance to battle the Nazis. The fight took place in the North Tyrolean Alps five days after Hitler's suicide (April 30, 1945) and led to the capture of Castle Itter, a last-ditch Nazi stronghold.

Chapter Twelve

I ver Olsen, born in Norway, raised in New Hampshire, had already been working in the U.S. Stockholm Embassy as a financial attaché, before he was tapped to join the War Refugee Board in the autumn of 1944. His immediate superior was Harry Dexter White (the controversial alleged Soviet spy), who was then an assistant to Secretary Morgenthau at the Treasury Department.

To build upon the work he had to do, there had been previous efforts by a Hilel Storch of the World Jewish Congress, whose efforts in Sweden had been overseen by the Scandinavian country's chief rabbi, Marcus Ehrenpreis.

Therefore, it was no surprise that the creation of War Refugee Board in the United States "met with instant [positive] response in Sweden."

This was doubtless in part due to Sweden's place on the Baltic shore and that its focus could be on the saving of intended victims within neighboring Latvia, Estonia and Lithuania. Other ties were linguistic between Finns, the Latvians and the Estonians, whose difficult languages had common roots.

But what about ties to Hungary, which were to loom so large in the person of Raoul Wallenberg? True, the Hungarian language did have an affiliation with Finnish, Estonian and Latvian, but Iver Olsen, who had instituted the "hazardous rescue across the Baltic to Sweden," subsequently was ordered to send an operative to Hungary, which in March 1944 had been preemptively occupied by their former allies the Nazis.

Jews were being expelled to Warsaw and the aforementioned mass conversion Christianity was taking place.

It was stated that "a few Jews have left Hungary with the help of the Gestapo."

In the Swiss journal *L'Action*, published in Lausanne on July 28,

1944, it was printed that the rescue of the Jews of Hungary to neutral countries cost 40,000 francs for an old Jew and 5,000 to 10,000 francs on a sliding scale for children. A warning was also given that an advanced payment was never returned "under any circumstances." The balance of payment had to be delivered to a German official who would take charge of the consignment of Jews at the Swiss-German border. Those Jews released on payment of ransom, if they had money left, could even order ground transportation to Basel or by plane to Lisbon.

Before the German invasion of its erstwhile Hungarian partner, the Hungarian Government was said "to be anxious to improve their reputation in the eyes of the democratic world."

There were 12,000 Jewish refugees in Hungary at the time and also 3,000 from Poland, 250 from Croatia and a few dozen from Romania. They were only allowed to stay in Hungary "in connection with possibilities of immigration to Palestine."

The Hungarian situation raised its head during the second month of the War Refugee Board's existence. There was an attack on the WRB's activities there in the Jewish publication, *The Day*, by Dr. Samuel Margoshes who authored a column called *News and Views*.

John Pehle's masterful putdown in response was: "Dr. Margoshes's article in *The Day* March 1, 1944, is based on a purported conversation between representatives of an anonymous organization and myself, which appeared in *The Forward* for February 26, 1944 . . . Since no such conversation ever took place, there is no occasion for me to comment on the inferences, deductions and arguments that Dr. Margoshes makes on the wholly erroneous assumption that it did. Neither Margoshes nor any member of the Jewish press made any attempt to check *with me* the authenticity of a conversation I am alleged to have had with persons who for reasons that must appear clear to all, remain unnamed."

The perils of dealing with the press were later brought all the more sharply in connection with another reference he made to Hungary. The confidentiality of his OFF-THE-RECORD remark to an Associated Press reporter was flagrantly violated.

His embargoed remark, printed in contravention of all journalistic ethics, was as follows: "About 200,000 refugees in Hungary, nearly all Jews, may not live through the next few weeks."

Next a big headline in the *New York Post* proclaimed "200,000 FACE MASSACRE IN A FEW WEEKS." Then followed a story by *Post* staff correspondent William G. Player Jr., who had covered a joint press conference held by John Pehle and Ira Hirschmann. Player began negatively, his lead being: "Pehle and Ira Hirschmann . . . special representative in Turkey, indicated that the Board's work is virtually finished . . . On this basis, it is considered quite possible that, on next January 22, the Board will quietly allow itself to go out of business." Cited was the so-called Russell Amendment passed sometime earlier by Congress, which made it law that a government agency could not go more than a year on presidential funds.

The purpose of such a restriction obviously was to prevent the Executive Department from making an end-run around the congressional budgeting power.

This particular press conference had been called by the WRB to mark Hirschmann's return from the Middle East.

Pehle opened it with a subtle slap at the quick demise predicted for the WRB. Its work would *not be done*, he emphasized, "as long as there were still Jews and members of other persecuted minorities to be rescued . . . from places like Hungary, Poland, Slovakia, etc., and Germany itself."

Hirschmann did add, however, that the job of getting Balkan refugees to Turkey and then to Palestine was pretty much finished. Nevertheless, when asked about Hungary, the two men said they didn't want to discuss that subject.

In the reporting on Iver Olsen's work in Sweden, there were mixed intimations. He was described as "unusually active," most likely a good thing but also grumpy at times, particularly with cause. One particular irritation was his discovery that the Estonian Underground with which he had to work was composed of confirmed anti-Semites. His "general view of Swedish politicians and businessmen was not very flattering." He thought Anglo-American policy in Sweden was a failure, Sweden supplying Germany's military as "its most potent satellite, most particularly millions of tons of iron ore."

Actually, Olsen had been operating in Stockholm as a spy a year before the WRB was initiated—an economic spy sent by the Treasury Department to report on the Scandinavian economy and, as a sideline, lend a hand to the OSS. Later, a book by Meredith Hindley, *The Strategy of Rescue and Relief*, documented the use of OSS intelligence by the War Refugee Board in Sweden.

There are several versions of who first contacted Raoul Wallenberg for his epic mission to Hungary. Was it Herschel Johnson, the U.S.

ambassador to Sweden, or was it Iver Olsen? It's known that part of Olsen's assignment was to find someone from the neutral country to move legally to Hungary to aid its beleaguered Jews. Yet Ambassador Johnson was reluctant to give up too much of his authority. He demanded to see Olsen's reports to Washington prior to their being sent and reserved the right to comment to D.C.

It was generally reported that Johnson made the ask to Wallenberg, possibly after Iver Olsen had chosen him.

Various German exchange proposals were made through Sweden as well as Switzerland. Germans claiming to be close to Ribbentrop and Himmler conducted talks in Sweden. It was said of them: "The final German offers in Sweden had the clear marks of surrender feelers."

Members of the Swedish Jewish Mosaic Community organization flew to Berlin for a meeting with Reichsführer Heinrich Himmler on April 21, 1945.

As reported by Olsen, "Himmler arrived at the meeting at 2:30 AM, having just driven 80 kilometers from Hitler's birthday party. Probably no more bizarre scene could be staged to record Himmler's unconditional surrender to world opinion—a two hour drive through wrecked German roads and a conference until dawn with a Jew from Stockholm."

Right afterward, Olsen went on, "a few thousand Jewish internees were released from Ravensbrück and taken to Sweden by the Sweden Red Cross. It was another last minute gesture by the Germans."

Olsen's stint in Sweden was not without its detractors. A particular contretemps had taken place in January, 1945, after a representative of the World Jewish Congress, a Dr. Zelmanovitz, asked James R. Mann, then in London on WRB business, to join the Dutch underground leader Salamon Adler-Rudel, who had just been to Sweden, and Dr. Baron, "a prominent English businessman," and one of the World Jewish Congress's leading figures. The meeting was an arrangement for Adler-Rudel to tell Mann "that the WRB 'had done nothing constructive in Stockholm' and for Dr. Baron to say: 'everyone in the United States thought that things were being taken care of mainly because the War Refugee Board was set up.'"

Adler-Rudel started off the meeting by asking why the War Refugee Board wasn't doing more. Mann responded by soliciting concrete suggestions. "Thereupon, he [Adler-Rudel] proceeded to deliver quite a criticism of Iver Olsen's work in Sweden. He referred to an article in the Swedish Communist newspaper at the end of November 1944 'which attacked the Baltic rescue plan and said it had only served to save Lithuanian refugees from the Russians all of whom were Nazis or collaborators.' He claimed the Baltic rescue hadn't saved a single Jew."

Olsen rejoined that Jews in the area stayed in hiding fearing the rescue plan was "just another German trick to trap them."

Adler-Rudel shot back that "the Jews would have come if the right people were running the boats but the ones doing it were collaborationists."

A Miss Laura Margolis of the Joint Distribution Committee, becoming aware of the charges against Olsen, declared to Sir Herbert Emerson and Patrick Malin of the Intergovernmental Committee of Refugees that the accusation was most unjustified.

She also applauded the sending of Raoul Wallenberg to Budapest.

Eventually, James Mann was to replace Iver Olsen at the Stockholm post.

Another friction that bedeviled Olsen's mission occurred when Ecuador without warning cancelled the passports issued by its office in Stockholm. There were also some happy endings such as being able through the WRB to inform a Mrs. Marie Fischel of Beverly Hills, California, that her son had arrived safely in Stockholm from Finland. She was also told he needed funds and could obtain a Treasury license to send them through the Federal Reserve Bank of San Francisco.

June 9, 1944, is given as the date that Olsen met with Raoul Wallenberg and a group of Swedish Jews. Raoul had been working for a Swedish ship owner, Sven Salén, and his Hungarian Jewish business partner Kalman Lauer through whom he connected to Iver Olsen and the War Refugee Board.

The Wallenberg family's wealth derived from the Enskilda Bank, founded by Raoul's great-grandfather, augmented by the Saltsjöbanan Railroad they built to the flourishing beach resort at Saltsjöbaden, where they also owned the famous seaside Saltsjöbaden Hotel. American influence on the family was strong. Raoul's great-grandfather had traveled to the United States before the Civil War and been impressed by its growth and spirit. So, too, had the most important figure in young Wallenberg's life, his grandfather. His own father, an officer in the Swedish Navy, had died of cancer three months before he was born at his family's summer home on the island of Kappsta, one of the isles of an archipelago bordering Stockholm.

Gustaf Oscar Wallenberg had traveled to America like his father before him and had stayed three years with two Navy friends and served in the merchant marine. "It is because what both my father and grandfather found in America that makes me so eager for you to get *your direction in life*," he wrote his seventeen-year-old grandson.

For all of his American chauvinism, Gustaf was a man of the world as well, a diplomat posted as Swedish ambassador to Japan and China and finally Turkey, where he retired in Constantinople. One of his grandson-directive missives sent to Raoul's mother Maj for him is datelined *Constantinople* in January 1929. A year later, the name of the Turkish capital was changed to *Istanbul*. Renamed by Kemal Atatürk, the city remained Gustaf Oscar's residence until his death in 1937, which ironically occurred while on a trip to Sweden.

In the meantime, grandson Raoul had begun travels of his own. His experiencing of America commenced with his enrollment at the University of Michigan in the fall of 1931. Four years later, he was still writing from Ann Arbor to Grandfather Gustaf, declaring: "I am now entirely done with school . . . My thoughts of Sweden have been lying dormant for three years and now suddenly they are breaking out in full bloom and I'm actually dreaming about home every night. I long to get back to see my parents [his mother and stepfather] and everybody else."

Incidentally, one of his classmates was Gerald Ford, the future U.S. president.

He did also tell his grandfather: "It felt very peculiar to end these pleasant and interesting years of study in America."

During one vacation, Raoul was able to visit Mexico. In Mexico City, he visited his half-sister Nita and husband Carl Axel Soderlund. The adventure of motoring in Mexico was aptly described. On the entire 320-mile trip from Monterey to San Luis Potosi, he and his friend Woodard from Owosso, Michigan, encountered only three cars and experienced half a dozen flat tires. "Oddly enough," Raoul wrote, "we haven't seen any rattlesnakes except a dead one. The flora has consisted of nothing but cacti and desert vegetation the entire week. We are filthy from the mud and the dust and wading in dirty water and I have let my beard grown just for fun. So far, I've had a great time and I'm in excellent health."

He did, however, touch upon one of the pitfalls of a prolonged sojourn overseas. "My Swedish is getting worse and worse and I no

longer have a written command of it. When my cousin Gosta Nisser
was here during the fall term, he told me I spoke Swedish with an
American accent."

Notwithstanding which, his travel time away from Sweden
continued. Raoul's grandfather, with whom he did meet personally
in Sweden in June 1935, was promoting a trip to Colombia, South
America, for him, where he knew "our [Enskilda Bank's] best
commercial attaché," A. C. W. Winqvist, who lived in Bogota. But he
especially waxed eloquently about Palestine and how the Jews were
transforming it. "For the past fourteen years," he wrote Raoul, "I have
been in close contact with one of the directors of the Dutch bank,
Ervin Freund. This man has just been appointed by the Amsterdam-
based bank to head up its office in Haifa. This city has been growing
exponentially and so has Tel Aviv as the centers of activity for Jewish
immigrants who have already amassed a large fortune, as much as
twelve million pounds sterling, in the banks of the area. Freund has a
first class pioneering spirit. Grandfather was contemplating a future
Swedish bank in the Orient and expected Ervin Freund to be its
foreign director. It is true we are not yet there but we will get there
eventually. Gustaf Oscar advised his grandson Freund had told him
that after Raoul's trip to Colombia, 'Have him come see me in Haifa.'
Having worked for a commercial firm in Bogota, you would then have
the best possible view of the activity inside a frontier bank."

Soon Raoul was writing Gustaf Oscar from a ship anchored
outside of Cape Town, South Africa. Once ashore in the famous city,
with two companions he continued his stay there for more than six
months. In Cape Town, he had a job, no doubt thanks to grandfather,
at a firm called Anderne, Scott, Thesend Ltd. He seemed to be
doing scut work of a financial type, and the firm dealt in lumber and
construction equipment. He pulled no punches about his reaction to
Cape Town. His office was "no bigger than a closet" and Cape Town
"a disappointment."

Within a short time, he left that job and took another with the
Swedish South African Company that sold "paper wood products,
imitation leather and lots of other thing," where one of his traveling
buddies Björn Burchardt was employed. The director was Carl
Frykberg, with whom he was able to have "much closer contact than
with the gentlemen at Thesends where he was lower than a supervisory
stamp licker." His new boss even took him to climb Table Mountain,

the city's most noted landmark, a seven-hour trek that left him stiff all over and with aching feet. He also related to Gustaf Oscar that he was moving out of the Hotel Ho Remilt, which was crawling cockroaches.

Just before Christmas of 1935, Raoul received a letter from Gustaf Oscar stating his wish for him to leave Cape Town and proceed to Palestine as soon as possible. "The work in Cape Town is secondary," he wrote and the experience Raoul would receive from Ervin Freund was of "primary importance." By January 20, 1936, Raoul would write that he planned to take an Italian ship to Haifa via Dakar, Gibraltar, Marseille, Genoa and Alexandria, Egypt. It would land him in Haifa a month earlier than his original intentions. He confessed that "I feel sad leaving South Africa."

En route, while waiting for a ship in Genoa, he managed a side trip to nearby Nice in France, where his grandparents were vacationing. Afterward, he wrote Gustaf Oscar: "It was good to see you and grandmother. I was especially pleased to see how well you looked." Included was also an awkward apology about an argument he and Gustaf Oscar apparently had about interrupting his stay in Palestine to go back to Sweden. Needless to say, Gustaf Oscar won that round.

Incidentally, a miscommunication had greeted him in Haifa. He hadn't been expected for another year. No problem, though. It was arranged for him to live in a boarding house, "Jewish, of course, and rather good."

Considering Raoul Wallenberg's World War II heroic efforts in saving many Jews in Hungary, his experiences in 1930s Palestine bear a special interest.

"Haifa is brand new," he wrote his grandfather, "except that there are still some Arab huts. There are three times as many Arabs as Jews in Palestine."

"The Jews here are afraid of the Arabs who are beginning to wake up and dream of an empire . . . It is truly a gamble on the Jews' part to try to settle hundreds of thousands of Jews in this dry, stony little place surrounded by and already teeming with Arabs . . .

"The people at my boarding house are mainly German Jews and very nice and funny. One day one of them told me his brother had been murdered by the Nazis "

Raoul was impressed by what the Jews were achieving in Palestine. "So long as Palestine contains a Jewish population," he opined, "it drips with milk and honey and can support a large population." He had been told by his Jewish friends that their goal was four million. Modern-day Israel has more than exceeded that then doughty-seeming number.

This foretaste in Raoul's youth of the Jews—some of them at least—and their yearning for a restarted homeland in Palestine, their culture's original birthplace, was no doubt in the back of this thirty-six-year-old Swede's mind when he met on June 9, 1944, with Iver Olsen. Kalman Lauer, his boss at the Meropa Trading Products Company had made the introduction possible. They met at the Hotel Salsjöbaden, the resort gathering place the Wallenberg family had created. Whether or not the credit for this first contact with the War Refugee Board was through Olsen or U.S. Ambassador Herschel Johnson is immaterial. History was about to be made. Raoul Wallenberg left for Hungary and undying posthumous fame on July 2, 1944, not quite a month later.

Of course, the War Refuge Board had been attuned to Hungary prior to Wallenberg's effort for them there. Leon Kubowitzsky, a top official of the World Jewish Congress, was in touch with John Pehle on April 7, 1944, regarding broadcasts to Hungarians urging the Jews in the country "to abstain from wearing the yellow badges and to destroy all registers which may reveal the identity of Jews who are in hiding or who intend to hide." All lists of Jews should be destroyed and the Gentile population should be called upon to help.

Immediate action by the War Refugee Board was entreated.

Similar urgency was requested in a message from Lawrence Lesser to John Pehle regarding Polish ships "tied up in Stockholm with food and clothing . . . originally intended for Poland to provide relief for civilians. The British have prevented their departure. Take steps to allow ships to sail." So read the directive that no doubt was forwarded at once to Olsen.

Sweden also became an entrepôt for medicines sought by the Norwegian Underground.

Per Anger, one of Wallenberg's biographers, offers a narrative that starts on March 19, 1944, when he was awakened in Budapest by a phone call from his boss at the Swedish legation there. Minister Ivan Danielsson told him: "The Germans are taking over the city. Come at once!"

This preemptive action by the Nazis, although long anticipated, was nevertheless a shock in the "lightning speed" with which it was accomplished. The Germans were fearful that the Hungarian Prime

Minister Miklós Kállay would make a deal with the Allies and open themselves to an occupation of American and British troops to forestall the Soviets, who were rapidly advancing on their country. Although allied with the Germans on the eastern front, Kállay was no Nazi stooge.

The previous evening at the opening in Budapest of a patriotic opera, Per Anger and Minister Danielsson had attended a reception given Nicholas Horthy, the son of the de facto ruler of Hungary. There they learned that his father, Admiral Miklós Horthy, had received an immediate summons to Hitler's headquarters in East Prussia.

Then wrote Anger: "Hungary was occupied in a single morning."

Naturally, Kállay was forced from office and replaced by a pro-Nazi General Sztójay as prime minister.

The Ministry of the Interior, in charge of police and security, was put in the hands of two vicious anti-Semites named László Baky and László Endre.

Per Anger's description of what followed conveys the sense of swiftness with which things instantly changed in Hungary: "Mass arrests of suspected persons were undertaken with the help of Germans, who in various guises had resided in Budapest before the occupation in collusion with the Arrow Cross.

"The surprise was total . . . Everywhere there were traitors. Perhaps the most typical was Horthy's own private detective, Peter Hain, who now revealed himself as the Germans' man and . . . was appointed head of the secret police."

Another player in this scenario was the chief of press relations in the Hungarian foreign ministry, Ullein-Reviczky, who had been appointed Minister to Sweden the previous year by the Kállay government. Secretly his job *had been* to negotiate a separate peace deal with the Allies for his Axis country. Following the Nazi occupation of his homeland, he was allowed to remain in Sweden and even organize a "Free Hungary" movement.

Concurrently, the Nazis in Hungary installed their usual SS extermination operation targeting Jews especially.

Adolf Eichmann arrived in Budapest. Although nominally under the direction of a Dr. Edmund Veesenmayer, called at the time the "most powerful man" in Hungary, Eichmann would far surpass him in reputation as a cold-blooded murderer.

Per Anger has commented: "We in Budapest became witnesses

to something we had not thought possible in modern times . . . the systematic extermination of an entire race." (Although consistent with the nomenclature of that time, Jews are an ethno-religious entity primarily but not exclusively of the Caucasian *race*). He goes on: "I will never forget the day the ordinances went into effect. One could see Budapest's Jews, that is, every third and fourth person one met, marked with a yellow star as a sign that they belonged to a despised pariah class that had been doomed to destruction. Against the dark clothing most of them wore, the six-pointed star of a poisonous cadmium yellow seemed luminous . . . In various cases desperate measures were taken to save Jews in our circle of acquaintance. One Swedish businessman for example declared himself ready to marry a Jewish woman who had been arrested. Some tried to hide Jewish friends in his house or hire them pro forma as servants. But nothing helped."

Anger's narrative continues that after hearing fifteen thousand Jews had been taken to a brickyard on the outskirts of the city, he went there "to see it with my own eyes." He describes thousands of Jews "standing or lying tightly together who had been kept there for a week without food or drink or shelter from the weather . . . a terrible sight." Outside the brickyard, non-Jewish inhabitants of the district watched "as silent, frightened spectators," while an SS officer wielded a long whip. A train arrived with cattle cars and was shifted onto a spur. "The doors were opened and as many Jews as possible—men, women and children—were forced into the cars with kicks and blows." Crammed into each car were eighty or so persons, twice the number allowed.

On the last day of June 1944, King Gustav V of Sweden sent a plea to Admiral Horthy, protesting the Hungarian treatment of its Jews. It was said that reports of the brickyard horrors had prompted his action, which was stated: "Having received word of the extraordinarily harsh methods your government has applied to the Jewish population of Hungary, I permit myself to turn to your Highness personally to beg in the name of humanity that you take measures to save those who still remain to be saved."

Horthy apparently heeded the request and stopped the deportations to the Nazi death camps. But at the Swedish legation, the Swedish officials were soon besieged by frantic Jews, seeking Swedish protection, mostly in the form of Swedish provisional passports.

When the Arrow Cross government announced they would not recognize such documents issued after March 19, 1944, the date of the

German invasion, the Swedes fabricated more of the passports but back-dated them. The crush of work on the Swedish mission was such that Minister Danielsson called for reinforcements from the Foreign Ministry.

His urgent request coincided with talks going on in Stockholm between the Foreign Office, the World Jewish Congress, and the War Refugee Board.

These negotiations led to the dispatch of Raoul Wallenberg to Budapest, with the added expense being secretly underwritten by the WRB.

Having been appointed secretary of legation at the Swedish Mission, Budapest, Wallenberg arrived on the 9th of June, 1944, "equipped rather oddly for a diplomat," Per Anger wrote. "He was carrying two knapsacks, a windbreaker and a revolver." Anger quoted him as saying: "The revolver is just to give me courage," and Anger added, "in his usual joking way."

The Swedish diplomat and his wife had known Raoul Wallenberg "for a long time," describing their friend as "a clever negotiator and organizer, unconventional, extraordinarily inventive, cool-headed and something of a go-getter." Per Anger also added that Wallenberg was very good at languages and well-grounded in Hungarian affairs. At heart, he was a great idealist and a warm human being."

Photos show Raoul Wallenberg as a slender, partly bald man in his early 30s, with an intelligent, kindly look about him.

He was likewise an innovator.

"What documents have you issued the Jews?" was his first question to Anger.

Shown the existent forms—the provisional passports, the visa certificates and a Red Cross protection letter, Wallenberg replied he had an idea for a new and possibly more effective document. *Provisional* passports were turned into *protective* passports bearing the Swedish colors of blue and yellow on their covers, as well as the three-crown emblem of the northern kingdom.

Then Wallenberg set about reorganizing the rescue operation in cooperation with Danielsson and set up a new organization staffed mostly by Hungarian Jews. He had also convinced the Hungarian authorities to exempt his workers from having to wear the Star of David. It proved impossible to transport bearers of these passports to Sweden, since they would have to pass through Germany, but

Wallenberg convinced the Hungarian Government not to deport them. They were allowed to live in "Swedish houses" on the Pest side of the Danube and eventually fifteen- to twenty-thousand Jews were living in them.

Wallenberg, who had felt his work was over, was on the verge of returning to Sweden.

Worse would soon follow. The Arrow Cross, assisted again by the Nazis, staged another coup, and this one, on October 15, 1944, was successful. That same day, the Swedish legation had arranged for all Swedish women and children to be sent home. Horthy had to yield and resign, whereupon with his son Nicholas and the rest of his family he was held prisoner in Bavaria at Hirschberg Castle. There, he and his family were liberated by the Americans, except for Miklós who had been separated by the Germans and spent time at Mathausen and Dachau.

Ferenc Szálasi, the Arrow Cross leader, was installed as prime minister. Eichmann and his gang of murderers came back to take up where they had left off.

Per Anger wrote: "And for Wallenberg a hectic and dangerous period now began. Of all the War Refugee Board's agents, he was the one who faced the most dire danger."

Sooner or later, the Arrow Cross, who hated the Swedish diplomat with a passion, would catch up with him in an unguarded moment.

Their new atrocities were beyond unspeakable. A specialty was to rob the Jews, make them strip, march them naked (in winter weather), shoot them on the river banks, and dump the bodies in the water, thereby turning a portion of the Blue Danube temporarily red.

Under Wallenberg's watch, previous to the Szálasi government, an "international ghetto" had been established as a protective measure for the Budapest Jews. These were the "Swedish houses," and there were thirty of them eventually.

In the near distance during the same period, the drumbeats of the Russian advance grew ever louder. The Nazis could no longer use trains and cattle cars to transport their victims to the death camps. So they walked them.

"Women in high-heeled shoes and men without overcoats were forced to walk 125 miles to Hegyeshalom and the Austrian-Hungarian border—a whole week in bitter cold and snow, without food or rest."

Into this maelstrom of murder plunged Per Anger and Raoul

Wallenberg. They were seeking those on the death marches who carried Swedish "protective passports."

They followed the columns, witnessed the prodding and blows from the rifle butts the guards delivered, carrying food that they passed to the "ashen-faced victims." Bodies littered the roads. They reached Hegyeshalom and saw how the survivors were turned over to the SS unit commanded by Eichmann. He counted them by numbers. "Four hundred eighty-nine . . . checked!"

But before this transfer occurred, Anger and Wallenberg were able to rescue about one hundred Jews. Some had the Swedish protective passports. Others were liberated through sheer bluff. Per Anger wrote: "Wallenberg would not back down. He made repeated trips like this and succeeded in bringing back more intended victims to Budapest."

The Swedes felt they were in a race against time, trying to hold out until the Russians arrived. They offered bait to the Szálasi regime that recognition of their government could be forthcoming. "The Hungarian foreign minister, the fanatical and half-mad Baron Kemény rubbed his hands together in glee at the thought he would soon be able to appoint himself the Arrow Cross's first emissary to Stockholm."

Per Anger stated frankly: "Our greatest worry was Wallenberg's safety. The Arrow Cross hated him openly and intensely." Eichmann personally told a staff member of the Swedish Red Cross his intention to have the "Jew dog" Wallenberg shot.

What happened next was worthy of a thriller movie script. Tension could not have been higher as the denouement in Hungary approached. Through the Swedish legation in Berlin, a complaint was made against the threat to Wallenberg, demanding that the "SS command be ordered to respect mission members and other employees." The Swedes had been told that Heinrich Himmler "set a great deal of store by Swedish-German relations."

In reply, Herr Doctor Veesenmayer replied that Eichmann had "good reason to criticize" Sweden's actions in Hungary on behalf of Jews and called Wallenberg's behavior "far too unconventional and unacceptable." But he also advised that Eichmann's threat against Wallenberg's life should be seen as only a warning.

The most terrifying part of the drama was the interim between the Russian "rescuers'" appearance on the outskirts of Budapest and the Nazis' evacuation of the Hungarian capital. There could be a period when, as Per Anger put it, "the Nazi rabble would have a free hand."

So Per Anger, along with his superior Danielsson, sought out the Hungarian Underground resistance movement and asked for protection of the Swedish mission. They received assurance of an armed force and also fortified themselves by acquiring a pair of Russian sub machineguns.

In the meantime, the Swedish legation had been taken over by the Arrow Cross.

Wallenberg ("the ingenious one," Per Anger called him) provided the solution to their dilemma. He had friends in the Hungarian Ministry of the Interior and assisted by them was able to enlist ten Hungarian gendarmes, who then arrived (while Wallenberg stayed in the background) and relieved Arrow Cross men of their "guard duty."

Russian bombs were dropping on the city and shells exploding ever closer, from the Red Army artillery.

Per Anger wrote that the last time he saw Raoul Wallenberg was on January 10, 1945. The latter had turned aside his countryman's plea for him to stay on the Buda side of the Danube and chose to remain on the Pest side, where he had his office.

Before parting, the two Swedes paid a daring visit to the SS headquarters. A harrowing trip by automobile was held up again and again by dead bodies, dead horses, fallen trees and rubble.

Then into the devil's den, itself, they brazenly rode, to the commanding SS general's office. Wallenberg sought nothing less, in addition to protection of the Swedish mission, than equal protection of the Swedish houses that were succoring Jews. Per Anger reported that "the SS general listened skeptically but found it hard to conceal that he was at the same time impressed by Wallenberg."

The final words that Per Anger heard from his heroic friend were: "I'd never be able to go back to Stockholm without knowing that I'd done all I could do to save as many Jews as possible."

No Greek tragedy could match the pathetic irony of this real-life saga. It is undoubtedly one of the main reasons why his story stands out so prominently among the many tales of heroism that grace the annals of the War Refugee Board.

In Wallenberg's case, he escaped the revenge of the Nazi murderers only to fall victim to the paranoia and ideological savagery of his would-be rescuers, the Stalinist Soviet Russians.

So there remain only the images he has left us.

Wallenberg would arrive at the Budapest train station with a list of protective passport holders and snatch them from the Germans simply by acting in an authoritative manner. He was known to have organized "special expeditions" in which Aryan-looking Jews dressed in Arrow Cross uniforms raided camps and prisons and liberated numbers of Jews, saying they were taking them to deport to German death camps.

Per Anger witnessed Wallenberg's stopping the deportations of several thousand Jews at train stations, who had been removed from the Swedish houses, and saving others from the death march to Austria, showing up and blustering that they were under Swedish protection.

He bribed Arrow Cross officials. He used threats of postwar execution for war crimes. Conversely, he would promise others to have them pardoned by the Russians.

When Wallenberg got wind of an Arrow Cross plot to exterminate all Jews left in the capital city by bombing the ghetto, he rushed to the German commander General Gerhard Schmidhuber and demanded he stop the massacre; otherwise, Schmidhuber would be swinging on a gallows after the Russians arrived.

The bluff worked and the SS general stopped the planned mass atrocity.

Aiding him surreptitiously was the wife of that same mad fanatic Foreign Minister Kemény, Baroness Elizabeth Kemény (she had Jewish ancestry), who influenced her dotty husband to approve the life-saving protective passports. Her denials that her husband was pro-Nazi and that he saved many Jews fell on deaf ears after the war and, he was executed by the new Soviet Hungarian Government as a war criminal.

One little sidebar about the Baroness were rumors she was linked romantically to Raoul Wallenberg. She actually felt forced to declare she had not been his mistress. In all the writing about Wallenberg, there is no mention of any lady love.

Memoranda left by Wallenberg reveal actual names and places involved in the tragedy of Hungary and give a flavor of these events.

He wrote: "The parents of one of my informants were sent away in the direction of Poland on July 1 [1944]. For some reason, the train was returned to the infamous camp at Békásmegyer—as a result, it was thought, of Archbishop Serédi's intervention at the time . . . According to his [Wallenberg's informant], his parents were then half dead. They were later taken to Poland."

Another informant visited the departure point at Kassa on May 25, 1944, and was shown around by the person in charge, a Baron

Fiedler, who reported that "following an escape by several Jews, he had ordered their relatives held up by their feet and beaten around the crotch as a warning to those following behind."

The entire family of the owners of the Manfred Weiss Company "was permitted to leave Hungary, kept in Austria for a month and allowed to move on to Lisbon." Baron Alfonz Weiss, the director, Frans Mauther and George Kornfeld, however, were held hostage in Germany. The Weiss Company had been leased to a Hungarian company, then sold to the Gestapo for twenty-five years. "The company has thus been turned over to the Gestapo-Waffen SS and not to the Goringwerke."

Wallenberg revealed that deportations to the death camps were now on a "*small scale*." Every effort is apparently made to preserve secrecy. "Jews were transported without wearing stars of David," and the Swedish envoy cites a group sent from the Ostbahnhof on July 26, 1944, at 8:50 p.m. Even Aryans—more than 1500 of them—"mainly intellectuals" were shipped out from Kistarcsa to Hegyeshalom and on to Germany.

Wallenberg does give credit to Horthy for stopping some deportations. The Germans were trying to shield him from knowing their activities. The king of Sweden's intervention with Horthy also has been confirmed for stopping the transports, Wallenberg wrote.

An internationally famous scientist, Wallenberg said, told him how he had been loaded into a train carriage with vicious blows from which he still displayed a wound on his cheek. The heat inside the sealed car in the next four and a half days was unbearable. One person died before the border with Austria was reached, and two persons had gone mad.

At the end of July, Wallenberg reported, 330,000 Jews had been deported as of that date.

Another memo of Wallenberg's from the Swedish legation stated: "Christian labor is difficult to come by. Even the Gestapo has had to employ Jews."

At the end of September 1944, Wallenberg did a summing up of expenditures spent on assisting Jews—money for soup kitchens run by the Jewish Council—money to the Jewish orphanage at Vilma-Kiraly . . . purchasing food . . . totaling 765,000 pengoes.

Under *Results Achieved*, Wallenberg included: "My entire staff and their families, around 300 individuals, have been exempted from wearing the Star of David and from forced labor."

Another report—this time from Iver Olsen to the WRB a month after the war in Europe ended in May 1945—gives an outsider's view of Raoul Wallenberg and his contribution to the work of the War Refugee Board.

"Sufficient facts now appear at hand to support the conclusion that the rescue and relief activities initiated by the War Refugee Board from Sweden . . . saved the way for the saving of perhaps 100,000 Jews. The work of Raoul Wallenberg, actively supported by Minister Danielsson and his staff . . . was nothing short of brilliant—to say nothing of being highly courageous . . . Minister Danielsson informed Minister Johnson and myself that during their last weeks in Budapest, Raoul Wallenberg had to hide in a different house he was so hotly hunted by the Hungarian Fascists and the Germans."

A final note of Wallenberg's to his mother carries the shrieking irony of Greek tragedy.

"I have a feeling that it will be difficult to leave after the Russian occupation, so I doubt I will get to Stockholm until around Easter."

Chapter Thirteen

A post-mortem on the Wallenberg phenomenon is perhaps obligatory here. He has risen in stature above many others in Nazi-occupied Europe, even in Hungary, who shared the same risks of death he did in helping Jews to escape wanton slaughter. What makes his deeds so stunningly exemplary?

Was it sheer numbers? We have seen that Iver Olsen's final postwar report to the War Refugee Board a month after the war in Europe ended imprinted the number 100,000 Jews (with a "perhaps" caveat) that Wallenberg saved. Another diplomat in Budapest during the same period, Carl Lutz of Switzerland, is credited with saving 50,000 Jews using the same *protective passport* device that proved so successful for Wallenberg.

It was commented years later at the opening of a performance of *Wallenberg, A Musical*, in New York City that "While Oscar Schindler is a household name (due to the Steven Spielberg movie of 1993) . . . Wallenberg who saved more people [given as 100,000 in six months] is virtually unknown."

Conceivably the mystery and controversy concerning his fate after the Soviet liberation of Budapest led to the fomenting of a legend.

As late as 1981, he was reported still being alive in a Soviet gulag.

One of the last—if not the last person—to see Raoul Wallenberg alive in his own country was the Chief Rabbi of Sweden Marcus Ehrenpreis. They apparently met on July 5, 1944, just before Wallenberg left for Budapest.

Rabbi Ehrenpreis was a controversial figure among Jews in Sweden. His roots were in Galicia, then a province of the Austro-Hungarian Empire, which he left in 1914 to become the chief rabbi of Bulgaria. After a few years in Sofia, he was invited to become Sweden's chief rabbi, a post he held until his death in 1951.

Later, an extraordinary accusation was made against him because of his alleged actions in Sweden after the Nazis took power in Germany in 1933 and Austria in 1938. It was charged that he successfully FOUGHT AGAINST bringing Orthodox refugees from Latvia and Lithuania to Stockholm after these countries were overpowered by the Hitlerians, thus condemning them to certain death. How could a Rabbi, never mind a chief rabbi, commit such a horrific act?!

Possibly Rabbi Ehrenpreis's most energetic accuser was Manfred J. Lehmann, a New York and Miami Beach businessman and Jewish scholar, who had been born in Sweden and immigrated to the U.S. in 1940. He, himself, had been ordained an Orthodox rabbi and presents a vivid portrait of an all-too-Jewish trait—tradition, fierce backbiting between different pockets of Hebrew believers—most prominently the ultra-Orthodox (or *haredi*) and the liberal-minded Reform group, with a body known as the Conservatives in the middle.

Manfred Lehmann well illustrated this often diehard enmity and power struggle between the Orthodox and the Reform. In his telling of a tempest-in-a-teapot disputation between the two factions during his father Han Lehmann's days in Stockholm in the pre-war 1920s, the language is intemperate from the start. Rabbi Ehrenpreis, in Rabbi Lehmann's words, is referred to as "a rabid Reform rabbi," trained at an Orthodox yeshiva in Galicia. "however, his life was the story of a turncoat . . . Whatever was left of authentic Judaism in Sweden disintegrated under his leadership," Lehmann charged.

He also asserted that in World War II, Rabbi Ehrenpreis was chastised in the Swedish Parliament for "doing less than Christians to save German Jews."

To get down to brass tacks, such fury between fellow Jews may well have stemmed in this incidence from a bruising event in the past that had made the rift forever bitter. As Rabbi Lehmann relates it, the Stockholm Orthodox, needing more funds to support their ritual bath (called a *mikveh* in Hebrew) asked the Reform group for 1,500 Swedish kronor. The claim was that Rabbi Ehrenpreis had originally agreed to provide the money but then reneged and made a "devastating attack against the *mikveh*." Years later, this petty (but not to the participants) brouhaha was still being vented.

Whether Wallenberg had any inkling of such a background when he took leave of Rabbi Ehrenpreis, who was also chairman of the Swedish Section of the World Jewish Congress, which helped fund the War Refugee Board, cannot be known Nor, naturally, could he foresee that the rabbi would die postwar in Saltsjöbaden, the seaside resort his family had helped develop.

Equally unknown of course was his own fate that lay ahead.

It might be argued that his bravado in accomplishing what he did in Hungary helped him to become legendary. There is a description of one of his daring acts that paints him as a sort of Swedish Scarlet Pimpernel in more modern times. A trainload of Jews was about to leave the Budapest central station for Auschwitz. Wallenberg arrived, climbed up onto the train roof and commenced handing out protective passports to Jews in cars that had not yet been sealed. The Germans ordered him down. The Arrow Cross started shooting at him. He was later to say he thought they were deliberately aiming too high, apparently impressed by his courage. After handing out the passports, he ordered the holders of them to leave the train and walk to nearby automobiles bearing Swedish colors.

Wallenberg saved dozens of intended victims this way. The Germans and Arrow Cross were so dumbfounded and flustered that they let him get away with their once-doomed victims. So too thought Sandor Ardir, one of his drivers, who provided the description of this dazzling act of the Swedish diplomat.

One of the people Wallenberg saved was sixteen-year-old Tom Lantos, who emigrated to the U.S. and later became an important U.S. Congressman from the State of California. He ended his fourteen terms by becoming chairman of the House Foreign Affairs Committee. Lantos said that his survival in Hungary "was due in part to Wallenberg and the protective passports . . . This was like my declaring you to be the prima donna of the Saint Petersburg ballet, it had no validity but these miraculous worthless pieces of paper worked."

One of his first acts as a Congressman was to introduce legislation that made Raoul Wallenberg an honorary citizen of the United States.

He also became a member of the International Raoul Wallenberg Foundation and was the first and to date only Holocaust survivor in the U.S. Congress.

As a Hungarian teenager, he escaped the labor camp where he'd been interned, fought with the underground in Budapest, and lived with his aunt in one of Wallenberg's Swedish safe houses.

Most likely at the initiative of Representative Lantos, the Congress of the United States posthumously awarded Raoul Wallenberg its Congressional Gold Medal.

Underlying ties between Wallenberg and the American World War
II effort contain various references to his alleged ties to the OSS (Office
of Strategic Services), the U.S. agency working with the underground
organizations in Nazi-controlled countries and Germany, itself.

Wallenberg's name apparently has been found in the U.S. National
Archives on a list of OSS operatives.

On November 7, 1944, it is claimed, the OSS Secret Intelligence
Branch in Bari, Italy, admitted that Wallenberg was an "unofficial
liaison" between the OSS and the Hungarian Independence Movement
(MFM).

Wallenberg was known to have ties to Gaza Soos, a high-ranking
officer of the MFM. Soos was only to be contacted through the Swedish
legation. Communications from this Hungarian Underground group
were sent to Stockholm, first to Iver Olsen who transmitted them
to Washington. Olsen, we have seen, had a strong hand in recruiting
Wallenberg for his dangerous mission.

There has long been speculation that the Soviets learned about
Wallenberg's connection to the OSS and considered him an American
spy. Since they were still allied with the U.S. at the time (January 1945),
his arrest by them had to be kept top secret, and even postwar, they
were denying they knew anything about the Swedish diplomat, alleging
they understood he'd been killed during the battle to liberate Budapest.

Dissatisfied with what they considered Soviet prevarication,
Wallenberg's mother and stepfather insisted he was very much alive—
even after the Russian Government later announced he had died in
Moscow's Lubyanka Prison in 1947. They searched and searched, and
finally in 1979 despairingly took their own lives, two days apart from
each other. At their request, however, the hope that Raoul really still
lived was to be kept until the year 2000.

It is interesting to discover that Raoul wasn't the first choice for
the Hungarian mission. It was offered to Count Folke Bernadotte, a
noted negotiator who was assassinated in that capacity several years
later by Jewish extremists, but the Hungarians rejected him. Kalman
Lauer, a member of the search committee, then suggested his business
partner Raoul Wallenberg, who knew Hungary and even spoke its
difficult language. Objections were raised that he was too young and
inexperienced, until Lauer wore them down with his insistence.

Wallenberg, true to form, set his own terms for doing the job.
Although he would hold the somewhat exalted diplomatic post of

first secretary, he wanted to avoid all paperwork and protocol. His memo to this effect was deemed "so unusual," it was sent to the prime minister, who consulted with the king before agreeing to Wallenberg's not unreasonable demands.

It didn't take him long in Budapest to arouse the intense ire of the SS under Adolf Eichmann and most particularly the dire hatred of the Arrow Cross.

Among survivors less known than Tom Lantos was Agnes Mandl Adachi, a young Jewish woman whom Wallenberg personally knew, since she worked at the Swedish legation. It seems that the Arrow Cross had devised a diabolical form of execution for its enemies. They would tie three victims together, cart them to the Danube, shoot the middle person and all three would topple into the ice-filled water, and the two left unscathed but tethered would presumably drown. However, Agnes, who was now hiding in the Swedish legation, would go to the site with doctors and nurses in cars. The Hungarian fascists were too busy "roping and shooting" to notice them. With three men to assist her, they would latch ropes to icicles that those in the water could cling to and be pulled out. It was estimated they saved fifty Jews from certain death this way.

Another among the rescuers of Jews in Budapest was Monsignor Angelo Rotta, the papal nuncio in Hungary. Previously in Bulgaria he had saved many of that Balkan country's Jews by supplying them baptismal certificates. But it was in the more frenetic period of 1944 to 1945, when transferred to Budapest, that his efforts became better known. He helped establish the Hungarian capital's International Ghetto, where at least 25,000 were sheltered. The Arrow Cross thugs did raid into the Ghetto and murder Jews there, particularly as the Russians inexorably advanced. Upon Wallenberg's arrival in Budapest, "Rotta relaxed his prerequisite of baptism [for Jews in return for help]. A lot of his [Rotta's] efforts . . . were successful because of his collaboration with Wallenberg."

It was Rotta who delivered the Vatican's first official protest against the treatment of the Jews in Hungary. "The Holy Father," he said, "deeply regrets the occurrences" and that Hungary's persecution was "creating conflict with Evangelist teachings."

Angelo Rotta, postwar, was awarded inclusion on the Israeli Government's prestigious honor list of Righteous Among the Nations.

Also noted for his rescue work in Hungary was the Italian

businessman Giorgio Perlasca, who saved more than five thousand Jews from deportation to the death camps.

He might have been as an unlikely candidate for this distinction, given his earlier record as a stalwart Italian Fascist. Prior to World War II, he fought in the conquest of Abyssinia and on the Franco side in the Spanish Civil War. In fact, although Italian, he was granted by the triumphant rightwing government in Spain a *safe conduct* pass to Spanish embassies anywhere in the world.

Perlasco had worked in the Balkans, purchasing meat for the Italian Army. In doing so, he held diplomatic status. However, once Italy surrendered to the Allies in September 1943, he chose to stay loyal to the king and the Badoglio government that had deposed Mussolini. His disillusion with Il Duce had long since set in.

On a trip to Hungary as diplomat in 1944, he was arrested by the Arrow Cross but confined in a special castle prison reserved for VIP prisoners. Escaping from this relatively cushy confinement, he took refuge in the Spanish Embassy in Budapest, calling upon his credentials of having fought for Franco. He even changed his first name to the Spanish *Jorge*. There is a memorial to him in Zaragoza, Spain, where he is referred to as *"el Schindler español."* He worked together with the Spanish consul Ángel Sanz Briz in smuggling Jews to safety. Involved with him, too, was a sympathetic Hungarian police officer named Batisfalvy.

Other no less heroic activists in Hungary 1944 to 1945 included Tom Veres who was sheltered in the Swedish legation, became active in Wallenberg' rescues, using his photographic skills to take full-faced passport pictures for the protective passes. Edith Ernesta was one of the super-Aryans employed in a Swedish villa located next door to Gestapo headquarters. A Mrs. Adachi, also a coworker, declared that Raoul Wallenberg had "the most beautiful eyes she'd ever seen." Others cited as helping in the effort were Prince Esterhazy, a Father Hummell and Tibor Baranski, later a Righteous Among the Gentiles designee, who had studied for the priesthood and also postwar was a member of the U.S. Holocaust Memorial Council. Baranski worked closely with Monsignor Motta Rotta and at the age of twenty-two was Executive Secretary of the Jewish Protection Movement, a Catholic organization in close touch with Wallenberg.

Those mentioned, plus Wallenberg and a Swiss attaché named Harold Feheler, met together in Budapest and sent a collective memo to the Royal Hungarian Government (which the Nazis had kept in place under a regent, their quisling puppet Szálasi). It sought to have them "impede transfers of Jews." Receiving no reply, a month later just before Christmas, they wired a second joint diplomatic cable.

Martyrs existed, too, for example Sára Salkaházi, killed by the Arrow Cross and decades afterward beatified. It was the first beatification in Hungary since that of King Stephen in 1083. Sára was shot alongside four Jewish women plus a fellow Christian coworker and dumped into the Danube River.

Restrained by the Germans and their own fierce anti-Semitism, the Szálasi fascists may have seen the dire future that lay ahead of them and did not deign to answer any pleas made to them. If such was the case, these thugs perhaps decided to enjoy their fleeting moments of total power in a state of gleeful madness in which wholesale murder seemed perfectly justified, and the more victims the better.

Comeuppance was not far off. Ferenc Szálasi, once a captain on the Hungarian Army's General Staff in peacetime, had secretly joined a racist party and then created a political party of his own—the National Will—a forerunner of the Arrow Cross, of which he became the ultimate leader. For the last three months of the war, Szálasi was Hungary's Chief of State.

Then he fled Budapest as the Soviets, with help from the Romanians who had changed sides, encircled the city. Fleeing north, the uprooted Hungarian dictator reached Szombathely, arriving on December 9, 1944. The following March he was in Vienna, then still in the hands of the Nazis. Eventually, he went to Munich.

His luck finally ended there in Bavaria. The Americans captured him. Per agreement with the Soviets, Szálasi was shipped back as a prisoner to Budapest, tried and found guilty of war crimes and hanged on March 12, 1944. Or rather he was somewhat gruesomely *hanged* Hungarian-style—essentially garroted (strangled) while tied to a post, a technique euphemistically called "the short drop."

Such straight-out justice could be savored by those who learned about it at the time.

But in the long run, while war memories faded, the ultimate triumph may have been achieved by the remarkable rise of the Raoul Wallenberg legacy. Even in this second decade of the twenty-first century, his memory is still celebrated.

A distant second-place rival has been ascribed to the Portuguese consul in wartime Bordeaux, France, who "came to be known as the Portuguese version of Raoul Wallenberg," according to Neill Lochery in his book, *Lisbon.* Sousa Mendes has been credited with having saved thirty thousand Jews. However, it is generally conceded that this is far too large a number, since he was early on recalled to Lisbon by an angry Oliveira Salazar, the Portuguese dictator.

In writing about this situation, author Lochery finally honestly admits: "It would be more prudent, if a little cynical, to regard Sousa Mendes as a 'Wallenberg Lite' rather than to talk of him in the same context as the Swedish diplomat."

Princeton professor Arno J. Mayer's 1988 book *Why Did The Heavens Not Darken?* joined in the chorus of kudos to Wallenberg. Example: "Raoul Wallenberg became exemplary in this regard. The young scion of a prominent Swedish family, Wallenberg resolved to use his position as an attaché of the Swedish legation to extend unsparing help to the imperiled Jews of Greater Budapest while arranging to issue special travel papers for them. The Swiss, Spanish and Portuguese engaged in similar if less intensive efforts and so did the papal nuncio, especially on behalf of baptized Jews (440)."

No mention that Wallenberg was in Budapest at the behest of the War Refugee Board and supported by its funding.

So plentiful have been the honors heaped posthumously on Raoul Wallenberg by countries across the globe that they cannot all be listed. Here is a sample:

- Nominated twice for the Nobel Peace Prize;
- Australia—made its first honorary citizen; an Australian postage stamp featuring him; Frank Vajda, naturalized Australian, one of those he saved;
- Canada;
- Georgia, under the Soviet Union;
- Germany, both East and West;
- Hungary—made an honorary citizen in 2000;
- Israel—made honorary citizen in 1986, and honored at Yad Vashem as Righteous Among the Nations;
- Peru—a park bearing his name in Lima;
- Russia—memorial in the courtyard of the Rudomno Library of Foreign Languages and Institute of Special Pedagogical and Psychology in Saint Petersburg;

- Sweden—memorial in Stockholm in 2000, presiding was UN Secretary Kofi Annan and his wife, who was Raoul Wallenberg's niece;
- United Kingdom—honored Wallenberg in 1997;
- United States—Made an honorary U.S. citizen, 1981, the only other person so honored being Winston Churchill; Raoul Wallenberg Plaza across from the United Nations building in New York City; a sculpture called *Hope*; Colorado, Connecticut, Illinois, Iowa, Maine, Maryland, Michigan, Nebraska, Nevada, New Jersey, New Mexico, West Virginia and Wyoming celebrate Raoul Wallenberg Day; there have been attempts in Congress to establish one in every State; 2012—Congress voted Wallenberg its Congressional Gold Medal.

In Hungary during the same period, additional attempts were being made *in relief and rescue*. Two names stand out here: Joel Brand and Rudolf Kastner, or in Hungarian, Rezsö Kastner. Their ties to the War Refugee Board were not—explicably so—broadcast to the world. Yet a mention does exist in the following paragraph from holocaustresearchproject.org: "Moshe Sharett and Ira A. Hirschmann, of the War Refugee Board who subsequently interviewed Joel Brand, were both impressed by him. Immediately they informed top Jewish Leaders in the Yishuv and to leading members of the American and British governments."

Some explanations: *Yishuv* is the term for the Jewish population living in Palestine prior to the establishment of the State of Israel. We are now into a complex drama—one might see it as a tragedy—that played out in the effort to save the surviving Jews of Europe and, as it turned out, all Jews living, sometimes for centuries, in Muslim countries. Moshe Sharett (his last name was originally Shertok) was a top official of the Jewish Agency, a rump Jewish government in Palestine, when the British controlled the Holy Land.

Thus, even before Raoul Wallenberg set foot in Budapest in the summer of 1944, and also prior to creation of the War refugee Board that January, the Jews in Hungary had set up a an organization in 1943 known as the Budapest Aid and Rescue Committee. This activity, too, predated the German occupation of Hungary of mid-March 1944. But it was just this act that galvanized the putative skeleton structure of Hungarian Labor Zionists into action.

Commanding the SS in Hungary was the later-to-become internationally infamous Adolf Eichmann. Knowing of Nazi venality, Rezsö Kastner set about trying to bribe one of Eichmann's staff into allowing six hundred Jews to proceed to Palestine in return for four million marks. This offer was refused, but Kastner didn't give up. He had contacts with the Abwehr, the German Army intelligence operation and used them to revive the exchange dialogue. By this stage of the war, high-ranking Nazis like Heinrich Himmler were looking to lessen their guilt by surrendering on the Western front (while continuing to fight in Russia). It wasn't money they wanted; it was war material like ten thousand trucks or necessities in short supply such as two million cakes of soap and two hundred tons of tea and coffee. Eichmann was actually planning more deportations, when Himmler ordered him in mid-May 1944 to contact Brand, who in turn asked for the Germans to show good faith by releasing 600 to 1200 Jews from their death camps.

Himmler essentially agreed in principle.

Intervening at this point was what can be termed a *bizarre* incident involving Joel Brand, who had gone to Turkey en route to Palestine to confer with Moshe Sharett, when he was arrested by the British and kept interned in Cairo.

The deportation of Jews from Hungary to the Nazi death camps thereupon recommenced.

Rudy Kastner, however, soon provided a new proposal that he used to help restart the talks.

It might be here that the War Refugee Board's hand can be deduced although never acknowledged. Money for the deal was proposed to come from the Joint Distribution Committee, which of course was the WRB's prime funder.

The American strategy in Washington was to string out these negotiations as long as possible to stave off the Nazis' actual intended extermination actions.

SS Major Kurt Becher was, we know, the Nazis' bargainer. Saly Mayer also became involved on the Allied side. Roswell McClelland, the WRB's man in Switzerland, was designated President Franklin Delano Roosevelt's "personal emissary." More than one thousand Jews, who were supposed to have been exchanged but were kept penned up at Bergen-Belsen, finally secured their release and were allowed to proceed to Switzerland.

Besides, the war in Europe was coming to an end.

On April 30, 1945, Hitler committed suicide.

The political complexities underlying much of this turmoil and continuing afterward especially concerned the ambiguous British policies regarding Palestine. There is no question that to placate the Arab population in the Holy Land, they unilaterally abrogated the Balfour Declaration proclaiming a Jewish homeland and kept Jewish immigration to a bare minimum as announced in the notorious White Paper of 1939. But where else postwar could the surviving Jews of Europe go? Back to Poland? Impossible? Back to Germany?—not likely. Back to their countries where they had suffered? No one wanted them in any numbers. People who had stolen their property resisted. Even in the United States (I know by experience) anti-Semitism persisted even after the Nazi defeat. So the saved Jews and their compatriots throughout the world took matters into their own hands. They created their own country of Israel and fought several wars to avoid the destructive promise of another Holocaust as proclaimed by Muslim factions.

By then, the War Refugee Board had ceased to exist. Since its work was technically done, the Truman administration supported its elimination.

But that story is yet to come.

My own personal brush with the events in Hungary was in Maine listening to a Jewish survivor of what happened there lecture and reading her book. She was Judith Magyar Isaacson, living in Lewiston, Maine, with her husband Irving Isaacson, called Ike by everyone, a captain in the OSS she met overseas after liberation from the Nazi camps I first heard her when a member of the Maine Legislature, and she spoke to us. Her maiden name of *Magyar* is also obviously how Hungarians refer to themselves in their own language.

The autobiographical book she authored, *Sarah's Seed*, published in 1990, contained two photographs of her taken in September 1987 at a reunion with fellow female inmates, who had been with her in the Hessisch-Lichtenau camp. In these printed snapshots, she is slender, even svelte, her blonde hair cut short, and possibly among the tallest of this group of survivors who had worked in a nearby munitions factory.

Her vivacity clearly shines through in her dazzling grin although she has then just passed sixty. Her earlier photos shows her with dark brunette hair, shoulder-length. Illustrated in her book is a group photo of women at a morning lineup, left standing wearing dresses, but bald, their heads closely shaven.

Kaposvár, the town where Judith Isaacson grew up, is described by her as "a speck on some maps, a void at most." To her, as she put it, "Kaposvár was my home, my universe." Before World War II erupted, it seemed like Kaposvár was an island of tranquility, despite the new intensity of Arrow Cross's activity. Judka Magyar's favorite teacher, Dr. Biczo, a non-Jew, simply wrote them off. "Some lunatic fringe, no doubt . . ." he told her. "Do you know, Magyar, how many Nyilasok [Arrow Cross] there are in all of Kaposvár? . . . No more than one hundred surely. In a population of thirty-five thousand . . . They pose no danger."

On the other hand, there was a professor named Kovary who was openly anti-Semitic. The students had secretly nicknamed him *Csutka*—Adam's Apple—because that protrusion was so noticeable when he ranted, and in Judith Isaacson's words years later, "bobbed up and down like a yo-yo."

In one memorable outburst in her class, Kovary outdid himself. "Tell me, you offspring of blushing idiots," he shouted at his students, "where did these worthless Jews come from? Stay mum and I'll flunk you out of here without another chance. One less Jewish intellectual to worry about."

He was answered, reluctantly if bravely, by a gawky, shy Jewish girl named Bode Winternitz, who said that "the Israelites in northern Hungary are descendants of the Khazars. We Jews of Somogy Country pride ourselves on our *Aryan* heritage."

"You improvising donkey with your elephant's trunk," the teacher spat out when she'd finished.

That was just too much invective, particularly the elephant's trunk analogy to the so-called Jewish nose, and the kids talked back. Particularly helpful for them was the contribution from non-Jewish classmates, perhaps a harbinger of the Righteous Gentiles to come. One Christian girl who rose to speak was Agi Toronyi, whose father was a prominent doctor in Kaposvár. "Professor, sir," she addressed Kovary, "we learned about the Khazars in first form. They were a nomad tribe who adopted Judaism before they joined the Magyars in the occupation of present day Hungary."

The *professor sir*, shot back: "The Khazars are gone. Wiped out! There isn't any mention of them in your textbooks."

But one Jewish kid wasn't allowing this prejudiced pedagogue to have the last word. Up jumped Evi Karpati who cried out passionately: "They weren't lost for a thousand years . . . We still had them in first form!"

The laughter this witty remark provoked was followed seconds later by the bells for recess. Professor Kovary stormed out of the room.

We are presented in *Seed of Sarah* with a vivid word picture of what it was like for young Jutka Magyar in the period just preceding the German invasion of Poland in September 1939.

"The year 1939 started with a jolt," she writes. "In January, my Uncle Feri [in the United States] sent us three affidavits . . . On the one hand, he promised to finance my college education; on the other, he discouraged us from coming altogether . . . 'Be prepared to work as a dishwasher,' he cautioned. He blamed the still lingering Depression for a lack of good jobs."

So began a series of anxious debates about what course the Magyar family should take. Jutka's father insisted they should leave Hungary. "Hitler means war," he declared. "I've got to get you out."

But when he went to the American Embassy in Budapest, he came back utterly frustrated. "Hungarians are on a five year waiting list. Five years with Hitler at the door."

Ironically, the father was considered Czech, since he'd been born in that part of the Austro-Hungarian Empire. He could go on the Czech quota but insisted his wife and daughter come with him and overstay illegally.

These very bourgeois females of the family protested: "They'll put us all in jail. Your father would turn in his grave."

"I was 18 when Hitler occupied Hungary," she informs us. Furthermore, she describes that morning of March 19, 1944. Planes were flying over Kaposvár. *The Americans!* she thought jubilantly. But after rushing to tell her mother, the planes were lower and more visible. Her parent silently pointed to the sky. The aircraft, it now could be seen, had the black *Balkenkreuz* imprinted on their wings.

On April 6, 1944, all Hungarian Jews and "Christians designated as Jews" were ordered to wear the yellow star on their left breast.

In short order, young Jutka was adjusting to the unhappy new situation or rather changing her very persona in order to cope. "The Germans' occupation soon transformed me from a law-abiding schoolgirl into a devil-may-care subversive."

The full brunt of the horror that had descended upon them was felt once the Magyar family had been ordered for deportation.

"It was a humiliating day," and Judith describes it in terse detail. "At the synagogue, male officials examined our packs, ruthlessly grabbing anything that took their fancy. Grandmother Vago presented her 'certificate for good hospitality,' but to no avail: we lost our soap, our hand-knit sweaters and Nana Klein's sealskin coat with her jewelry in the shoulder pads. In a separate room we women underwent searches by police matrons. Did they really think I would hide gold in my vagina? The military police picked up all furloughed Jews at the synagogue, to rejoin their forced labor units. It was a last-ditch attempt by the Hungarian Government to keep them within our borders . . . Just before nightfall, we rode, standing up, in an open motorcade to the municipal stables of my hometown."

Her next horrendous experience was to be packed into a group of seventy-five people inside a smelly cattle car. She was sitting on her backpack when an SS officer bolted the door from outside. The train started up. Nobody had any idea where they were headed. Jutka was able to peer through a splintered crack in one wall. She watched the station sign for Kaposvár appear and disappear. She told her mother: "I never want to see Kaposvár again."

The next railroad placard she saw after more than three days of travel, during which one woman went mad, was an unfamiliar name: Auschwitz.

The first thing Jutka noticed when the car door opened was a strange odor "like burning skin . . . like chickens singed of feathers."

Then, the selection process began. Women of forty or older and children under sixteen were parted from the others. Jutka's mother lied and said she was thirty-eight. Both she and Jutka were sent to one side. The rest were told they were going "to the showers."

Next, the two women had their heads shaved.

Jutka ran into a bald schoolmate and at first sight they didn't recognize each other. The girl, named Evi, was supposed to be on her honeymoon.

They were taken off to Birkenau Lager (a subsidiary of Auschwitz) and placed in BIII barracks. The sardonic nickname for it was "Mexico"—the poorest of the poor. A German guard referred to it as a *Vernichtungslager*—an *annihilation camp*. The word was that no one lasted there more than three weeks.

Jutka met another friend from Kaposvár named Ilona. The two of them contemplated suicide, just rushing headlong into the electrified fence that surrounded them. Magda, another friend who joined them, thought hanging would be easier.

Unexpectedly, Jutka was given the chance to be a *kapo*—Jews who assisted the Nazis and received better treatment. Equally unexpectedly, Jutka turned the offer down. "Without the whip," (and the armband as well she'd been given) she could declare, "I felt free! (80)"

A clipping from a German newspaper dated July 22, 1944, mysteriously came into the hands of the prisoners. It reported the attempted assassination of Hitler two days earlier.

When friend Evi asked if the item had reached them through "someone from the underground," she was immediately warned: "Never refer to them."

At perhaps the most dreadful moment of their enslavement, Jutka and her mother found themselves facing the diabolically sadistic Doctor Joseph Mengele, who was about to separate them. Instead of obeying, Jutka and her mother ran. Mengele went for his pistol, but his attention was deflected by a "statuesque blonde" prisoner appearing before him, and they miraculously escaped.

Once more these three were put on a train. Neither food nor water, but without the packs they were able to lie down.

A day or so later, they arrived at Hessisch-Lichtenau and assigned to become laborers working on manufacturing artillery shells.

It was a heart-stopping moment when she was singled out at the morning lineup, identified by the kommandant because of the blue kerchief she was wearing over her shorn pate. What she couldn't know then was that he had ordered his female Jewish kapo: "*Suchen zie mir ein saueres madchen . . .*" Find me a clean girl.

Her immediate terror was that she would be raped by that uniformed brute in "puffed out breeches."

The kommandant drove her to a nearby house now lighted as dusk fell. She was told to wait inside the entry.

The suspense was no doubt beyond excruciating, until a young German woman appeared and pointing at Judka's filthy dress, humphed: "Are you the clean girl we were supposed to get?"

What might be termed "comic relief" put an end to this intolerable mental torment. From a nearby bedroom, the kommandant barked, "What's keeping you, *liebchen?*"

The answer: "I must instruct her."

Instruct in sex?

No. Teach Judka how to wash, wax and polish the dwelling's beautiful parquet floors.

It seemed that the "clean girl" the Nazi wanted was a "cleaning girl."

But the reprieve lasted only overnight. The next day Jutka was shipped back to the ammunition factory to work. and another Jewess took her place to clean for the kommandant. There seemed to be some favoritism here.

The next blind bullet Jutka dodged would have been fatal, it turned out. The kommandant announced: "Two hundred prisoners are needed at a nearby camp," and then added, "for easier work. Anyone over 35 or disabled may also volunteer."

Jutka's gut instinct was to stay. But in the end, she and her mother and a friend Magda did volunteer. The rest of this story illustrates the instant life-or-death choices faced by these inmates in the unknown unraveling of their fate.

The kapo in charge of them was a woman named Manci. Suddenly, she turned to Jutka's mother and muttered: "Grab your daughters, Mrs. Magyar [Magda was posing as Jutka's sister] and run!"

The trio dashed back to their barracks. The transport of 206 women left without them. None of those "volunteers" were ever heard from again.

Liberation did not come easily. When the Germans retreated, they took their captives with them—in cattle cars once more. Just ahead of the Americans advancing in Germany, the railroad cars passed through Weimar, the scene of a short-lived German republic after World War I and before Hitler. Off they continued to Leipzig, a major city farther east. This was in April 1945. The Nazis were exulting over the sudden death of FDR on April 12. One of them crowed in Jutka's presence, "Roosevelt is dead. Our Führer will win!"

In an American bombing raid on Leipzig, the woman who had taken over Jutka's brief role as the *cleaning girl* was killed. "I gazed at her scorched corpse in dread," was Jutka's aghast comment.

For two and a half days, Jutka and her companions were in limbo. The Germans had fled, but the Americans hadn't yet arrived.

On April 20, 1945, the Yanks did appear.

In all the confusion and euphoria that accompanied their rescue,

Jutka met a Captain Bergman who was working for U.S. Army Intelligence. His nickname was Ike—like General Eisenhower, it was pointed out.

There was still some spook stuff going on, and finally this American who confessed that *Bergman* was only his nom-de-guerre. He was really Irving Isaacson, "in peacetime a lawyer in Maine," he said.

Summing up in a sense were the opening lines of Judith Isaacson's last chapter:

"I spent my nineteenth birthday, July 3, 1944, in the stables of my hometown, Kaposvár, before deportation to Auschwitz.

"On my twentieth, became engaged.

"I observed my twenty-first at my in-laws' summer place in Popham Beach, Maine, a married woman, five months pregnant."

Auschwitz, which Judith survived, has in the eyes of the world turned into a sort of shorthand for the entire Holocaust experience. Lesser-known sites like Hessische Lichtenau contain atrocities equally hideous but on a smaller numerical scale. These latter for the most part have turned into mere footnotes or single-line geographical names on any listing of war-crime locations. Interestingly, at Auschwitz, the single largest grouping of Jews were those from Hungary—438,000.

Knowledge of Auschwitz in the outside world commenced on one such list—published in July 1942 by the London-based *Polish Fortnightly Review* that named twenty-two camps.

In March 1943, a message from the Polish Underground reported that Jews were being killed at Auschwitz.

On June 1 that same year, the *London Times* published an article "about Nazi brutalities to Jews at Auschwitz."

January 1944, the month when the War Refugee Board was forming and beginning its activities, a coded cable from Poland explicitly stated "that children and women are put in cars and lorries and taken to the gas chambers [in Auschwitz-Birkenau]. They are suffocated with the most horrible suffering, lasting ten to fifteen minutes. Daily 10,000 people were murdered in this fashion, 650,000 Jews all told to date, and their bodies burned to ashes in three large crematoria."

The muted reaction to this hard-to-believe news was followed by the media coverage soon given to four prisoners who had escaped from that deadly complex—Rudolf Vrba and Alfred Wetzler in April 1944, followed by Arnost Rosin and Czelaw Mordewicz in May. Their collected information was printed under the title of *The Auschwitz*

Protocols. Rudolf Kastner received a copy but kept it under wraps while he was negotiating with Adolf Eichmann. But on June 18, 1944, the BBC broadcast a program about Auschwitz and two days later, *The New York Times* started a three-part series unveiling the existence of the gas chambers.

It was also in June 1944 that the War Refugee Board was briefly brought into the picture. They received the request from Jacob Rosenheim of the Agudas Israel World Organization for the Allies to bomb the railway lines leading to Auschwitz. John Pehle sent it on to John McCloy, the number-two man at the War Department. It was later bruited that Pehle had his doubts about the proposal's viability. John McCloy had no doubts. He rejected it out of hand as an *impractical* move that would cause a diversion of bombers from more important tasks.

Via the WRB, a plea came from the World Jewish Congress in Geneva to bomb the gas chambers, themselves, and not just the railroad tracks. This, too, was opposed by McCloy.

As a political cliché in the U.S. goes: those involved "just kicked the can down the road," did nothing. The rightness or wrongness of this peremptory decision has been argued ever since.

In addition to his many publications, Neil Rolde is a long-time public servant, philanthropist, Renaissance man, and gentleman. The renowned Maine historian grew up in Brookline, Massachusetts. He earned a BA at Yale and a master's in journalism at Columbia University. He worked as a film scriptwriter before moving to Maine with his wife of fifty-four years, Carlotta Florsheim, to raise their family. In York they brought up four children and now enjoy family visits with their eight grandchildren.

The author has won book awards from the Maine Historical Society, the Maine Humanities Council, and the Maine Writers & Publishers Alliance. Most of Neil Rolde's books involve the history of his beloved Maine and its people. With a wealth of historical knowledge about politics, the author has recently turned his skill and wit to blogging current political incidents in a historical context at neilroldeauthor.com.

Rolde's public service includes six years as assistant to Maine's Governor Kenneth M. Curtis and sixteen years as representative in the Maine State Legislature. He was the Democratic candidate for U.S. Senate in 1990. The author has served on many state boards and commissions, including the Maine Health Care Reform Commission, the Maine Historic Preservation Commission, the Maine Humanities Council, and the Maine Arts Commission.

For bibliographic references, links and further information, please visit www.polarbearandco.com/neil-rolde.

www.ingramcontent.com/pod-product-compliance
Lightning Source LLC
Chambersburg PA
CBHW031128090426
42738CB00008B/1007